ABRAHAM LINCOLN AND TREASON IN THE CIVIL WAR

CONFLICTING WORLDS:
NEW DIMENSIONS OF THE AMERICAN CIVIL WAR

T. Michael Parrish, Series Editor

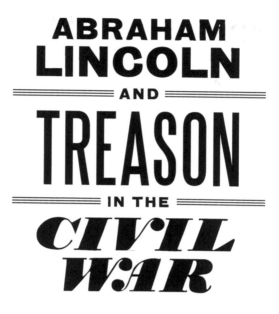

ABRAHAM LINCOLN AND TREASON IN THE CIVIL WAR

THE TRIALS OF JOHN MERRYMAN

Jonathan W. White

LOUISIANA STATE UNIVERSITY PRESS
BATON ROUGE

Published with the assistance of the V. Ray Cardozier Fund

Published by Louisiana State University Press
Copyright © 2011 by Louisiana State University Press
All rights reserved
Manufactured in the United States of America

DESIGNER: Michelle A. Neustrom
TYPEFACE: Adobe Minion Pro
BINDER: Acme Bookbinding

Frontispiece: John Merryman of Hayfields. (Guy Edison Kagey, *Sherwood Church:
Sketches of the History of Sherwood Parish, Cockeysville, Baltimore County,
Maryland, 1830–1930*. Baltimore: Read-Taylor, 1930)

LIBRARY OF CONGRESS CATALOGING-IN-PUBLICATION DATA

White, Jonathan W., 1979–
Abraham Lincoln and treason in the Civil War : the trials of John Merryman /
Jonathan W. White.
 p. cm. — (Conflicting worlds: new dimensions of the American Civil War)
Includes bibliographical references and index.
 ISBN 978-0-8071-4214-1 (cloth : alk. paper) — ISBN 978-0-8071-4215-8 (pdf) —
ISBN 978-0-8071-4216-5 (epub) — ISBN 978-0-8071-4217-2 (mobi) — ISBN 978-0-
8071-4346-9 (pbk. : alk. paper)
 1. Merryman, John, 1824–1881—Trials, litigation, etc. 2. Lincoln, Abraham,
1809–1865—Views on civil rights. 3. United States—History—Civil War, 1861–1865—
Collaborationists. 4. Habeas corpus—United States—History—19th century. 5.
Treason—United States—History—19th century. 6. Traitors—United States—History—19th century. 7. Civil rights—United States—History—19th century. I. Title.
 E458.8.W58 2011
 973.7—dc22

 2011015406

The paper in this book meets the guidelines for permanence and durability
of the Committee on Production Guidelines for Book Longevity
of the Council on Library Resources. ∞

~

*For my Father, who was born in Baltimore during another war,
and my Mother, who was born in the Land of Lincoln.*

~

By the *principles* of the American revolution, *arbitrary power may* and *ought* to be resisted, even by *arms* if necessary. The time may come, when it shall be the *duty* of a *State,* in order to preserve itself from the oppression of the general government, to have recourse to the sword; in which case, the proposed form of government declares, that the *State* and every of *its citizens* who *act under its authority* are guilty of a direct act of treason;— reducing, by this provision, the different States to this alternative, that they must *tamely* and *passively yield* to *despotism,* or *their citizens* must *oppose it* at the *hazard* of the *halter* if unsuccessful: and reducing the citizens of the State which shall take arms, to a situation in which they must be *exposed* to *punishment,* let them *act as they will;* since, if they *obey* the authority of their *State government,* they will be *guilty of treason against the United States;* if they *join* the *general government,* they will be *guilty of treason* against *their own State.*

—LUTHER MARTIN
to the Legislature of Maryland,
November 29, 1787

In the divided condition of public sentiment a conviction for treason no matter how clearly the crime may be proved is extremely difficult.

—JUDGE ADVOCATE GENERAL JOSEPH HOLT
to U.S. attorney for the District of Maryland William Price,
March 12, 1863

Contents

Acknowledgments

Several colleagues and friends read this manuscript in its entirety and offered substantial criticism and comments. I thank Mark Neely for first reading this as a six-page "research note" and for encouraging me to give this project the attention it deserved. Mark has been a mentor and a scholarly example since I was an undergraduate at Penn State. Bruce Ragsdale gave me the opportunity to conduct in-depth research on the *Merryman* case when I was an intern at the Federal Judicial Center in 2005. Bruce has been a constant source of wisdom and good advice as I proceeded with this project. James Henretta and Whit Ridgway both helped guide me through graduate school at the University of Maryland, and I appreciate their thoughts on this project both in its dissertation form and later as a book manuscript. Michael Burlingame and Allen Guelzo, both of whom I met recently at several Lincoln events, offered kind and helpful comments on the book. Finally, Michael Parrish kindly introduced himself to me at the first biennial meeting of the Society of Civil War Historians in June 2008 and has been a ready source of advice, encouragement, and information as I have worked on this and other projects. I thank Mark, Bruce, James, Whit, Michael, Allen, and Mike for each reading and commenting on the manuscript. I also thank Herman Belz, Mark Graber, and Leslie Rowland for their comments and advice on the portions of this manuscript that derive from my dissertation. And I thank Jo Ann Kiser, who is a terrific copy editor.

I gratefully thank several archivists, librarians, and curators, without whom I could not have completed this project: Richard Sommers of the U.S. Army Military History Institute; Jonathan Stayer of the Pennsylvania State Archives; Ed Papenfuse, Owen Lourie, and Jen Hafner of the Maryland State Archives; Jefferson Moak and Gail Farr of the National Archives at Philadelphia; Bill Davis of the Center for Legislative Archives at the National Archives; Johnnie Gray, the Interlibrary Loan specialist at Trible Library at Christopher Newport University; Stephen Bachmann of the Historical Society of Dauphin County; Linda Corbelli, Sara Sonet, and Catherine Romano of the Library of the Supreme Court of the United States; Catherine Fitts, Lauren Morrell, and Steve Petteway of the Curator's Office at the Supreme Court (I also thank Catherine for getting me a ticket to hear oral arguments in *Samantar v. Yousuf* at the Supreme Court on March 3, 2010, a case that has some similarities to the indemnity cases discussed in chapter 5); Bob Schmidt of the University Archives at the Miami University of Ohio; James Summa of the New York State Library; Tom Lowry, whose Index Project, Inc., facilitated my research for chapter 4; and the always helpful staffs at the Library of Congress, the National Archives, the Historical Society of Pennsylvania, the Maryland Historical Society, the Baltimore County Historical Society, the Enoch Pratt Free Library, the Baltimore County Public Library, and the special collections librarians at the University of Maryland, Duke University, and the University of Virginia. I also thank several individuals who helped me with certain aspects of my research: my friend Richard Boles, who is completing his Ph.D. at George Washington University; Jasmine Bumpers of SUNY-Albany; Donald Sailer of the staff of Dickinson College's "House Divided" Project; and Sean A. Scott, assistant editor of the Papers of Abraham Lincoln Project, who found John Merryman's June 1861 letter from Fort McHenry (see the Epilogue) and who also graciously tracked down another set of letters at the National Archives for me.

I thank Matthew Pinsker for convincing me to pursue a project related to the *Merryman* case. I found John Merryman's 1863 letter to Simon Cameron (see chapter 5) during the summer of 2007 but did not do anything with it for more than two years. I met Matt at a Lincoln Symposium at Eastern University in October 2009 and told him about the letter. He convinced me that I should write about it sooner rather than later.

I thank my good friends Mark Bieszka, Jeremy Rein, Jason Hummel, Jonathan and Jacquie Tuke, and Rebecca Trego for graciously hosting me during several research trips to Washington, D.C., and Baltimore; Ben Peets for hosting me in California; and Dave, Irene, and Jake Lepley for hosting me in Carlisle. I thank Sean McClure for opening a Chick-fil-A across the street from my office at CNU, where I spent many hours working on this book.

I thank Matt Aversa, the general manager of the Hayfields Country Club, for giving me a tour of John Merryman's beautiful estate; Jim Bailey for taking me through Fort McHenry; and Dave Pindell, Suzie Merryman, and Deb Stipa for showing me around Sherwood Episcopal Church, a church that John Merryman attended and helped build. I also thank Fran Merryman for sharing some family stories and photographs with me.

I thank Bob Colvin, Phil Hamilton, and Elizabeth Busch for allowing me to teach a course on the history of treason in America at Christopher Newport University while I was working on this manuscript. I thank my history and American studies students at CNU for helping me think through various issues related to treason in American history.

I thank Lewis Lehrman for his support of my research through the Lehrman Institute, the Gilder Lehrman Institute of American History, and the Lehrman American Studies Center. I thank the Jack Miller Center and Provost Mark Padilla for funding my postdoctoral fellowship at Christopher Newport University. I thank Nathan and Elizabeth Busch, co-founders of the Center for American Studies at CNU, for giving me the opportunity to pursue my research and writing. The Center has been a wonderfully collegial and intellectually engaging place to begin my career as a professor. While I was a graduate student at the University of Maryland, the History Department funded a research trip to London, where I read letters from the consul at Baltimore to the British Foreign Minister. In 2006, the Huntington Library in San Marino, California, graciously granted me a C. Allan and Marjorie Braun Fellowship. The University of Maryland, the Earhart Foundation, and the Lynde and Harry Bradley Foundation also funded my graduate work, during which I conducted some of the research for this book.

I thank my parents, Bill and Eileen White, and my siblings, Dave, Mary Ellen, and Kathy, for always being supportive of my career. Finally, I thank my wife, Lauren, for having patience as I worked on this book and for accompanying me on research trips to Annapolis, Baltimore, Carlisle, Cockeysville, College Park, Harrisburg, Philadelphia, Princeton, and Washington, D.C. Thank you for being an ever-faithful companion and friend.

ABRAHAM LINCOLN AND TREASON IN THE CIVIL WAR

INTRODUCTION

*J*ohn Merryman, a Baltimore County farmer, was arrested by Union military authorities at 2:00 a.m. on May 25, 1861, on vague and imprecise charges of treason against the United States. Merryman was suspected of being a pro-secession militia officer who had burned railroad bridges around Baltimore about a month before his arrest. On April 19, 1861, the streets of Baltimore had been awash in blood as an angry mob attacked soldiers from Massachusetts and Pennsylvania that were passing through the city on their way to Washington, D.C. Four soldiers and twelve civilians fell dead amid the chaos; dozens more were wounded. Following the riot, state authorities ordered members of the Baltimore police and the Maryland militia to destroy railroad bridges around Baltimore to prevent more northern troops from passing through the city. Leading a local band of cavalrymen, John Merryman burned several strategic bridges. This act, which prevented northern recruits from reaching the endangered national capital, was treason.

While imprisoned at Fort McHenry, in Baltimore harbor, Merryman petitioned Chief Justice Roger B. Taney for a writ of habeas corpus. This court order would require the arresting officer to bring "the body" of the prisoner before Chief Justice Taney so that Merryman could either be charged with a crime and lawfully recommitted to prison or be set free. Merryman and his lawyers believed the writ would either secure his freedom or have him turned over to civil authorities to be tried according to Article III of the Constitution and the provisions of the Bill of Rights that secure procedural safeguards to accused criminals. On May 26, Taney issued the writ, but President Abraham Lincoln ignored it. As a consequence, the military continued to hold Merryman in close confinement at Fort McHenry.

On June 1, 1861, Chief Justice Taney delivered a written opinion in *Ex parte Merryman* that blasted Lincoln's handling of the matter. The arrest of a little-known farmer from Baltimore County thus led to a clash of enormous proportions between the chief justice and the president. This "collision," as it was called at the time, has been the subject of numerous essays, books, and articles regarding the nature of executive power in wartime, the definition of treason, and the rights of accused criminals to due process of law. Yet these accounts are based on a woefully incomplete understanding of what was transpiring in the 1860s as judges, lawyers, politicians, traitors, and ordinary civilians battled over the meaning of treason, the rights of the accused, and the power of the government to protect itself in times of national emergency.

Historians love to tell the Merryman story. Great literature rarely provides better drama—the nation had been sundered, an ordinary man sat wallowing in a dungeon,[1] soldiers were hastening to battle, vicious mobs roamed city streets, storm clouds were ominous, and the president and chief justice stood locked in an epic constitutional struggle that might determine the fate of the young republic. Yet the account, as it is often told, leaves more questions than answers. One remarkable fact is that historians who write about *Ex parte Merryman* have very little idea as to who John Merryman was or what he did to merit arrest. While we know that Merryman was a man of southern sympathies, we have yet to learn what actually motivated him to act illegally in April 1861. Moreover, what exactly was Chief Justice Taney doing in Baltimore? What effects did *Ex parte Merryman* have on military policy? And finally, what became of the main actors in this drama after Merryman was released from Fort McHenry in July 1861? The answers to these questions reveal a great deal about the treason, civil liberties, and habeas corpus issues that arose during the Civil War. These questions, however, have been too often overlooked or cursorily dealt with because historians and political scientists who write about *Ex parte Merryman* have relied almost entirely on the published reports of the case in *Federal Cases* and the *Official Records* rather than on the original manuscript court records.

～

In a recent volume commemorating the two hundredth anniversary of Abraham Lincoln's birth, historian Mark E. Neely, Jr., selected Taney's opinion in *Ex parte Merryman* as one of "three documents . . . critical to understanding President Abraham Lincoln's record on civil liberties." Neely went on to call *Merryman* "one of the most poorly understood decisions to come from the Supreme Court."[2] Neely's assessment is partially correct. *Merryman* is one of the most significant judicial decisions of the Civil War era. In fact, *Merryman* is the first case listed on the federal judiciary's "Landmark Cases Related to Understanding Terrorism Cases" website.[3] But the case is also very "poorly understood." *Merryman* was not a Supreme Court decision, as many historians and political scientists contend. Nor was it simply a routine circuit court case. The story is much more complex and deserves a complete retelling.

Historians still know very little about why exactly John Merryman was arrested by the military in 1861. According to James M. McPherson, Merryman "was a wealthy Maryland landowner and lieutenant in a secessionist cavalry company that had torn down telegraph lines near Baltimore." Geoffrey Stone describes Merryman as "a cavalryman who had allegedly burned bridges and destroyed telegraph wires during the April [19] riots."[4] According to Judge Frank J. Williams, Merryman was "a dissatisfied resident" of Maryland who "spoke out vigorously against the Union and in favor of the South, and he recruited a company of soldiers for the Confederate army and became their lieutenant drillmaster."[5] Paul M. Angle characterizes Merryman as "a citizen of Baltimore with Southern sympathies." Michael Vorenberg describes him as "a Maryland militiaman who had been imprisoned without trial for recruiting soldiers for the Confederacy in an area where Lincoln had suspended habeas corpus rights." Law professor James F. Simon identifies Merryman as "a wealthy landowner, state legislator, and cavalry officer from Cockneysville [*sic*], Maryland, who was accused of burning railroad bridges and destroying telegraph wires in northern Maryland after the April 19 Baltimore riot." Peter Charles Hoffer sums up the *Merryman* case this way: "In 1861, President Abraham Lincoln ordered the arrest and military trial of a confederate sympathizer named John Merryman and at first refused to honor a habeas corpus that Chief Justice Roger Taney granted." Presuming Merryman's guilt, but without ever stating what overt act of treason Merryman had committed, Hoffer concludes, "Merryman was in fact levying war against the United States, and could, without much of a stretch, have been indicted in the federal courts for the offense."[6] The point is clear: Merryman used his position as an officer in a Maryland militia unit in some way to impede the Union war effort—most likely by burning railroad bridges and cutting telegraph lines, possibly by speaking out against the Union, perhaps by recruiting soldiers for the Confederacy—but historians are vague as to what exactly he did or what he was even charged with doing.

This book is an attempt to understand more fully who John Merryman was, what he did to harm the Union, and how his actions impacted Lincoln's war and reconstruction policies. In the process, we will examine the difficulties that faced Union authorities who were responsible for dealing with suspected traitors in areas that were swarming with disloyalty. Unlike most accounts of the *Merryman* case, this book does not limit its scope to the spring and summer of 1861. Rather, it explores John Merryman's interactions with the federal government and with federal officials for the duration of the war and into the postwar period. In a sense, John Merryman's story will serve as a lens through which we can explore the development of President Lincoln's habeas corpus policy in 1861, Chief Justice Taney's reaction to Lincoln in *Ex parte Merryman,* the role of the courts in handling matters related to disloyalty and civil liberties, and the successes and failures of Congress's attempt to settle the habeas corpus issue in March 1863.

Chapter 1 describes the background of Lincoln's habeas corpus policy in the spring of 1861. Maryland seemed to be tottering on the brink of secession, and Baltimore disunionists were lashing out violently against federal soldiers. Lincoln had to act quickly to keep Maryland from seceding. Facing a rebellion of unprecedented scope and vigor, the president decided to suspend the privilege of the writ of habeas corpus. Article I of the Constitution permits the writ to be suspended "when in Cases of Rebellion or Invasion the public Safety may require it." Suspension of habeas corpus meant that federal authorities could arrest and detain civilians without charges, thus leaving the prisoners without legal recourse. As a consequence, Lincoln could order his military commanders to arrest and indefinitely detain Maryland civilians when doing so would help to keep that very consequential border state in the Union.

Amid the political and social turmoil in Maryland, Union military authorities ordered the arrest of one John Merryman, a secession-sympathizing farmer and militia officer in Baltimore County. Chapter 2 traces Merryman's story from the time of his arrest in May 1861 until his release in mid-July. The chapter also explores the conflict that emerged between President Lincoln and Chief Justice Taney over the military arrest and imprisonment of Maryland civilians. The public disagreement between these two high government officers set the tone that debates over the suspension of habeas corpus would take for the next four years of the war (and, in fact, for the next century and a half). Lincoln persistently claimed that public safety required him to suspend the writ and that the Constitution permitted the president to use the law of war in time of war. His detractors, by contrast, accused him of violating his oath of office and of acting tyrannically.

Most historians leave the *Merryman* case in July 1861, when John Merryman was released from Fort McHenry. Ignoring the subsequent few years of Merryman's life, however, causes historians to miss several important and often overlooked aspects of the legal history of the Civil War. Chapter 3 traces the Lincoln administration's efforts to prosecute Merryman and several other Baltimoreans suspected of treason. Merryman was indicted for treason in the federal courts, not once but twice. But it was nearly impossible to bring these prosecutions to a successful conclusion, in part because Chief Justice Taney presided over the federal circuit court in Baltimore, in part because it would be difficult to find a Maryland jury willing to convict their neighbors of a capital offense, in part because of the heavy burden the Constitution requires for treason convictions, in part because of the overwork and possible negligence of the federal prosecutors in Baltimore, and in part because of the Lincoln administration's hesitancy to make martyrs of disloyal citizens in a loyal state. All of these factors combined to make the successful prosecution of Maryland traitors highly unlikely during the Civil War.

Because of the difficulty Lincoln faced in attaining treason convictions and because of the vast amount of treason confronting the government—not only in the South but also in the North—the Lincoln administration came to rely heavily on other methods for dealing with civilians suspected of disloyalty. Throughout the war Lincoln used the military to arrest, try, and punish thousands of northern and border state civilians. This policy was a natural outgrowth of the habeas corpus policy that he developed in the first months of the war.[7] The problem, however, was that Lincoln's actions seemed to violate the letter of the Constitution. The placement of the suspension clause in Article I led many observers to believe that only Congress could suspend the writ of habeas corpus. Moreover, others claimed that even if the president could lawfully suspend the writ, Lincoln's use of military commissions to try civilians was illegal because it violated the procedural rights guaranteed to persons accused of criminal acts by the Fourth, Fifth, and Sixth Amendments in the Bill of Rights. In other words, some of Lincoln's critics believed that suspension of habeas corpus meant that a person could be arrested without charges but that they did not lose their right to a civil trial before a jury of their peers.

Initially Congress refused to take a stand on Lincoln's actions in regard to civil liberties. Both houses debated the issues at stake in *Ex parte Merryman* in July and August 1861, but few congressmen were willing either to confront the president or to condone his actions. By the midpoint of the war, however, Congress could no longer ignore the civil liberties issues that had emerged amid the friction and abrasion of the conflict.

Chapter 4 takes a slight detour from the Merryman story to examine how Congress sought to legislate regarding the rights of civilians in wartime. On March 3, 1863, Congress enacted the Habeas Corpus Act, or Indemnity Act, in an attempt to resolve the nation's civil liberties problems. The act had several important provisions. First, it authorized Lincoln to suspend the writ of habeas corpus during the rebellion, when the public safety required it. Second, the act sought to stop the use of military tribunals in the North and instead to have civilians tried in civil courts. Third, the law offered protection to Union authorities who were being sued for wrongful arrest by northern civilians whom they had detained. In the end, the Habeas Corpus Act proved a dismal failure, offering little protection to Union authorities and no protection to suspected traitors. Chapter 4 concludes by arguing that Lincoln consciously ignored the act because he believed its terms would inhibit his ability to prosecute the war effectively. Moreover, he believed that he, as president, possessed the authority to interpret the Constitution's suspension clause irrespective of what Congress or the courts had to say. Lincoln would determine just what the suspension of habeas corpus entailed, and he essentially decided that the suspension included the temporary interruption of the procedural safeguards of the Bill of Rights as well.

Chapter 5 returns the focus to John Merryman and explores the legal consequences of the military arrest of civilians. As early as August 1861, Maryland civilians who had been arrested by the military sought damages from high-ranking government and military officials for wrongful arrest, illegal search and seizure, and assault and battery. These suits had been part of the impetus behind the passage of the Habeas Corpus Act of 1863 and also explain why it was commonly referred to as the Indemnity Act. Between 1863 and 1865, John Merryman filed two suits against the Union commander who had detained him at Fort McHenry, claiming $50,000 in damages for wrongful arrest (such an amount would be equivalent to almost $900,000 today). These civil suits, in fact, reveal more about the wartime habeas corpus issue than the famous *Ex parte Merryman* proceedings do. John Merryman's arrest was just one of many that state and federal judges were powerless to stop during the Civil War. The civil proceedings, however, exposed the deep fears that plagued Union authorities who oversaw the arrest of civilians. Suits for damages could have a paralyzing effect on Union officials—in fact, just one year after Merryman's arrest the military officer who had overseen Merryman's incarceration was too afraid to reenter the state of Maryland because he feared that *he* would be arrested by state authorities for his earlier role in the Merryman affair.

While Union authorities initially rejoiced with the passage of the Habeas Corpus Act, they soon found that it did not provide adequate protection. During the latter half of the war, and well into Reconstruction, damages suits hamstrung the Union war effort and made federal leaders wary of prosecuting the war perhaps as vigorously as they should have. Civilians used these suits as a way to strike back at the government after their release from prison.[8] In a very real sense, these suits gave southern-sympathizing northerners an opportunity to aid their rebel friends without taking up arms, burning bridges, or committing any other overt act in support of the southern Confederacy. The damages suits involving John Merryman, in short, expose the many weaknesses of the Habeas Corpus

Act as well as some of the deeper problems of disloyalty in the loyal states during the Civil War. As we will see in chapter 5, Merryman's suit against a Union officer for wrongful arrest even impacted President Lincoln as late as March 1864 as he was striving to craft a policy for reconstruction of the Union. Indeed, the post-1861 legal proceedings involving John Merryman reveal the political tensions and legal considerations with which wartime officials and military officers were forced to contend.

~

The broader context of the *Merryman* case has been so poorly understood for a century and a half, in large measure, because the historians, lawyers, and political scientists who have written about *Ex parte Merryman* have done so without consulting the original manuscript court records. A previously unpublished letter by John Merryman in which he gave some insight into his motivation for burning railroad bridges (the letter is reproduced in chapter 5) also sheds new light on the very consequential habeas corpus case that bears his name. Legal histories of the Civil War era typically rely too heavily on published court reports. If this book has a subsidiary point to make, it is to remind legal scholars to delve more deeply into unpublished case materials and to rely on more than the published court reports, even those reports that contain substantial supplementary documentation, as *Ex parte Merryman* does.

Up to this point, historians have simply recounted *Ex parte Merryman* as a story about the monumental clash that arose between President Lincoln and Chief Justice Taney in the summer of 1861. In truth, the Merryman story sheds light on nearly every aspect of the treason, disloyalty, habeas corpus, and civil liberties issues that arose during the Civil War. John Merryman's arrest by the military and the subsequent conflict between Lincoln and Taney were only the opening salvos of a protracted string of legal battles that not only determined the fate of Merryman's life, liberty, and property but also had a significant impact on how the president and Congress attempted to stem the rising tide of disloyalty in the North. The various legal proceedings involving John Merryman, in short, reveal the magnitude of the disloyalty problem that faced Lincoln and the Union during the Civil War. Merryman's criminal indictments in the federal courts in Baltimore, which were not dismissed until 1867, reveal not only the difficulty that the Lincoln administration faced in dealing with traitors in loyal states but also the importance of effective patronage to managing the Union war effort. Finally, the civil cases seeking damages that involved John Merryman expose the failure of Congress to protect either those accused of being traitors or those who were trying to save the Union in the midst of great struggle.

In 2008, Mark E. Neely, Jr., rightly observed, "In the case of *Ex parte Merryman,* the political future of the United States was at stake." Similarly, Harold M. Hyman calls *Merryman* "the single most important item of opposition literature" to emerge during the Civil War.[9] The importance of the *Merryman* case in American history and law cannot be overstated.[10] Indeed, the questions raised by the Civil War trials of John Merryman continue to arise in America today: Where is the balance to be found between individual liberty and national security? What rights, if any, should Americans give up in wartime? Under what circumstances, if any, are military commissions lawful? Should the judicial branch defer to the political branches during national emergencies? Can the executive branch determine the constitutionality of its own wartime actions? What legal protections do political and military officers need in order to wage war effectively? Should those making war against the United States be able to claim rights under the U.S. Constitution? These questions were on the mind of Lincoln and his cabinet; they echoed in the halls of Congress and in the corridors of the Capitol; they were argued and adjudicated in courtrooms throughout the nation. They continue to be debated in all of these places today.

In order to set the context for John Merryman's story, we must begin with the city of Baltimore on the eve of the Civil War. As men and boys throughout the North hastily mustered into militia units and armed themselves to fight the South, the citizens of the Monumental City boiled with anger and anxiety at the thought of "Yankee invaders" and "Northern scum" treading their streets toward the capital of Washington, D.C.

1

"BALTIMORE IS TO BE THE BATTLEFIELD OF THE SOUTHERN REVOLUTION"

The Baltimore Riot and the Formation of Lincoln's Habeas Corpus Policy

When Abraham Lincoln received word on April 14, 1861, that Fort Sumter had fallen into Confederate hands, he set to work with his cabinet to formulate a policy that would sufficiently respond to the crisis. Seven Deep South states had already seceded from the Union. Now these so-called Confederate States had attacked the nation's flag, affronted the national honor, and forcibly seized federal property. The president needed to respond decisively. On April 15, Lincoln issued a proclamation calling forth seventy-five thousand militiamen from the states and summoning Congress to convene in special session on July 4, 1861.[1]

Lincoln's proclamation was greeted with disillusionment and anger across the Upper South. His call for troops was evidence to Virginians that he really sought the "subjugation of all who would not subscribe to the creed of the conqueror." On April 17, the Old Dominion State voted herself out of the Union. Arkansas, North Carolina, and Tennessee soon followed. For Lincoln, the slaveholding border states of Delaware, Maryland, Kentucky, and Missouri now needed to be held at all costs. Indeed, Lincoln believed that losing the border states would mean losing "the whole game."[2] If Maryland fell to the rebels, the national capital would be impossible to defend.

Maryland, a border slave state, sat in a precarious position in the spring of 1861. Geographically, Maryland linked the North to the nation's capital. Strategically, northern soldiers could not reach the District of Columbia except by train through Maryland. The Philadelphia, Wilmington and Baltimore Railroad ran from Philadelphia to Baltimore, while the Northern Central Railway Company's lines linked Harrisburg to Baltimore. From the west, the Baltimore and Ohio brought travelers to the Monumental City. Passengers on these trains could then head south to Washington on the Baltimore and Ohio Railroad from Camden Station, near the harbor.

Between November 1860 and April 1861, Maryland governor Thomas H. Hicks did all he could to keep his state in the Union. When secessionists urged him to call the state legislature into session, he refused, fearing that the legislators might vote the state out of the Union. Secessionists were furious with Hicks, while some Unionists praised him for his "masterly inactivity." Still, Hicks was a timid and sometimes vacillating man who may have been in over his head. In response to Lincoln's proclamation calling for troops, Hicks informed Secretary of War Simon Cameron that in light of Maryland's divided sympathies and the strength of secessionists in the state, "I think it prudent to decline (for the present) acting upon the requisition made upon Maryland for four regiments."[3]

But other states heeded Lincoln's call. On April 18, 1861, five companies of Pennsylvania troops passed through Baltimore on their way to Washington, D.C. A crowd gathered around the soldiers as they marched through the city toward the railroad depot at Camden Station. The soldiers carried their muskets capped and half-cocked, giving the impression that they were loaded and ready to fire. As a consequence, the mob chose not to attack the troops while they were marching. Once the Pennsylvanians had boarded the train for Washington, however, "the angry mob hurled a shower of bricks, clubs, and stones" upon the soldiers. "In the midst of the confusion," wrote nineteenth-century historian Samuel P. Bates, "an attempt was made to detach the engine from the train and run it away. This was only prevented by the determined character of the engineer and his assistants, who drew revolvers, and threatened to shoot any who dared to make the attempt. At length, amidst the demoniac yells of the crowd, the train moved off, carrying the volunteers safely beyond the reach of their desperate assailants." Fortunately this attack resulted in only "slight injuries" to the soldiers. Baltimore mayor George William Brown claimed that but for the "great efforts" of the city authorities "a fearful slaughter would have occurred."[4]

Once the soldiers had departed, Governor Hicks and Mayor Brown sent an urgent note to Lincoln: "A collision between the citizens & the Northern troops has taken place in Baltimore and the excitement is fearful. Send no ~~more~~ troops here. We will endeavor to prevent all bloodshed." Hicks and Brown then informed Lincoln that they had called out "the troops of the State in the City . . . to preserve the peace. They will be enough." Lincoln grossly misunderstood this missive. Rather than take it as a request that Lincoln send no more federal troops through Baltimore, the president interpreted the letter to mean that state and local authorities would be able to protect other Union soldiers who might be brought through the city.[5]

Tensions increased in Baltimore as another contingent of troops approached. Railroad executives telegraphed Secretary of War Cameron to stop sending troops through the city.[6] But Cameron would have none of their yellow-bellied Unionism. "Governor Hicks has neither right nor authority to stop troops coming to Washington," fumed Cameron. "Send them on prepared to fight their way through, if necessary."[7]

Violence erupted in Baltimore on Friday, April 19, when the Sixth Massachusetts Regiment and one thousand unarmed Pennsylvania volunteers attempted to pass through the city on their way to Washington, D.C. The troops entered Baltimore in thirty-five railroad cars that arrived at President Street Station on the east side of the harbor at about 10 a.m. The cars had to be detached from the locomotive at the station and drawn by teams of horses about one-and-a-half miles to Camden Station, where they would be attached to different locomotives and sent southward to Washington. As the soldiers arrived in Baltimore they saw angry crowds gathering outside their train windows.[8]

The first six cars, carrying Companies A, B, E, F, G, and H of the Sixth Massachusetts (roughly four hundred men), made it to Camden Station without much trouble. The next car, carrying Company K, however, was pelted with stones and shards of iron. "Stones, brickbats, 'april' shells, and missiles of all kinds were hurled into and through the car windows, through which could be plainly seen the uniformed occupants, who although armed made no offensive attempt at defense," remembered one witness years after the riot. "It was an awful melee and a wild mob of crazy men and boys shrieking with fearful oaths their desire to annihilate the hated 'Yankees.'" Another witness recalled: "The soldiers bore the pelting of the pitiless mob for a long time . . . & more than three of them were knocked & shot down before they returned the assaults." Indeed, it was only after one Bay State soldier had his thumb shot off that an officer finally gave the order to fire. The soldiers had been ordered "not [to] fire into any promiscuous crowds, but select any man whom you may see aiming at you, and be sure to drop him." The boys of Company K aimed their muskets and side arms through the broken car windows, firing into the chaos around them. Suddenly the car came to a halt because the mob had torn up the tracks and laid anchors, sand and other debris in its way. As the rioters were destroying the track, one James Whiteford of Baltimore yelled, "Rally boys! The cars ought to be stoned," and "Kill the damned sons of bitches." The Massachusetts men were forced to exit the car and fight the mob as they marched the remaining quarter mile to Camden Station.[9]

The remaining 228 Massachusetts soldiers at President Street Station formed ranks and marched toward Camden Station, leaving behind the thousand unarmed Pennsylvanians. They marched through the city exchanging volleys with civilians who hid in upstairs windows. Four Bay State soldiers fell dead, two from gunshot wounds, one who was knocked down and beaten to death, and one who was "mortally wounded by stones and other objects which fractured his skull." Another thirty-six were wounded. Henry S. Durkee, a citizen who lived on Orleans Street, recalled the horrors he witnessed: "Saw a soldier in the gutter & two men kicking him almost to death. . . . The police officers were holding him down while the men were kicking him." Another Marylander, who later enlisted in the Union army remarked: "At the depot they were attacked by the mob. [Police] Officer George Jones assaulted John Hoffman & broke his head with a spontoon, crying 'You black son of a bitch you came here to fight us white men.'" Another witness saw Jones "run . . . after one of the soldiers & strike at him with a club."[10] Eventually about six hundred Massachusetts men reached Camden Station and boarded a train to Washington.

The role of the police in the riot has been a matter of some dispute. Baltimore mayor George William Brown claimed that he and Police Marshal George P. Kane did their best to escort the men safely to Camden Station. Corroborating Brown's account, the colonel of the Sixth Massachusetts later reported that Brown had seized a musket from one of the frightened soldiers and shot a rioter with it.[11] Other witnesses described the scene as more of a police riot. "The police acted in such a way that I told some of them they were heading the mob," testified John Ehrman to a federal grand jury. "One [man] asked a policeman why he did not arrest a rioter; he replied I will arrest *you*." Other bystanders corroborated this account: "Police arrested only Union men who were trying to keep down [the] riot," testified Constable John Plummer. "Wm. Eckart a police man was in the cars with [an] axe breaking open boxes at the orders of the crowd," recalled another man. He concluded that the "Police rather encouraged the riot." Rev. Andrew Schwartz of the United Evangelical Church on Eastern Avenue observed that "the police instead of arresting the rioters crudely arrested the poor wounded flying volunteers—*police had no numbers on their hats.*"[12]

While the Massachusetts soldiers slogged through Baltimore, the Pennsylvania boys found themselves stranded at President Street Station without uniforms, arms, or protection. Benjamin Upton of Britton Street "returned to [the] Depot [and] saw men who said they were recruits from Phila.—the crowd were beating them desperately. Saw Richard Price with a stick in his hand striking & encouraging others—was more excited than I ever saw him in my life." Finally, at about 2:00 p.m. the Pennsylvania soldiers were able to board a train back to the City of Brotherly Love. In addition to the four Massachusetts soldiers, at least a dozen civilians were killed in the melee.[13]

Baltimore secessionists could not contain their rage. "Let any more Northern troops attempt passage of this city and not one will live to tell the story," seethed Jabez Pratt, a Baltimore businessman who had been born in Massachusetts. A Baltimore County newspaper echoed this sentiment with a grotesque call to arms: "Organize at once and take every precaution to prevent the passage of these murderers over Maryland soil. Beat your 'plow shares into swords, and your pruning hooks into spears,' and leave the dead carcasses of your intended murderers as dung upon your soil, rather than permit them to pass over it." Indeed, in the wake of the riot, Baltimore police marshal George P. Kane showed his true colors. "Fresh hordes will be down on us tomorrow," he telegraphed future Confederate general Bradley T. Johnson. "We will fight them and whip them, or die."[14]

On the afternoon of April 19 a crowd of secessionists gathered at Monument Square. They raised the Maryland state flag and several prominent leaders took the stand. Severn Teackle Wallis and Columbus O'Donnell gave pro-secession speeches. Next came the mayor. "In my speech," recalled Mayor Brown, "I insisted on the maintenance of peace and order in the city. I denied that the right of a State to secede from the Union was granted by the Constitution." Brown's speech was greeted with "groans and shouts of disapproval by part of the crowd, but I maintained my ground. I deprecated war on the seceding States, and strongly expressed the opinion that the South could not be conquered." The crowd then called for Governor Hicks. According to one pro-South observer, "He was frightened to death & wanted to go to the Fort [McHenry] to place himself under the protection of its guns." The governor declared his desire for preservation of the Union. The crowd reacted with vitriol toward the timid chief executive, who hastily added: "I bow in submission to the people. I am a Marylander; I love my state and I love the Union, but I will suffer my right arm to be torn from my body before I will raise it to strike a sister state." Another report of the speech quoted Hicks saying: "If separate we must, in God's name let us separate in peace; for I would rather this right arm should be separated from my body than raise it against a brother."[15]

Meanwhile, back in Washington, April 19 was a hectic day at the White House. A constant stream of visitors called on the president, while Lincoln's private secretary, John Hay, "had to do some very dexterous lying" to persuade Mary Lincoln that rumors of assassination plots against her husband were unfounded. After tea, two men arrived from Baltimore assuring the president "of the entire fidelity of the Governor and the State authorities." Lincoln showed the men the letter he had received from Hicks and Brown the previous day. General Winfield Scott exclaimed that "Gov. Hicks has no authority to prevent troops from passing through Baltimore," and Secretary of State William H. Seward concurred that Hicks had "no right." The two visitors told Lincoln that they feared that the North would strike a crushing blow against Baltimore in retaliation for the Pratt Street Riot, but Lincoln reassured them: "Our people are easily influenced by reason. They have determined to prosecute this matter with energy but with the most temperate spirit. You are entirely safe from lawless invasion."[16]

On the night of April 19 several Maryland leaders, including Baltimore police marshal George P. Kane, met at the home of Mayor George William Brown to discuss how to prevent more federal soldiers from traveling through the city. While accounts of the gathering vary, it is clear that the participants all opposed the passage of more Union troops through the state and desired to find a way to impede their route. Burning railroad bridges seemed the most efficient way. Mayor Brown insisted that unless the troops were somehow stopped, "a terrible collision and bloodshed would take place, and the consequences to Baltimore would be fearful, and that the only way to avert the calamity was to destroy the bridges." Some members of the meeting claimed that Governor Hicks verbally authorized the burning of bridges. According to Brown, Hicks had replied: "It seems to be necessary." But Hicks later denied giving explicit consent. One Maryland journalist reported that Hicks "sought refuge in Mayor Brown's residence and passed the night there. Fearing an attack on the city it was determined by the Police Commissioners to cut off communication with the city by the destruction of the rail road bridges. Marshal Kane went to Brown's to consult him & they determined to get the assent of Hicks. He had gone to bed. The two went into his room and told him that the threatened danger to the city necessitated such a step. They asked his advice. He did not wish to give it. He rolled and groaned. Brown insisted and declared he would not act without explicit orders from him. Hicks twisted the sheet over his head rolled over agst. the wall and moaned rather than exclaimed 'Oh! Yes. Go and do it.'"[17]

Word spread quickly that the city and state governments had authorized the destruction of railroad bridges and telegraph wires around Baltimore. Colonel Isaac R. Trimble led a group of Baltimore policemen and city guards to burn bridges along the Philadelphia, Wilmington, and Baltimore line, while Captain J. G. Johannes and Police Marshal George P. Kane led men to burn bridges of the Northern Central. Within hours of the meeting at the mayor's house multiple bridges were ablaze. One watchman at a railroad bridge in Canton recalled the scene: "On [April] 20th soldiers came down and stopped & the police came on [the] bridge. I asked what they were doing. They said its none of my business. I told them I was the watch man and begged them not to burn it. Nine of them seized me & took me to throw me into the river. I took out a stick & eight run—one held on & took me to Trimble." Other watchmen were offered beer or were arrested by the police so that the bridges could be torched.[18] By the morning of April 20 the Marylanders had successfully severed the transportation and communication lines around Baltimore and into Washington, D.C.

Many northerners expressed alarm at the actions of the Maryland authorities. Writing from Philadelphia, U.S. district judge John Cadwalader told an old family friend in Maryland that in ceding the District of Columbia to the United States, the state of Maryland had given up its right to impede the passage of federal troops to the national capital. "The purpose for which military forces of the United States may pass through Maryland cannot be rightfully questioned by her people, or by her government," wrote the judge. "She ceded the present district of Columbia to the United States as the seat of *their* Government. Of course, the cession carried with it the unqualified right of passage, including that of transporting troops, to and from the district, through the State." For Marylanders to "oppose or question the right would be simply preposterous." The state government, according to Cadwalader, must "open the passage, and keep it open" so that the federal government could accomplish its own purposes.[19]

Americans raised on tales of the Revolution noted the "curious coincidence" and the "significant augury" of Massachusetts men being murdered in city streets on April 19. "The Old Bay State is wrought up to the highest pitch," wrote former U.S. senator Nathaniel P. Tallmadge. "She is the first in the field, and will be the last to leave it. On the 19th of April 1775, Massachusetts, at Lexington, spilt the first blood of the Revolution. On the 19th day of April 1861, she spilt the first blood at Baltimore, on her way to defend the National Capital." Just as it had been for their fathers and grandfathers, the hard hand of war was becoming an ever-real possibility. "It is evident," predicted one Baltimore newspaper, "that Baltimore is to be the battlefield of the Southern revolution."[20]

Meanwhile, the streets of Washington "were full of the talk of Baltimore." Many in the capital felt completely severed from the North. "Here we are in Washington, cooped up by the cutting off by the crazed secessionists of Maryland of all communication with [the] North either by mail, railroad, or telegraph," noted one Washington official. The president felt some consolation when the Sixth Massachusetts arrived from Baltimore on the evening of the nineteenth. "Thank God, you have come," he told them, "for if you had not Washington would have been in the hands of the rebels before morning." The Bay State soldiers drilled on Pennsylvania

Avenue and kept their quarters in the Capitol. Back at the White House, Lincoln spent the next few days greeting visitors from Maryland, each of whom presented different demands to the president.[21]

On April 20 and 21, Lincoln met with Mayor Brown and several "penitent and suppliant crowd[s] of conditional Secessionists from Baltimore" who begged that no more northern troops be sent through their city. They warned the president that the Baltimore mob "was thoroughly unmanageable" and that the soldiers must reach Washington by some other route. Mayor Brown also informed Lincoln that between two and three thousand Union soldiers were camped about fourteen miles north of Baltimore, at Cockeysville, Maryland, and that the presence of these troops had Baltimore "wild with excitement." (The troops had been forced to encamp there since the railroad bridges near Cockeysville had been burned.) Trusting the wisdom and experience of his visitors, Lincoln agreed to order the soldiers back to Pennsylvania. He also agreed to transport federal soldiers around rather than through Baltimore in the future. But he added to one of the delegations, "If I grant you this, you will come to-morrow demanding that no troops shall pass around."[22]

Sadly, Lincoln was right. The president's secretary, John Hay, noted in his diary on April 22 that the "whining traitors from Baltimore were here again this morning." By now the president had heard enough of their treasonable appeals. "You, gentlemen, come here to me and ask for peace on any terms, and yet have no word of condemnation for those who are making war on us," he told them. "You express great horror of bloodshed, and yet would not lay a straw in the way of those who are organizing in Virginia and elsewhere to capture this city. The rebels attack Fort Sumter, and your citizens attack troops sent to the defense of the Government, and the lives and property in Washington, and yet you would have me break my oath and surrender the Government without a blow. There is no Washington in that—no Jackson in that—no manhood nor honor in that." Lincoln assured the callers that he had "no desire to invade the South; but I must have troops to defend this Capital. Geographically it lies surrounded by the soil of Maryland; and mathematically the necessity exists that they should come over her territory. Our men are not moles, and can't dig under the earth; they are not birds, and can't fly through the air. There is no way but to march across, and that they must do. But in doing this there is no need of collision. Keep your rowdies in Baltimore, and there will be no bloodshed. Go home and tell your people that if they will not attack us, we will not attack them; but if they do attack us, we will return it, and that severely." Another report of the conversation quoted Lincoln as saying, "*I will lay Baltimore in ashes.*"[23]

Lincoln's initial, conciliatory approach toward Maryland seemed to be giving way under the pressures of stress, danger, and exasperation. For several days Unionist visitors had been telling Lincoln that Baltimore "had to be leveled to the earth" and "laid in ashes." While dining at the White House one evening, U.S. treasurer Francis E. Spinner opined, "The only good use for traitors is to hang them."[24] The president now appeared ready to adopt more drastic measures.

Nevertheless, Lincoln kept his word to Mayor Brown. On April 21, the president ordered the Pennsylvania soldiers stationed at Cockeysville to return to the Keystone State.[25] Prior to their departure, a local resident named John Merryman apparently "offered to render . . . the troops any service required; and if necessary would slaughter his cattle to supply them with food." When word of Lincoln's order arrived at their camp, the soldiers packed up their belongings and prepared to go home. Secessionist leaders in Maryland also responded to Lincoln's order. Major General George H. Steuart, the pro-secession militia commander at Baltimore, ordered a local militia unit, the Baltimore County Horse Guards, to follow the soldiers back to Pennsylvania and "destroy all bridges, and break up the road at intervals of a mile or two between Cockeysville and the state line."[26] The Horse Guards quickly mobilized for action. Captain Charles H. Ridgely delivered Steuart's written order to First Lieutenant John Merryman. On the morning of April 23, the Horse Guards galloped off to fulfill their orders as the Pennsylvania boys took the train back across the Mason-Dixon Line. When later asked if the bridge burnings had been "done publicly and openly; and [as] a matter of general notoriety," one member of the unit answered: "I don't know whether it was a matter of general notoriety; it was done in the day time—it was not done secretly." The Horse Guards, in other words, obeyed the orders because they ostensibly believed their actions would prevent further bloodshed in their state.[27]

With sword drawn and brandishing a pistol, Lieutenant Merryman led a contingent of the Horse Guards, ordering his men to burn bridges and cut telegraph wires as the Pennsylvania troops retreated northward. According to witnesses, Merryman claimed "discretionary power" to burn the bridges and "would have destroyed Gunpowder bridge even if [he] had had no authority to do so." Two watchmen at one of the Northern Central's bridges claimed that Merryman "compelled them, with pistols pointed to their breasts, to cut wood, and carry oil for the purpose of burning the bridges." They also heard him "utter sentiments against the Government." At another bridge, Merryman ordered the watchmen "to overturn a cask of water placed there for the protection of the bridge in case of fire." He then poured camphene onto the bridge and lit the fire himself. Like the other members of his company, Merryman claimed that he was obeying orders intended to prevent bloodshed in Maryland by keeping more federal troops from passing through the state. When, on Wednesday, April 24, someone confronted Merryman about the Horse Guards' actions, the angry lieutenant allegedly drew a revolver and retorted, "Damm you, what is it your business, we act under orders."[28]

Accounts of Merryman's behavior during this expedition conflict with the report that he was willing to slaughter his prize-winning cattle to feed the Pennsylvania soldiers. In fact, several local residents observed Merryman trying to intimidate the troops during their encampment. One witness claimed that Merryman shouted: "G—d—m them, we'll stop them from coming down here and stealing our slaves," while another claimed that Merryman "ordered [the] Pennsylvanians to leave the County." According to J. H. Smith, a resident of Wiseburg, Baltimore County, Merryman boasted that the Pennsylvania soldiers "were so badly scared that several of them fell dead when they heard that the Baltimoreans were coming."[29]

Merryman's hyperbole may not have been so far from the truth. His actions apparently affected the troops encamped outside of his home. One soldier from the First Pennsylvania Regiment later recalled: "During the night at Cockeysville we had a number of alarms. The Baltimoreans came near our camp by [the] thousands, and all kinds of wild rumors were being circulated through camp. It was reported that ten thousand Baltimoreans were armed and equipped and marching against us." Fear quickly spread among the green recruits. "One man of Company 'E' became very much frightened, he lay on the ground moaning, 'My God, we will all get killed.'

I grabbed him and held him up between myself and the supposed enemy; and made a kind of shield of him for self-protection; berated him for his cowardice. I, too, was badly frightened but no one knew it but myself."[30]

The Horse Guards patrolled the area throughout April 1861. They arrested several prisoners during this time, including a Pennsylvania deserter and a Baltimore County Unionist. The deserter claimed to be "looking for work" but the Horse Guards "supposed he was a spy." They kept him overnight at Hayfields before transporting him to the public jail at Towsontown. The Unionist, William Lovell, was a carpenter who had said at a local tavern that "the troops ought to have gone through Baltimore." Sergeant Charles Cockey and Corporal Harry Gilmor entered the home of one John Bosley at 11:00 p.m. on April 24 to look for Lovell. Lovell testified that Cockey "drew a pistol and stated that if I made any resistance he would shoot me." Cockey and Gilmor then bound Lovell's arms and forced him to walk three miles to Hayfields. Upon arriving they found Merryman and a dozen other members of the Horse Guards sitting in their uniforms. Merryman approached Lovell and "told me that he had heard that I had been talking too much and that the County was very much excited, that they had their men all through the County, and that they could not have any more such talk." The Horse Guards detained Lovell for the night at Hayfields.[31] It was an ironic moment that can be appreciated only in hindsight: John Merryman, as a militia officer, oversaw the arrest and detention of a Maryland civilian for speaking disloyally against the southern cause.

With the railroad bridges destroyed and Union soldiers unable to pass through Baltimore, federal authorities had to establish a new route from the free states to the capital. General Benjamin F. Butler determined to bypass Baltimore by ferrying soldiers from Perryville to Annapolis and then sending them by rail to Washington. The only problem was that Maryland secessionists had burned railroad bridges near Annapolis as well. Union soldiers set up their quarters at the Naval Academy to guard the city and rebuild the railroad lines, ever vigilant for trouble from local secessionists. "I can sleep on the floor with my sabre and knapsack on with my minie rifle by my side loaded all of the time as well as I can in bed," wrote one Massachusetts soldier to his mother. To the soldiers, the railroad burnings were only a minor setback: "We have taken possesion of the road and are laying down the rails and there are aplenty of machionest in the troops

[who] are putting the Engines together." General Butler placed Annapolis under martial law and "told the mayor if one man belonging to our troops was killed or hurt he would burn a strip a mile wide each side of the rail road track."[32] Within a short while Union soldiers were steadily reaching Washington thanks to Butler's ingenuity in Annapolis.

On April 22, Governor Hicks announced that he would call the Maryland legislature to convene at Annapolis on April 26. Two days later Hicks changed the location to Frederick. The "extraordinary state of affairs existing at the present moment" and Hicks's desire for "the safety and comfort of the members of the Legislature" required the change of location. In truth, there was no telling if General Butler would use his troops at Annapolis to harass or arrest members of the legislature. Situated in western Maryland, Frederick was also more Unionist than Annapolis. Hicks likely hoped that the strong Unionist sentiment there would encourage the legislature to keep from acting rashly. Still, many in the legislature were sympathetic toward the South and resented Hicks for his delaying tactics. They might yet decide to vote Maryland out of the Union.[33]

With pressure mounting all around him, Lincoln determined to take the bold step of suspending the privilege of the writ of habeas corpus. Article I, section 9, of the U.S. Constitution declares, "The Privilege of the Writ of Habeas Corpus shall not be suspended, unless when in Cases of Rebellion or Invasion the public Safety may require it." With Congress out of session, a rebellion in progress, and the Maryland legislature assembling possibly to vote Maryland out of the Union, Lincoln knew he had to take action. While he did not believe it would be "justifiable; nor, efficient" to disperse or arrest the legislators before they acted against the Union, he commanded General Scott "to watch, and await their action, which, if it shall be to arm their people against the United States, he is to adopt the most prompt, and efficient means to counteract, even, if necessary, to the bombardment of their cities—and in the extremest necessity, the suspension of the writ of habeas corpus." Two days later, Lincoln gave Scott explicit authorization to suspend the writ: "You are engaged in repressing an insurrection against the laws of the United States," he told his commanding general. "If at any point" along "the military line" between Philadelphia and Washington "you find resistance which renders it necessary to suspend the writ of Habeas Corpus for the public safety, you, personally or through the officer in command at the point where the resistance occurs, are authorized to suspend the writ."[34]

This was a broad and expansive grant of power—one which Lincoln arguably did not possess the authority to dispense. Because the suspension clause was in Article I of the Constitution, legal authorities in the early republic and antebellum period had assumed that only Congress could suspend the writ.[35] Lincoln's letter of April 25 signified the delicacy with which he approached the suspension issue—the implication being that he might actually feel more comfortable leveling Baltimore than suspending the writ there.[36] But a mere two days later he gave that power not only to his commanding general but also to subordinates in the military.

While Lincoln was grappling with this delicate constitutional issue, Union forces were massing in Annapolis under General Butler. By the second week of May, the railroad bridges around Baltimore had all been repaired. Union troops were now poised to flood into Maryland. On May 13, amid a torrential rain, federal forces under Butler seized control of Baltimore. Butler encamped his troops on Federal Hill with his cannons facing the city. "If I am attacked to-night," he informed the commander at Fort McHenry, "please open upon Monument Square with your mortars." The following day Butler issued a proclamation to the people of Baltimore informing them that loyal citizens and their property would not be molested, but that "rebellious acts must cease." To that end, Butler authorized the confiscation of arms and munitions that might be used by the rebels, he forbade any military drilling within his jurisdiction, and he outlawed the display of any Confederate flags or symbols.[37] On May 14, Butler ordered the arrest of Maryland legislator, secessionist, and inventor Ross Winans. "I . . . thought that if such a man, worth $15,000,000 were hanged for treason," Butler later explained, "it would convince the people of Maryland, at the least, that the expedition we were on was no picnic."[38]

Back in Washington, General Scott was furious at Butler's actions. "Your hazardous occupation of Baltimore was made without my knowledge and of course without my approbation," he wrote to Butler. "It is a God-send that it was without conflict of Arms."[39] On May 15, Scott replaced Butler with General George Cadwalader, a Philadelphia lawyer and veteran of the Mexican War. Upon Cadwalader's arrival at Fort McHenry, Butler headed southward to Hampton Roads, Virginia, where he took command of Fortress Monroe. Butler would again become embroiled in controversy there when he welcomed fugitive slaves at the fort and declared them contraband of war.

On May 16, Assistant Adjutant General E. D. Townsend sent a message to Cadwalader at Fort McHenry: "Herewith you will receive a power to arrest persons under certain circumstances, and to hold them prisoners though they should be demanded by writs of habeas corpus. This is a high and delicate trust, and, as you cannot fail to perceive, to be executed with judgment and discretion. Nevertheless, in times of civil strife, errors, if any, should be on the side of safety to the country." Cadwalader replied that he would execute this power "with prudence and discretion, and with the best judgment I am capable of giving the subject."[40]

The following day, Lincoln wrote out a brief memorandum concerning military arrests in Maryland and the District of Columbia: "Unless the *necessity* for these arbitrary arrests is *manifest,* and *urgent,* I prefer they should cease."[41] But they did not cease. Ross Winans was released on May 16, but other arrests soon followed. One arrest in particular, that of John Merryman—the Baltimore County farmer who had in one breath offered his prize cattle to the Pennsylvania troops and in another cursed them for wanting to steal his slaves—would lead to a "collision" between the president and chief justice of the United States that would impact American jurisprudence for at least a century and a half.

2

"A COLLISION OF CIVIL AND MILITARY AUTHORITY"

The Arrest and Incarceration of John Merryman

The Merryman family had been present in Baltimore County since the middle of the seventeenth century. The Merryman clan grew and spread throughout the county during the eighteenth and nineteenth centuries, owning several significant estates such as "Merryman's Lot," "Merryman's Beginning," "Merryman's Addition," "Merryman's Pasture," "Brotherly Fellowship," "Merryman's Delight," "Merryman's Inclosure Rectified," and "Merryman's Discovery." John Merryman of Hayfields, as he is now known, was born at Hereford Farm on August 9, 1824, just eleven months after his parents, Nicholas Rogers Merryman and Ann Maria Gott, were married. John's mother died in 1829, when he was only four years old. In 1832, Nicholas remarried. John had one sister (who died in infancy) and two half brothers.[1]

In 1839, John Merryman took a job at a hardware store in Baltimore City. Two years later, he moved to Puerto Rico, where he worked in a counting house owned by one of his uncles. He returned to Maryland in July 1842 "to take charge" of his family's farms in Baltimore County; soon thereafter he moved to Hayfields, the 560-acre estate owned by his relative Colonel Nicholas Merryman Bosley. In 1844, John married Ann Louisa Gittings, the nineteen-year-old daughter of Elijah Bosley Gittings and Ann Lux Cockey. Together, John and Ann would have eleven children, ten of whom survived to adulthood. In 1847, Merryman inherited Hayfields from Colonel Bosley, who happened to be not only Merryman's close relative (sometimes called his uncle) but also his wife's great uncle. Bosley had owned the estate since 1811 and had periodically purchased adjoining lands to increase its size. Hayfields was known throughout the state for its beauty. Indeed, in November 1824, the Marquis de Lafayette stopped in Maryland—in between visits to Thomas Jefferson and John Adams—to present Colonel Bosley with "a handsome silver tankard" on behalf of the Maryland Agricultural Society "for the best cultivated farm."[2]

Hayfields continued to flourish under John Merryman's attentive eye. One Pennsylvania visitor to Cockeysville in 1861 noted that Hayfields was a "noble looking mansion, located on an eminence in full-view from the hotel, and but a short distance from Cockeysville." He continued: "The grounds are extensive, and naturally beautiful—fine farm-land, with an inexhaustible supply of limestone. In fact we have never seen finer grain soil or finer looking crops of grain and grass than are to be seen on the whole route of the Central road from York to Cockeysville. Mr. Merryman is a man of considerable property—in fact of great real estate. He is said to be a very clever neighbor, an ambitious politician, but very liberal, and living up to his large income."[3] Merryman was proud of his agricultural pursuits. He was an active member of the Maryland State Agricultural Society, serving as its president from 1857 to 1861, and he served as a trustee of the Maryland Agricultural College—now the University of Maryland at College Park—for about ten years beginning in the 1850s.[4] Merryman raised prize-winning Hereford cattle, the first of which he purchased in 1856 from William Sotham and Erastus Corning, whose name is largely remembered today as the recipient of an 1863 letter from Abraham Lincoln regarding the suspension of habeas corpus.[5]

When Merryman inherited Hayfields in 1847, the inventory of Colonel Bosley's estate showed the "livestock" on his property as including 5 yoke of oxen, 10 cows, 40 hogs, 5 breed sows, 55 sheep, 17 lambs, 10 horses, 4 adult male slaves, 4 adult female slaves, and 2 slave children. Merryman family lore holds that Colonel Bosley drew out the plans for the Hayfields mansion in the ground with his cane and that the home was built by his slaves in the early nineteenth century.[6] By 1860, slavery was on the decline in Baltimore County. Census records from that year indicate that John Merryman owned five slaves, signifying that he had a moderate financial interest in the peculiar institution. In 1860 most slave owners in Maryland owned only one slave; half of the slave owners owned fewer than three slaves; three-quarters of the slaveholders owned fewer than eight;

and 90 percent owned fewer than fifteen. The median slaveholding was three bondsmen. Thus, John Merryman owned slightly above the average number of slaves for a Maryland slaveholder on the eve of the Civil War; but he was not among the largest slave owners in Baltimore County.[7]

John Merryman, like other antebellum southern landowners, played an active role in the state militia system. In 1847, he was commissioned third lieutenant of the Baltimore County Troops. On February 2, 1861, Governor Thomas H. Hicks of Maryland commissioned him first lieutenant of the Baltimore County Horse Guards, a cavalry unit made up of "states' rights gentlemen" that had been formed under Charles H. Ridgely in January 1861 "for the defense of their homes and state."[8] On the night of April 19, Ridgely's band of horsemen, led by Lieutenant Merryman, marched to Fort McHenry to guard "against an anticipated attack from secessionists." When no attack materialized, they returned home to Baltimore County. Over the next few days, the Baltimore County Horse Guards kept picket duty along the York Turnpike between Towsontown and Cockeysville.[9] A company of about twenty-five men under Lieutenant Merryman's command burned several bridges of the Northern Central Railway and cut telegraph wires on the morning of April 23, 1861, as the Pennsylvania troops retreated from Cockeysville back to their home state. Most historians have assumed that Merryman's actions had been on the night of April 19–20; in fact, they came three days later. Merryman's efforts as a militiaman brought him under the scrutiny of Union authorities in the spring of 1861.[10]

On April 27, the War Department divided the seat of war into three military districts. The Department of Pennsylvania included Pennsylvania, Delaware, and sections of Maryland north of Washington, D.C., and Annapolis.[11] Under this jurisdiction, General William High Keim, the second ranking officer in the Pennsylvania militia (although he had only been commissioned on April 20), ordered Colonel Samuel Yohe of the First Pennsylvania Volunteers "to seize the arms of the company near you and arrest the captain if in arms against the Government." On May 21, Yohe ordered a subordinate to "be cautious in your movements and be well satisfied that the captain or any of them are spreading secession sentiments and using their influence in favor of the Southern Confederacy. By all means get the arms. . . . If you arrest the captain take him to General Cadwalader's department. Do not be precipitate. Act coolly and deliberately but determinedly."[12]

On May 22, Assistant Adjutant General Fitz-John Porter ordered Yohe to arrest "any armed bodies of men outside of Baltimore collected with hostile intent . . . by surprise, if possible, and hold them subject to future orders. Men not known to be friendly, drilling at night, or secretly, must be looked upon with suspicion of hostile intent and treated accordingly."[13]

Of all of the Baltimore County Horse Guards who might have been arrested, it appears that John Merryman was chosen because of the disfavor he had earned among his neighbors. According to one local memoir, Unionists in Baltimore County "took a special pleasure in trying to get" members of the Horse Guards "individually and collectively into trouble." Perhaps knowing that the federal soldiers were intent on arresting any troops drilling in the vicinity of Baltimore, "they laid what they thought would be quite a successful plan to capture the Captain and company, who they expected to . . . drill on a certain day." The Unionist plotters "engaged the cooperation of several bodies of [Union] troops from Baltimore & different places in Baltimore County, to effect this result." Unfortunately for the plotters, a Cockeysville Unionist and county judge named John H. Price thought that Captain Ridgely was "too fine a fellow and too good a man to be made the victim of such a mean plot." Price informed Ridgely of the scheme and Ridgely informed his men so that the drill was not held.[14]

Thus, while Keim and Yohe had originally called for the arrest of "the captain" of the Horse Guards, local sentiment would not allow for Ridgely's arrest. Instead, the Horse Guards' first lieutenant, John Merryman, was selected. Merryman appeared to be less popular than Ridgely among his Unionist neighbors. One resident of Baltimore County informed a federal colonel that Merryman had been singled out only "to subserve the petty malice of some personal enemy in his neighborhood." Indeed, Colonel Yohe found ten residents of Baltimore County—including Judge Price of Cockeysville—to testify about Merryman's treason. "As regards Mr. Merryman's case there can be no doubt about his complicity with the Secessionists," wrote Yohe, "and proof sufficient can be had in his neighborhood to establish his guilt."[15]

According to the *New York Tribune*'s Washington correspondent, two men from Cockeysville "informed us, and their character is sufficient voucher for the statement, that no more overbearing, intolerant, and bitter secessionist lives than John Merryman, and that his neighbors would rejoice to hear that he had been hanged as a traitor, as he richly deserves to be. He not only personally superintended the burning of the railroad bridges but he had been active in warning out of the State all those whom he considered as opposed to secession. During the reign of terror, he wrote a notice to a number, and one poor fellow has since died from an illness caused solely, as they say, by excitement brought on by Merryman's threats and persecution."[16]

If such was true, it was now time for Merryman to be held accountable. In fact, rumors that Merryman and other secessionists, like Baltimore police marshal George P. Kane, would be arrested had been swirling around Baltimore since the second week of May.[17] Colonel Yohe prepared the men of the First Pennsylvania for action. On May 25, at 2:00 a.m., a military force entered Merryman's home at Hayfields, arrested him, and sent him to Fort McHenry, in Baltimore harbor. That Merryman was arrested in the middle of the night leaves one to doubt that he was "in arms against the Government," at least not at the time of his arrest.

The military officers at Fort McHenry seemed ambivalent about what exactly their prisoner was charged with doing. In truth, they had not been informed of why they were detaining him.[18] They knew he was suspected of committing some sort of treasonous acts that included "holding a commission" in a militia unit that was hostile toward the government. General George Cadwalader, the commander at Fort McHenry, further claimed that Merryman had "made open and unreserved declarations of his association with this organized force as being in avowed hostility to the Government and in readiness to co-operate with those engaged in the present rebellion against the Government of the United States."[19] But nothing in these original "charges" accused Merryman of burning railroad bridges or cutting telegraph wires, the accusations usually cited by historians. The military's justifications for holding Merryman exhibited a surprising level of ambiguity and lack of specificity as to what exactly John Merryman stood accused of having done.

From prison, Merryman was allowed to contact his counsel and friends. "We learn that Mr. M is well treated in the Fort," reported the *Baltimore County Advocate,* "and that members of his family have free access to him."

Through his lawyers, Baltimore city counselor George M. Gill and the prisoner's brother-in-law, George H. Williams, Merryman immediately petitioned Chief Justice Roger B. Taney, a fellow Marylander, for a writ of habeas corpus. This writ, one of the bulwarks of freedom for Englishmen, required the arresting officer to bring "the body" of the prisoner before a court so that the prisoner could either be charged and sent back to prison or be released. Merryman petitioned Taney for the writ because Taney's jurisdiction as a circuit justice included the U.S. circuit court in Baltimore. On Sunday, May 26, Merryman's petition was delivered to Taney at his home in Washington, D.C. The aged judge immediately traveled north to Baltimore and convened a court session to hear the case. The chief justice issued the desired writ, ordering General Cadwalader to bring "the body" of Merryman from Fort McHenry to his courtroom at the Masonic Hall in Baltimore at 11:00 a.m. the following day.[20]

About two thousand people crowded outside the Masonic Hall on the morning of Monday, May 27. As the chief justice passed by, walking slowly while leaning on his grandson's arm, "the crowd silently and with lifted hats opened the way for him to pass." The northern press reported that 150 men, "armed to the teeth," had lined the courtroom to force Merryman's release if he was brought into court.[21]

At 11:00 a.m. sharp Taney took his seat in the courtroom. After a few minutes, one of General Cadwalader's subordinates appeared before the court in full military regalia. He presented to the court a letter from the general that explained why Merryman could not be brought before Taney at this time. Merryman was charged with "various acts of treason" and was an officer in a military company that was armed against the United States. Moreover, Cadwalader argued, the president had authorized him "in such cases to suspend the writ of Habeas Corpus for the Public Safety." Cadwalader echoed his earlier correspondence with the War Department: "This is a high and delicate trust and it has been enjoined upon him that it should be executed with judgment and discretion, but he is nevertheless also instructed that in times of civil strife errors, if any, should be on the side of safety to the Country." Cadwalader then asked Chief Justice Taney to postpone any further action in this case to avoid further embarrassment to the national government.[22]

Cadwalader's letter was the first time that Taney had heard of the suspension of habeas corpus. As might be expected, he was indignant and he immediately ordered an attachment against Cadwalader for contempt. The following day the U.S. marshal went to Fort McHenry to deliver the attachment, but he was denied admittance to the fort, so he returned to the court with the attachment still in hand. Taney informed the marshal that he could summon a *posse comitatus* to aid in the seizure of General Cadwalader, but as the military force was vastly superior to any force the marshal might be able to muster, the chief justice released him from any further duties in the case. Taney stated that he had issued the attachment for contempt because the president did not possess the authority to suspend the writ of habeas corpus (nor may he authorize a military commander to do so); furthermore, the military had no right to arrest and detain a civilian except when aiding the judicial authorities of the United States. Taney then stated that he would file a written opinion in the case and ensure that a copy was given to the president.[23]

Because General Cadwalader refused to bring Merryman before the court, Chief Justice Taney was unable to pronounce any opinion upon the merits of Merryman's arrest. Thus, Taney had to limit himself to the question of who had the power to suspend the writ of habeas corpus. In his written opinion, which the chief justice delivered to a "crowded" courtroom on June 1, Taney argued that Merryman's arrest and detention were illegal because they had been done without a warrant or any specific charges. He censured Lincoln for never declaring martial law or officially suspending the writ of habeas corpus, but he also argued that only Congress could lawfully suspend the writ. In short, Taney believed "that the president has exercised a power which he does not possess under the constitution." Moreover: "He certainly does not faithfully execute the laws, if he takes upon himself legislative power, by suspending the writ of habeas corpus, and the judicial power also, by arresting and imprisoning a person without due process of law." Taney chastised the military authorities for "thrust[ing] aside" the judicial powers in Maryland when there was no danger of obstruction of justice by the civil authorities (although Taney must have been aware that the civil authorities had ordered the burning of the railroad bridges). And he reprimanded the military for undertaking the judicial function of defining the legal concepts of treason and rebellion, as well as for ignoring the protections of the Bill of Rights.

Taney concluded on a sorrowful note: "Such is the case now before me, and I can only say that if the authority which the constitution has confided to the judiciary department and judicial officers, may thus, upon any pretext or under any circumstances, be usurped by the military power, at its discretion, the people of the United States are no longer living under a government of laws, but every citizen holds life, liberty and property at the will and pleasure of the army officer in whose military district he may happen to be found." The chief justice then added a stern admonition to the president: "I have exercised all the power which the constitution and laws confer upon me, but that power has been resisted by a force too strong for me to overcome. . . . It will then remain for that high officer, in fulfillment of his constitutional obligation to 'take care that the laws be faithfully executed,' to determine what measures he will take to cause the civil process of the United States to be respected and enforced."[24]

When Taney finished delivering his opinion, the crowded courtroom expressed "great indignation" against Lincoln. Andrew Sterrett Ridgely, a prominent Baltimore lawyer and the son-in-law of Reverdy Johnson, "was very decided in his views and was willing to form one of a posse comitatus to proceed to the Fort, demand the prisoner and sustain the majesty of the law." Confederate sympathizers throughout Maryland also seized upon Taney's opinion in the *Merryman* case to fan the flames of hostility against Lincoln.[25]

Newspaper reaction to the Merryman affair was swift and pointed. Republican papers held that executive discretion trumped the judicial power in wartime. The *New York Tribune* said that Chief Justice Taney— "the hoary apologist for crime"—had issued the writ without any necessity or warrant, but only because he wanted to side with the traitors. In time of peace, the editors of the *Tribune* conceded, a writ of habeas corpus ought to be issued, but it is "not a weapon of war." "The attempt to rescue [Merryman] by writ of habeas corpus was wholly unnecessary, and eminently unpatriotic. No Judge whose heart was loyal to the Constitution would have given such aid and comfort to public enemies." Merryman was certainly a traitor; he therefore should be confined at Fort McHenry until it was safe to release him or commit him to a civil trial. In the meantime, the courts ought not to interfere. "The times are perilous," continued the editors of the *Tribune*. "We advise [the judges of the Supreme Court] to attend to their appropriate duties in the Courts, and leave the task of overthrowing this formidable conspiracy against Liberty and Law to the military and naval forces of the United States." The editors concluded that Taney was "the leader of the Secessionists of Maryland" and a "rebellious judicial autocrat," whose opinion was "as full of aid and comfort for the traitors generally as an egg is of meat."[26]

Similarly, the *New York Times* accused Taney of wanting "to bring a collision between the Judicial and the Military Departments of the Government, and if possible to throw the weight of the judiciary against the United States and in favor of the rebels," for Taney was "at heart a rebel himself." The *Times* found the controversy between the courts and the military unfortunate: "A collision of civil and military authority is always to be, if possible, shunned; because the majesty of law must, in all cases, succumb to the necessities of war, and the respect which the magistracy must assert for itself in a period of peace, is impaired by the sight of a fruitless struggle for supremacy at a period when military law is in the ascendant. In the case of John Merriman, the interposition of Chief Justice Taney can only be regarded as at once officious and improper."[27]

Even some nonpartisan presses were critical of the chief justice. The *New York World*—in 1861 a politically independent paper, though later to become a Democratic organ—criticized Taney for the injudicious tone of his courtroom remarks toward the president: "It is consistent neither with dignity nor courtesy for one high public functionary either to lecture another on the necessity of doing his duty or to give notice of such an intended lecture." The *World* further chastised Taney for writing an opinion that was "so obviously intended as a grave inculpation of the President of the United States" and for seeking "to weaken and undermine the confidence of the country in the President. In the midst of a rebellion which threatens the very existence of the government, its highest judicial officer volunteers the weight of his influence and of the influence of his high position in favor of the rebels."[28]

Moderate newspapers acknowledged what they saw as Taney's correct legal reasoning but stated that his decision in *Merryman* was untimely. One such editor believed that Taney's opinion was "correct . . . but ignoring the emergency."[29] The *National Intelligencer,* in Washington, D.C., which had supported the Bell-Everett ticket in 1860, argued that "every reader will give to this opinion the consideration it deserves, as well for the high source from which it emanates as for the cogency of the legal argument it contains." In a sense, Taney's opinion would be for the future rather than the present—to "stand as a warning in more peaceful times yet to come that here is an act the necessity of which was its justification, and which is not to be made a precedent at any time when the public exigency is less pressing."[30]

Many Democratic papers, by contrast, reprinted Taney's opinion and lavished it with praise. The *Crisis,* in Columbus, Ohio, argued that the military should interfere in civilian affairs only if the judiciary had failed to do its duty. Moreover, the editors of the *Crisis* worried that the nation had reached a "point in our history when men on mere *suspicion* of *political opponents,* are deprived of their liberty, and incarcerated in our jails, or held by military power." The judiciary was on the verge of being "converted into mere partisan assemblies" with newspaper editors acting as judges and the government administering "*vengeance* instead of *justice.*"[31] The *New York Weekly Journal of Commerce* saw the Merryman affair as "a collision between the law as it stands recorded, and its sworn administrators." Its editors pointed out that the writ was not intended to protect the loyal only, but also those accused of treason:

> The remark of one of the New York papers that the writ was "originally intended to secure the liberty of loyal men," and that "it would be a gross perversion of its powers to employ it as the protecting shield of rebels," is a specimen of the very tyranny which the writ of *habeas corpus* is designed to overcome. The writ was originally and always intended as a defence of the subject against the tyranny of the government; and nowhere is such defence more needed than under a government like our own. The article in the Tribune, to which we refer, is the grossest perversion of right and of free principles that ever disgraced the pages of a New York paper. Says the Tribune,—"of all the tyrannies that afflict mankind, that of the Judiciary is the most insidious, the most intolerable, the most dangerous."!!

To the editors of the *Journal of Commerce,* all of Lincoln's constitutional abuses justified the South in the course of action it had taken. If Lincoln so freely deprived northerners of their constitutional rights, southerners, of course, could expect only worse. The *Brooklyn Daily Eagle,* another Democratic paper, simply remarked that the "collision" between Taney and the military was not a "conflict of laws" but "a conflict between law and illegal violence, in which law suffered total defeat" because military commanders, at their own discretion, could arrest civilians suspected of "political offences," and "the Supreme Court of the United States is summarily set aside by order of President Lincoln."[32]

Upon reading the reports of the *Merryman* proceedings in the newspapers, General Cadwalader's brother, John, who was a U.S. district judge in Philadelphia, wrote out a private legal opinion on the case. Judge Cadwalader argued that the appropriate question was "not . . . whether the writ of habeas corpus is, or should be, suspended, but whether the case is a proper one for the enforcement of the mandate of such a writ." In other words, Judge Cadwalader agreed with Taney that only Congress could suspend the writ, but he believed that if his brother had responded in a different way, the collision between the president and the judiciary might have been avoided. According to the judge, General Cadwalader should have claimed that Merryman—as a militia officer—was being held as a prisoner of war who had been arrested for being "mustered in hostile array" against the United States. Judge Cadwalader, a Democrat, believed that if his brother had made such a claim then Chief Justice Taney "might have refused to award the habeas corpus" to Merryman or even "might . . . have excused [General Cadwalader for] not bringing in the body." But since Merryman was being held by the military as a civilian prisoner, the judge believed "it was absolutely necessary for [Taney] to issue the writ." "Legal Process," he concluded, "cannot be thus delayed where any question of right, and particularly the right of personal liberty, is concerned."[33]

Judge Cadwalader anonymously sent the opinion to his brother. As a judge, he desired to see the civil law upheld in time of war. In fact, for years following the war, Cadwalader family lore had it that "if Judge John had issued the writ, he would have damn well made his brother obey it."[34] But the judge's opinion could have little impact on the situation. On the one hand, General Cadwalader could not recant his letter to Taney in which he claimed Merryman as a civilian prisoner who was charged with various acts of treason. On the other hand, Chief Justice Taney was unlikely to accept a claim from the military that Merryman was being lawfully detained as a prisoner of war. Taney's decision in the case had been motivated by several factors. To be sure, Taney saw himself as upholding the majesty of the law. At the same time, Taney's private animus toward Lincoln and the "Black Republicans" exudes from his written opinion. Privately, the chief justice also hoped that the southern Confederacy would be allowed to go in peace.[35] His personal opinions, therefore, had a significant impact on his judicial decision. Despite the soundness of Judge Cadwalader's legal reasoning, Chief Justice Taney was unlikely to come to any conclusion that would have justified the military in continuing to detain a civilian prisoner.

Nevertheless, Taney privately professed to want no collision with the president. "I certainly desire no conflict with the Executive Department of the Government; and would be glad, as you will readily suppose, to pass the brief remnant of life that may yet be vouchsafed to me in peace with all men, and in the quiet discharge of every-day judicial duties," wrote the aged chief justice. "Yet, I trust I shall always be found ready to meet any responsibility or any consequence that my official duty may require me to encounter." While he was alarmed and saddened by the reaction of much of the North to Lincoln's suspension of the writ, he still found it gratifying "to see the judiciary firmly performing its duty and resisting all attempts to substitute military power in the place of judicial authorities." The *Merryman* case had placed a "grave responsibility" upon the old Democrat. "But my duty was plain—and that duty required me to meet the question directly and firmly, without evasion—whatever might be the consequences to myself."[36]

Taney made it clear to observers in the courtroom that he would stand on principle even if so standing made him vulnerable to dangerous physical or partisan attacks. He told the British consul in Baltimore "that he had been brought up to study, & revere, the English Common Law, and that, pained as he was to be so obliged, at such a moment, he would not shrink from asserting its glorious principles, which were likewise those of the Constitution of the United States." When Mayor George William Brown of Baltimore approached the bench to thank Chief Justice Taney for the position he was taking, the judge replied, "I am an old man, a very old man, but perhaps I was preserved for this occasion." "Sir, I thank God that you were," rejoined the mayor.[37]

This occasion for which Taney was preserved proved to be a major turning point in the Lincoln administration's dealings with the courts. Taney believed that he would be arrested. Rumors circulated throughout the North that he had resigned, or that his functions as a judge would be suspended. "There is a fear abroad among the rebels that . . . [Taney] will suddenly find himself in the embraces of the strong arm of that same military power which he is so defiant of," editorialized the *New York Tribune*. The *New York World* suggested that a civil trial for Merryman would be preferable, but if Taney did not impartially fulfill his duty as a trial judge, then Congress could impeach him.[38]

But none of these things happened. Taney continued to sit as a judge; articles of impeachment were never brought against him; he was never arrested. Instead, Lincoln simply ignored both the judge and his opinion. The president then directed Attorney General Edward Bates to write an opinion on suspension of habeas corpus, which, of course, justified all of the president's actions.[39] Finally, on July 4, 1861, Lincoln publicly defended the course he had taken in a message to Congress, which he called into session on the nation's eighty-fifth birthday.

In answer to Taney and his other critics, Lincoln argued that the momentous issue of civil war "presents to the whole family of man, the question, whether a constitutional republic, or a democracy . . . can, or cannot, maintain its territorial integrity, against its own domestic foes." Or put another way, "Must a government, of necessity, be too strong for the liberties of its own people, or too weak to maintain its own existence?" In Lincoln's mind, it was neither of these things. The people's liberty would be protected, but the government would also flex its muscle enough to stamp out treason and insurrection. "So viewing the issue," said Lincoln, "no choice was left but to call out the war power of the Government; and so to resist force, employed for its destruction, by force, for its preservation."[40]

At this point Lincoln explained the course of action he had taken. After calling out the militia for the nation's defense, he authorized his commanding general, Winfield Scott, to suspend the writ of habeas corpus and, at his own discretion, to detain "such individuals as he might deem dangerous to the public safety." This authority, according to Lincoln, was exercised "sparingly." Still, because Lincoln's actions were being challenged in the courts and by the Democratic press, Lincoln felt obliged to answer his detractors with the constitutional grounding for his actions. He re-minded the nation that all of the laws were being resisted in a large part of the Union. Lincoln wondered if those laws should all be allowed to fail even if he could preserve them by violating one single law. "To state the question more directly," continued the president, "are all the laws, *but one,* to go unexecuted, and the government itself go to pieces, lest that one be violated? Even in such a case, would not the official oath be broken, if the government should be overthrown, when it was believed that disregarding the single law, would tend to preserve it?" But Lincoln denied that any law had been broken, for the Constitution allowed the writ to be suspended "when in cases of rebellion or invasion, the public safety may require it," and Lincoln certainly faced a case of rebellion. For those who claimed that only Congress could suspend the writ, Lincoln replied that "the Constitu-tion itself, is silent as to which, or who, is to exercise the power; and as the provision was plainly made for a dangerous emergency, it cannot be be-lieved the framers of the instrument intended, that in every case, the dan-ger should run its course, until Congress could be called together; the very assembling of which might be prevented, as was intended in this case, by the rebellion."[41]

In this passage Lincoln appealed to the intentions of the framers, thus showing his desire to construe the meaning of the Constitution in accor-dance with their understanding. But the text was ambiguous. It declared that the writ could be suspended, but it never clearly stated by whom. Considering the circumstances—a rebellion gaining momentum and Congress out of session—Lincoln deemed it necessary, expedient, and constitutional to authorize suspension of the writ himself. In so doing, he asserted himself as a final arbiter on the meaning of the Constitution, independent of what Taney or any other member of the judiciary had to say. Lincoln, in effect, gutted *Ex parte Merryman* of any legal significance and determined that as long as the war lasted *Merryman* would have no practical effect.

~

One significant point of disagreement among historians and political sci-entists is whether Roger Taney heard *Ex parte Merryman* as a U.S. circuit judge or as a Supreme Court justice in chambers. Throughout the nineteenth century, federal law required Supreme Court justices to "ride circuit." For several months each year, each justice traveled throughout his assigned judicial circuit, holding U.S. circuit court sessions with the local federal district judges in each judicial district within the circuit. The district courts and circuit courts were both trial courts, although the circuit courts generally handled cases of greater significance, as well as some appeals from the district courts. Section 14 of the Judiciary Act of 1789 authorized the judges of the district, circuit, and Supreme courts to issue writs of habeas corpus.[42]

As we have already seen, Chief Justice Taney's circuit included the District of Maryland. At Baltimore, the chief justice and U.S. district judge William Fell Giles presided together over the U.S. Circuit Court for the District of Maryland. Giles, a fifty-four-year-old Maryland Democrat, had been appointed to the federal bench in 1853 by President Franklin Pierce. Chief Justice Taney heard Merryman's petition without Judge Giles present on the bench. At issue is whether Taney presided over the *Merryman* proceedings as a circuit judge or as a Supreme Court justice.

Jeffrey Rosen, Melvin I. Urofsky, Craig R. Smith, Douglas L. Wilson, and others contend that Taney issued his ruling in *Ex parte Merryman* as a circuit judge.[43] Others disagree. Brian McGinty writes: "Although the precise capacity in which the decision was made is not entirely clear, the better view seems to agree with Taney that it was a decision of the chief justice 'in chambers.' . . . When Taney issued the writ in *Ex parte Merryman,* the full Supreme Court was not in session, and he explicitly stated that he was acting in chambers. Interestingly, Judge Giles's absence during the *Merryman* hearing is explainable if the decision was an in-chambers decision of the chief justice. If it had been a circuit court decision, Giles would have had every right to participate, and would normally have done so. If it was an in-chambers decision, however, he had no right to participate."[44] (Judge Giles's absence does not necessarily mean that *Ex parte Merryman* was a Supreme Court decision in chambers. Section 4 of the Judiciary Act of 1802 allowed a U.S. district judge or a circuit justice to hold sessions of a circuit court in the absence of the other judge.)[45] Mark Neely writes in a similar vein: "Taney made it plain that he was issuing the opinion from the Supreme Court 'in chambers' and that his jurisdiction to hear the case stemmed from the provision of the Judiciary Act of 1789 giving Supreme Court justices as well as federal judges original jurisdiction in habeas corpus cases for federal prisoners." Daniel A. Farber agrees: "Technically, he did not issue it in his capacity as a judge 'on circuit' but rather as an 'in chambers' opinion of the chief justice."[46] James G. Randall offered a carefully nuanced interpretation: "The Merryman decision was not that of the Supreme Court; but it was an opinion of one member of the Court, Taney, in a case which he heard while on circuit. Furthermore, it was in chambers, not in open court, that the decision was rendered."[47]

For as significant a case as *Ex parte Merryman* is, it seems it would be important to be clear as to whether this was a Supreme Court decision, the opinion of a Supreme Court justice in chambers, or the decision of a circuit judge. The confusion derives from the fact that Taney wrote "At Chambers" on his opinion, insinuating that he heard the case as the chief justice of the United States rather than as a justice riding circuit and serving as a circuit judge. Ironically, the most common source historians cite regarding the *Merryman* case, West Publishing Company's *Federal Cases,* did not include "in chambers" or "at chambers" in its report of the case. Rather, West's editors began their report: "TANEY, Circuit Justice," which was language they created out of whole cloth.[48] The compilers of *Federal Cases* likely omitted the "at chambers" notation because they believed it would have forced them to exclude the case from the series they were producing (*Federal Cases* was limited to only U.S. district court and U.S. circuit court cases). Historians who have noted Taney's "at chambers" reference have found it in other contemporary sources.

It is thus not unreasonable to assume that Taney was acting in his capacity as a Supreme Court justice in chambers.[49] But the original manuscript court records reveal further details that cast doubt on the "Supreme Court" interpretation. When Merryman and his lawyers petitioned Taney, they addressed their petition "To the Honorable Roger B Taney Chief Justice of the Supreme Court of the United States and Judge of the Circuit Court of the United States in and for the District of Maryland." *Federal Cases*—the source most relied on by legal scholars—reports the petition as being addressed "To the Hon. Roger B. Taney, Chief Justice of the Supreme Court of the United States." The reason for this discrepancy is that Taney crossed out the latter half of the address to make it appear as though the petition had been addressed to him only as "Chief Justice of the Supreme Court of the United States."[50] The petitioners, however, had understood themselves to be petitioning him as a justice on circuit.

Merryman's lawyers were likely aware that Supreme Court precedent required them to petition Taney as a justice riding circuit rather than as a member of the Supreme Court. In 1807, Chief Justice John Marshall had ruled for the Supreme Court in *Ex parte Bollman* that the high court could issue writs of habeas corpus only as part of its appellate jurisdiction—that is, to petitioners who were detained by the ruling or order of a federal trial court. (Marshall's holding in *Bollman* was in keeping with his earlier decision in *Marbury v. Madison* [1803] that Congress could not extend the original jurisdiction of the Court beyond what Article III of the Constitution stipulated.) It thus followed that Merryman's lawyers addressed Taney not only by his highest formal title but also by the title that had practical import in this case. It was Taney who hoped to obfuscate the public's perception of the case. Historian Bruce A. Ragsdale aptly notes, "Taney appears to have represented himself as Chief Justice to the extent that he could without asserting the authority of the Supreme Court, which he knew would have had no jurisdiction in the case." According to Ragsdale, Taney "appeared deliberately to raise the profile of the *Merryman* case with suggestions that he was acting in his capacity as Chief Justice rather than as a judge on the circuit court of Maryland."[51] Hence the confusion among observers at the time and scholars since who referred to and still refer to the case as a Supreme Court decision.

Taney's handwritten draft of his *Ex parte Merryman* opinion reveals the evolution in chief justice's thought as he worked and reworked his landmark decision. In the first draft, Taney required Cadwalader "to produce the prisoner before the court in order that I may examine" the case. Taney crossed out "the court" and inserted "a judicial tribunal" in pen. Taney then crossed out "a judicial tribunal" and "I" and inserted in pencil "a justice of the Sup. Court" and "he" so that that sentence now read, "requiring him to produce the prisoner before a justice of the Sup. Court in order that he may examine . . ."[52] While the final version was technically correct—Taney was a justice of the Supreme Court—the first and second drafts were more forthright. Taney made these changes so that he could appear as a Supreme Court justice in chambers rather than as a justice riding circuit, but the initial drafts reveal Taney's awareness that he was presiding over a session of a circuit court.

Other court records confirm that the case was a circuit court decision in which Taney attempted to exploit his position as chief justice. *Federal Cases* reports that at the court session on May 28, Taney said he would "put my opinion in writing, and file it in the office of the clerk of the circuit court, in the course of this week." The manuscript version reveals that Taney had originally pledged to "file it in the office of the Clerk of the Supreme Court," but that he crossed out the word "Supreme" and replaced it with "Circuit." Taney was careful not to file *Ex parte Merryman* as an official Supreme Court decision precisely because it was not a Supreme Court decision. The clerk of the circuit court followed Taney's instructions. "Be it remembered that on this 3d day of June in the year aforesaid," stated the clerk, "the papers and proceedings in the foregoing case were filed in this court and recorded and a copy thereof are hereby transmitted to the President of the United States."[53] The fact that the records are still with the clerk's office at the U.S. District Court for the District of Maryland, rather than in the records of the Supreme Court in Record Group 267 at the National Archives, is clear evidence of *Ex parte Merryman*'s provenance as a lower federal court decision.[54]

~

Taney's handling of the *Merryman* proceedings had a notable effect on how the military dealt with other accused bridge burners. On May 30, three other men from Cockeysville—George E. Worthington, Alfred H. Matthews, and Harrison Scott—were arrested by the military for their part in the acts of the previous month. Rather than imprison them within Taney's circuit at Fort McHenry, however, General Keim sent them north of the Mason-Dixon Line and imprisoned them "in the common jail" in York County, Pennsylvania. The three men secured Merryman's brother-in-law, George H. Williams, and prominent Philadelphia Democrat George M. Wharton as their counsel. Williams and Wharton petitioned the judges of the U.S. Circuit Court for the Eastern District of Pennsylvania, Justice Robert C. Grier and Judge John Cadwalader (the general's brother), for a writ of habeas corpus in each case. The U.S. attorney in

Philadelphia reported to Attorney General Edward Bates that these bridge burners were acting "in imitation of the Merriman case."[55]

When the case came before the court on June 4, the bridge burners' attorney, George Williams, "was not present, the reason alleged for his absence being the fear of personal violence from a mob." In fact, Williams had returned to Baltimore after hearing rumors that the military had been authorized to hang him if he appeared in court. Just before leaving Philadelphia, however, Williams learned that the three detainees had been released and sent home, thus negating any need for further judicial action. At the hearing, Wharton informed Cadwalader of these developments. According to one spectator in the courtroom, "Judge Cadwalader, in reply, said that, unless Mr. Wharton called the case up for some purpose, he had nothing before the court."[56] The *Merryman* proceedings had taught the military to avoid unnecessary collisions with civil authorities when possible. The military shrewdly removed the three bridge burners from Taney's jurisdiction and then released them from prison before another court could issue any major pronouncements in their cases.

3

"PROSECUTE YOUR BEST CASES—NOT THE WEAK AND DOUBTFUL"

The Difficulty of Punishing Disloyalty in the Loyal States

John Merryman's arrest was only one of many to come in Maryland during the Civil War. Union authorities quickly found that "arbitrary arrests" —which were in fact rarely arbitrary—were a useful tool for silencing dissent and stopping the spread of disloyalty in a region that often seemed to be teetering on the edge of rebellion. Fearing that there were many influential "malcontents in Baltimore" who would never support the Union, Attorney General Edward Bates warned, "To keep them quiet we must make them conscious that they stand in the presence of coercive power." The federal government willingly exercised that power in Maryland throughout the Civil War. Between April and September 1861, the Union military clamped down on the disloyal elements of Baltimore society. Rather than risk arrest and imprisonment, many Maryland secessionists moderated their tone in public. "There is a Lot of Rebels in Baltimore," observed one Massachusetts soldier in July 1861, "But they Dont dare do anything."[1]

Union authorities in Washington believed that disloyal elements in Baltimore's city hall needed to be removed in order to maintain peace and order in the city. On June 24, 1861, General Winfield Scott issued an order authorizing the arrest of Baltimore's four police commissioners and Police Marshal George P. Kane, all of whom were suspected of being secessionists. The order stated, "It is the opinion of the Secretary of War, and I need not add my own, that the blow should be early struck, to carry consternation into the ranks of our numerous enemies about you." In partial compliance with this order, General Nathaniel P. Banks detailed 1,800 Union soldiers to arrest Kane at his home. At 2:00 a.m. on June 27, the soldiers marched to Kane's house and called up to him to come down from his bed. Kane appeared at his front door "partially dressed" and was "at once seized" and sent to Fort McHenry. When the Baltimore police commissioners subsequently attempted to retaliate by disbanding the police force, Banks fulfilled the remainder of his orders and had them arrested as well, at 4:00 a.m. on July 1. Later that year, the military arrested about thirty "disloyal members" of the Maryland General Assembly, the mayor of Baltimore, a Maryland congressman, and other civilians from the state. The Lincoln administration believed that these arrests were necessary to prevent the state from seceding. Simon Cameron, who was secretary of war at the time, would later claim not to have given the orders for the arrest of the police. While this was perhaps technically true, Cameron appeared—at least in Scott's order—to have directed and approved of what transpired.[2]

In July 1861, Congressman Henry May of Maryland introduced a resolution in the House of Representatives asking Lincoln to give "the grounds, reasons, and evidence, upon which the Police Commissioners of Baltimore were arrested, and are now detained as prisoners at Fort McHenry." The House adopted the resolution with an amendment to ask the president for the information only "if in his judgment not incompatible with the public interest." Seizing the language from this nonbinding resolution, Lincoln replied to the House that "it is judged to be incompatible with the public interest at this time to furnish the information called for by the resolution."[3] The Marylanders thus continued to sit in prison without knowing the cause of their arrest.

On July 4, 1861, Secretary of War Cameron visited John Merryman and the other civilian prisoners at Fort McHenry. Cameron assured incarcerated Police Commissioner Charles Howard and his son, newspaperman Frank Key Howard, that the political prisoners would be given suitable quarters while held in confinement. Charles and Frank Key Howard were, ironically, the son-in-law and grandson, respectively, of Roger B. Taney's brother-in-law, Francis Scott Key, who had written "The Star-Spangled Banner" while watching the British bomb Fort McHenry in 1814. Cameron also reportedly informed Merryman that he "was to have been discharged" and that "the order for his discharge had in fact been written" but that "in the press of business" the secretary had accidentally "overlooked" it. "When Merryman applied for the writ of *habeas corpus*," according to

Severn Teackle Wallis, a Maryland legislator who would later be arrested for disloyalty, the Lincoln administration "became offended, withdrew the order, & he has been since held & indicted for treason, because of his effort (as they say) 'to bring the Judiciary in conflict with the Executive.' In other words, he has been *punished* for using a lawful right, secured to him by the constitution."[4]

About one week after Cameron's visit to Fort McHenry, John Merryman was turned over to federal civil authorities and indicted for treason in the U.S. District Court for the District of Maryland.[5] Because treason was a capital offense, his case was remitted to the U.S. Circuit Court for the District of Maryland.[6] Merryman's case was one of about sixty treason cases before that court.[7] The judges who would preside over these cases were Roger B. Taney and William F. Giles, the U.S. district judge for the District of Maryland. Republicans likely hoped that Merryman would hang, while Democrats professed to want his case "disposed of by the courts in proper form."[8]

On July 10, 1861, a federal grand jury in Baltimore, "composed entirely of unconditional Union men," returned an indictment for treason against Merryman. The U.S. attorney for the District of Maryland, William Meade Addison, based the Merryman indictment on a printed indictment that he had prepared for the many treason indictments brought against those who had participated in the Baltimore Riot of April 19. Where changes needed to be made, Addison crossed out words in the printed indictment and inserted new words, by hand, describing the acts of treason that John Merryman was accused of committing. As was typical for eighteenth- and nineteenth-century treason indictments in the United States, Addison borrowed language from the old English law of treason. The indictment prefaced the charges by saying that Merryman, "wickedly devising and intending the peace and tranquility of the United States of America to disturb, and to stir, move, excite, levy and carry on war, insurrection and rebellion against the United States of America . . . unlawfully, falsely, maliciously and traitorously with force and arms, did compass, imagine and intend to raise and levy war, insurrection and rebellion against the United States of America."[9]

The indictment, which spans eight pages, charged Merryman with traitorously assembling with "five hundred persons and upwards, armed and arrayed in a warlike manner" to levy war against the United States, and with traitorously adhering to those in rebellion against the United States. The indictment specifically charged Merryman with committing two overt acts of treason: 1) burning "six bridges on . . . 'the Northern Central Railroad,' with intent then and there to hinder, delay and prevent the passage and movement of military troops" to defend the nation's capital; and, 2) destroying telegraph wires "with the intent to prevent the speedy and rapid transmission of intelligence & thereby embarrass, obstruct[,] hinder and delay the said United States . . . in the prompt adoption of the measures necessary for the defence of the United States."[10] One of the seventeen witnesses against Merryman, Samuel Worthington, would later be held liable for burning railroad bridges as well.[11]

U.S. attorney Addison knew that when writing a treason indictment he had to be careful and thorough in constructing the charges. After all, if Aaron Burr had been charged differently in 1807, he might have been convicted rather than acquitted. As a consequence, Addison explained to Attorney General Edward Bates: "I adopted the plan of adding counts for *'levying war,'* when the act committed was *'aiding & abetting'*" so that all of his bases were covered.[12]

Despite Addison's painstaking work, Merryman's case never went to trial. On July 13, 1861, Merryman appeared in court before Judge Giles and, with the assistance of several friends, posted $40,000 bail. He went home a free man.[13] Chief Justice Taney then purposefully thwarted the prosecutions in *U.S. v. Merryman* and the other sixty treason cases in Baltimore, in part because he empathized with the defendants' southern sympathies and in part because he believed that it would be impossible to conduct fair and impartial trials while Maryland was under martial law. Taney informed Judge Giles that a district judge could not hear capital cases without the circuit justice present as well.[14] Old and infirm, Taney was unable to attend many of the circuit court's sessions, thus forcing the cases to be continued from term to term.[15]

Over time, President Lincoln came to doubt the loyalty of his federal prosecutor in Baltimore. When initially dispensing patronage in Maryland, in April 1861, Lincoln decided not to fill the slot of district attorney for the District of Maryland, but to leave the position with William Meade Addison, a Douglas Democrat who had been appointed in 1853 by President Franklin Pierce. Lincoln likely believed that retaining a northern Democrat in an important office might demonstrate to uneasy Marylanders that he was willing to keep their state in the Union by conciliation. "May I say to you that in my judgment the removal of Mr. Addison would be injurious to the cause of the *Union* in Maryland," one Baltimorean had told the president. Reverdy Johnson and other prominent Unionists agreed.[16]

Maryland abolitionists, however, were dissatisfied with Lincoln's decision. Worthington G. Snethen of Baltimore warned General Winfield Scott that indictments for treason would go nowhere "so long as Addison is the U.S. District Attorney." Instead, "a true-hearted, loyal man, ought to be put in Addison's place."[17] In August 1861, Lincoln solicited General John A. Dix's opinion of the U.S. attorney in Baltimore. Dix replied that Addison was not "what I should call an efficient man." While Dix saw Addison as "a gentleman of the most unexceptionable social, moral & religious character, and a fair lawyer," he was not "an active or an energetic man" and his residence outside of Baltimore had caused him to be absent on occasions when he was needed.[18] General Nathaniel P. Banks offered a more dire prediction: "If the Government expects impartial trials or judgments, it is absolutely necessary that the prosecuting attorney should be a zealous efficient and capable law officer," he told Attorney General Bates. "Without this a trial will be a mockery of justice, both as it regards the law of the court and the verdict of juries. It is of vital importance that the rights of the Government should be firmly protected in this regard, and I cannot deny that I feel great solicitude in the present condition of affairs, as to the result of any trial in which the interest of the United States may be involved."[19]

By the summer of 1861, Lincoln began to rethink his decision not to appoint a new U.S. attorney in Baltimore. In October 1861, Attorney General Bates informed Lincoln that *if* he was going to remove Addison from office, "it ought to be done with little delay, because the Court will sit in Baltimore a week from next Monday, and there are several indictments for treason pending therein." During the winter of 1861–62, Addison endured a "long & severe illness" that prevented him from doing his duties as a federal prosecutor. Now the president had an easy excuse to replace him.[20]

In May 1862, President Lincoln removed Addison from office and appointed William Price U.S. attorney for the District of Maryland. An antebellum Whig, Price had opposed Lincoln's candidacy in 1860 (presumably in favor of the Bell-Everett ticket), but once the Rail Splitter was elected, Price stood publicly and firmly in support of the president-elect and the Union. A fierce political fighter—he had once fought a duel with a sitting congressman—Price spoke publicly in January 1861 in favor of military coercion of the seceding states. By the time of the war, Price had a reputation in Maryland as an eminent statesman (he was the second choice of the Maryland legislature for U.S. Senate in 1862, losing narrowly to Reverdy Johnson). When the Lincoln administration decided to replace Addison, Attorney General Edward Bates called Maryland governor Augustus Bradford to Washington to inquire who should be appointed. Bradford was adamant that Price be the man.[21]

Upon receiving his commission, Price immediately felt the press of business. His office did not even have a complete set of the *U.S. Statutes at Large.* Unlike his predecessor, Price asked Attorney General Bates for funds to hire assistants. "The treason cases are of great interest and ought to be thoroughly tried, if tried at all," he informed his superior. But Price worried that he would not be able to win convictions with Taney on the bench. "You are aware that from the constitution of the court," he reminded Bates, "if the Chief Justice should be on the bench, the treason cases will have to be made very plain & conclusive if we expect a conviction."[22] Price well knew that even with incontrovertible evidence and solid legal arguments the chief justice could still use his position to thwart the government's efforts in prosecuting treason cases.

In truth, Price was overwhelmed by the numerous cases pending in the courts.[23] Many defendants and their families had been asking whether the government intended to prosecute the cases on the docket. If not, they wanted the charges dropped. From his vantage point, Price also wondered what to do about the cases of civilians who had been arrested by the military. "Take the instance of Geo. P. Kane," he wrote to Attorney General Bates, "who was indicted for treason but the process for his arrest, was not served by reason of his confinement in Fort Warren. Am I to issue process by removal & have him taken & held to bail? Or let the matter rest for the present?"[24]

Bates did not have "an exact answer" for Price. In fact, Price could not have proceeded against Kane even if he had wanted to, for Kane had been released from Fort Warren in 1862 (after fourteen months' imprisonment) and had become a Confederate agent in Richmond and Canada.[25] But the perplexing question remained: Was it better to have prisoners freed from military prison and indicted in civil court, where they would be released on bail and possibly acquitted by a jury, or was it preferable not to pursue the treason cases and to keep alleged traitors indefinitely confined in military captivity?

Bates let it be known that he wanted the cases tried, so the U.S. attorney moved forward with his preparations. Price spoke with a member of the grand jury about obtaining the notes the juror had taken during the grand jury's investigation in 1861. "He was ready to hand me the testimony," Price informed Bates, "but Judge Giles whom he consulted, advised him, that such a course would be improper, and now he hesitates about letting me have his notes, as promised." Price told the grand juror "that as District Attorney I had a clear right to know what the testimony adduced before the Grand Jury was," but his entreaties were to no avail. Bates believed the grand juror's refusal was "very suspicious" and "very like a designed concealment of information which might be important to the success of the prosecution."[26] But such was the situation that faced federal prosecutors when they sought to punish treason in an area teeming with disloyalty. If the strict constitutional requirements for treason trials did not make things difficult enough for Price, the presence of southern-sympathizing Democrats on the bench made the process of trying and convicting alleged traitors even more challenging.

Because he had not been present when Addison had drawn up the initial charges against Merryman and the other alleged traitors, and since he could not get copies of the testimony the grand jury had heard when the indictments were being drawn, Price decided to ask the court to quash the treason indictments currently pending before Taney and Giles. According to the *Baltimore Sun,* Price publicly declared the 1861 indictments "defective" and moved that they be quashed, which the court did on May 6, 1863.[27] Price's motion to quash the indictments was likely a ploy so that he could examine the witnesses himself to ascertain the information he needed to move forward with the prosecutions.

In July 1863, Price drew up new treason indictments against Merryman and fourteen of the Baltimore rioters (Price dropped the charges against about forty-five of the Baltimore defendants). The charges against Merryman now spanned twelve circumlocutory pages. The new indictment lowered the number of Merryman's accomplices from five hundred to one hundred (which was still an exaggeration). It also described Merryman's actions with more specificity. For example, it listed the six bridges that he participated in burning and it specifically accused him of violating President Lincoln's April 15, 1861, proclamation calling out the militia. The overt acts of treason—burning railroad bridges and cutting telegraph wires—remained essentially the same.[28]

The 1861 indictment had been self-contradictory as to when Merryman had committed his overt acts of treason, variously accusing Merryman of committing treasonous acts on April 19 and 23. This discrepancy was the result of carelessness on Addison's part. Because the printed indictments had been prepared for those accused of rioting, they all had "April 19" printed in the charges. As Addison made his changes to Merryman's indictment, he changed some of the "April 19" dates to "April 23," but he missed six of them. As a consequence, the 1861 indictment against Merryman was, in fact, "defective." Price was much more careful in the 1863 indictment to uniformly accuse Merryman of committing treason on April 23.

With new indictments in hand, U.S. attorney Price was now ready to proceed against the Baltimore rioters. But Chief Justice Taney and Judge Giles continued to delay the cases. A frustrated Price asked Attorney General Bates whether another circuit justice could be called upon to sit in Taney's place since the chief justice was ill and obviously not recovering. Bates threw up his hands in exasperation: "I do not find that I have any authority, power or duty in the premises," he replied to Price. "I do not see that I can, with official propriety, take any step touching the question whether the judges shall or shall not hold terms of their Courts, at the times and places appointed by law."[29] The assignment of circuit duties was a matter that belonged exclusively to the judiciary and could not be interfered with by the political branches of the government.[30] Chief Justice Taney was also irritated by Price's request. "Mr. Price the District Attorney has written to me suggesting that from the great mass of business in the Circuit court that I should appoint some other Judge of the Supreme court to take my place at the approaching Term," Taney wrote privately. "I have declined doing so, as I hope to be well enough to perform the duties myself."[31] Of course, the octogenarian jurist would never again be well enough

to perform his circuit riding duties. Thus, federal prosecutors were powerless to force their cases to trial if the judges were hell-bent on thwarting
them. Over the next few years, Price would learn just how difficult it was
to prosecute treason cases in courts in which the presiding judges were
sympathetic with the South.

~

The acts of southern sympathizers in Maryland forced the Lincoln administration to grapple with several difficult questions related to the prosecution of alleged traitors in the North. First, the administration had to decide
whether it was better to try alleged traitors in civil or military courts, or
simply to hold them indefinitely and without charges in military prisons.
Throughout the war, Lincoln permitted many border state civilians to be
arrested and detained by the military, and as we will see in chapter 4, a
number of these civilians were also tried by military tribunals.

While most of the war-related arrests in Maryland were handled by
the military, the administration allowed for a select group of prisoners—
mainly those who had been involved in the events of April 1861—to be
prosecuted in the federal courts.[32] Once the administration decided to indict suspected traitors in civil tribunals, federal prosecutors had to determine what charges to bring against them. Related to this question was the
problem of determining whether the federal definition of treason encom-
passed all acts of disloyalty against the United States or only certain types.
In other words, did some acts of disloyalty not amount to high treason?
And, if not, with what crimes should disloyal civilians be charged? Finally,
Lincoln had to learn how to wield the weapon of presidential amnesty
in the loyal border states. Pardon and amnesty were powerful tools that
the commander-in-chief could use to secure Marylanders' loyalty to the
Union in the same way that he could use it to restore the states of the
southern Confederacy to their allegiance.

If John Merryman and the Baltimore rioters were to be tried in a civil
court, they had to be charged with treason. By the spring and summer of 1861
—when Merryman and the Baltimoreans had allegedly committed their
disloyal acts—Congress had not yet passed legislation defining crimes of
disloyalty less than high treason.[33] As a consequence, the only option for
trying these men would be to indict them for treason against the United

States. Federal prosecutors in Baltimore would thus face the most difficult legal challenge of their careers. No person had been convicted of treason in a federal court since the presidency of John Adams.

Many of the difficulties facing federal attorneys in the prosecution of treason cases were placed upon them by legal constraints written explicitly into the U.S. Constitution. Treason is the only crime defined in the Constitution: "Treason against the United States, shall consist only in levying War against them, or in adhering to their Enemies, giving them Aid and Comfort." The next sentence states that treason must be an "overt Act," thus precluding judges or politicians from declaring that conspiracy or words might be deemed treason. In defining treason narrowly the Framers hoped to depoliticize a crime that for centuries had been partisan in nature. In early modern England monarchs could define treason however they chose and force judges to convict the accused simply to eliminate political opposition. In Elizabethan England, judges had held rioting against public policy or the general execution of the laws to be treason. This process of construing a defendant's words or nontraitorous actions to be treason became known as "constructive treason."[34]

The Founding Fathers hoped to prevent partisan and constructive meanings of treason from taking root on American soil. "The doctrine of *constructive treasons,* created by servile judges, who held their office during the pleasure of the king, was used by them in such a way as to enable the sovereign safely to wreak vengeance upon his victims under the guise of judicial condemnation," wrote William Whiting, solicitor of the War Department, in 1862. "If the king sought to destroy a rival, the judges would pronounce him guilty of constructive treason; in other words, they would so construe the acts of the defendant as to make them treason." The power to define treason or determine who was a traitor, under the old English law, "was in its nature an *arbitrary* power."[35] By incorporating a limited and precise definition of treason into the Constitution, the Framers hoped to keep arbitrary and constructive definitions of treason out of the United States.

The limited constitutional definition of treason notwithstanding, British treason law provided precedents that helped introduce the doctrine of constructive treason into American jurisprudence. In the 1790s, several unrelated groups of disgruntled Pennsylvania farmers lashed out violently against the imposition of federal taxes in their neighborhoods. The leaders of these insurrections were arrested and prosecuted for treason in the federal courts. Their convictions rested on earlier English doctrines of constructive treason; the judges in these cases held that rioting and violent resistance to a federal law amounted to the king of crimes. Under the precedents of the Whiskey Rebellion (1794) and Fries Rebellion (1798) cases, the Baltimore rioters and bridge burners could have easily been convicted of treason. During the first half of the nineteenth century, however, the federal courts narrowed the definition of treason to require an actual levying of war with intent to overthrow the government. When a group of fugitive slaves and free blacks rioted to prevent the capture of four fugitive slaves in Christiana, Pennsylvania, in September 1851, a federal judge held that such a riot did not amount to treason because the riot was not part of a larger conspiracy that sought violently to destroy the government. The Christiana precedent would prove a stumbling block for the prosecution in *U.S. v. Merryman* and the cases of the Baltimore rioters.[36]

Securing indictments against rioters for treason was only the first and easiest step. Once the rioters were indicted, government attorneys had to convince local jurymen to convict their peers of the most heinous political crime against the nation. Failure to bring convictions would be embarrassing to the Lincoln administration, while trials and convictions might undermine the war effort by making martyrs of the accused. Writing in July 1861, Attorney General Edward Bates noted that it would be "better [to] let twenty of the guilty go free . . . than to be defeated in a single case. . . . Success in the selected cases is very desirable, but a multitude of cases is not only not desired, but feared, as tending to excite popular sympathy and to beget the idea of persecution." Lincoln also tended toward leniency. In 1862 he noted that "the severest justice may not always be the best policy." Thus, due to fear of embarrassment, the possible creation of martyrs, limited resources, and larger fish to fry, the executive branch tended not to pursue many actual treason cases in the courts.[37]

Indeed, Attorney General Bates discouraged local district attorneys from prosecuting too many treason cases. It would be more effective, in Bates's view, to try northern traitors for lesser crimes than treason:

> It is not desirable to try many cases of treason. It is a crime hard to prove, being guarded by a variety of legal technics [*sic*]. And even conviction makes the convict all the more a martyr in the eyes of his

partisans. In a clear case against a person of eminence, of notoriety, I would be glad to see a conviction for the public effect rather than the punishment of the individual. But it would be unfortunate to be defeated in many such cases. It is far better policy I think when you have the option to prosecute offenders for vulgar felonies and misdemeanors than for romantic and genteel treason. The penitentiaries will be far more effectual than the gallows. Prosecute your best cases—not the weak and doubtful. It will not do for us to be habitually beaten.[38]

Bates understood that numerous treason trials were not the most effective way to bring wayward citizens back into their allegiance to the Union. Arresting prominent citizens for treason might renew the vigor of the northern antiwar movement.[39] Imprisoning northern dissenters for lesser crimes, however, could prove a more effective way to quell dissent and increase support for the northern war effort. Nevertheless, prudence required that some northern citizens be tried for treason to keep before the public a clear understanding of what was at stake.

Privately, Bates had "no doubt . . . of the guilt of some at least, of the accused parties" in Baltimore, but he "doubted whether the popular feeling in the City & the State is such as to warrant the expectation of a fair and impartial jury." Moreover, he "seriously feared" that Chief Justice Taney and Judge Giles were "biased against the prosecution, and strongly sympathize with the accused."[40] Bates contemplated postponing the prosecution of the Maryland treason cases, but once he was convinced that an impartial jury could be had, he ordered U.S. attorney Price to move forward with the prosecutions. As it turned out, Taney's chronic illnesses successfully thwarted the treason cases so that they never would go to trial anyway.

The difficulty in prosecuting treason cases led the Lincoln administration to use a two-pronged approach toward suspected traitors. On the one hand, it was much easier to use the military to detain those suspected of disloyalty than to go through the time, expense, and uncertainty of a civil trial. John Merryman and the Baltimore rioters were the anomalies; most Marylanders arrested for disloyalty were held by the military without being charged in a civil court. On the other hand, Lincoln used his pardoning power as an antidote to the strong hand of military justice. Amnesty could help draw rebels back to their allegiance to the United States. Forgiveness, as articulated in the presidential pardoning power, was a healing device that the framers had purposefully written into the Constitution for times such as these.

During the ratification debates of the 1780s, Alexander Hamilton argued that presidents needed the power to grant pardons so that they could undermine the strength and momentum of traitorous movements. "In seasons of insurrection or rebellion," he wrote in *The Federalist* No. 74, "there are often critical moments, when a well-timed offer of pardon to the insurgents or rebels may restore the tranquillity of the commonwealth; and which, if suffered to pass unimproved, it may never be possible afterwards to recall." To be sure, Hamilton had envisioned much smaller insurrections—like Daniel Shays's Rebellion in western Massachusetts in 1786—in which the president could act more quickly than Congress to offer consequential pardons. But the principle still applied. "Humanity and good policy conspire to dictate, that the benign prerogative of pardoning should be as little as possible fettered or embarrassed," wrote Hamilton.[41] President Lincoln (and later, President Johnson) could avoid the legislative bickering that members of Congress could not. And when they felt that a large-scale offer of pardons could help bring peace and tranquility, they used their power to restore the nation, just as Hamilton had envisioned they might.

With this historical context in mind,[42] and being confronted by the reality that "many persons have committed and are now guilty of treason against the United States," Lincoln issued a Proclamation of Amnesty and Reconstruction on December 8, 1863. Under the terms of the edict, Lincoln promised presidential pardon to any low-ranking rebel who would take an oath of future loyalty to the United States and pledge to support all Union war measures relating to emancipation. In accordance with the proclamation, the Attorney General's Office informed William Price that "there is nothing in its terms to exclude persons indicted for treason at Baltimore from availing themselves of its benefits."[43]

In March 1864, several Maryland traitors decided to attain their freedom by taking Lincoln's oath. Hazel B. Cashell, a Montgomery County farmer who had been indicted for treason for directing rebel soldiers to cattle owned by the United States during the Gettysburg campaign, requested to take the oath and was granted permission. On March 15, 1864,

Cashell signed Lincoln's amnesty oath of allegiance and had the charges against him dropped. Others decided to follow suit. Unfortunately for the Baltimore traitors, Lincoln soon came to the conclusion that he did not want to grant amnesty to persons indicted for treason in the federal courts. On March 26, 1864, the president clarified his December proclamation, saying that it did not apply to those who were imprisoned by civil or military authorities or who had posted bond for good behavior. "Prisoners excluded from the amnesty offered in the said proclamation," Lincoln stated, "may apply to the President for clemency like all other offenders, and their applications will receive due consideration." Baltimore Republicans praised Lincoln for his second proclamation. The *American and Commercial Advertiser* said it "will prevent such abuses of the Amnesty act as have occurred in one or two cases . . . where a party actually under indictment for aiding and assisting the enemy, was allowed to take the oath and escape punishment."[44]

Lincoln's amnesty proclamations are noteworthy on three accounts. First, the president was offering pardon to criminals who had not yet been convicted—who, in fact, were still at large and still committing offenses against the United States.[45] Lincoln hoped, in effect, that rebels would renew their allegiance if they were promised not to be punished upon their return to the Union. Second, Lincoln's policy was in keeping with his understanding of the conflict as a rebellion rather than a civil war. The president, in this view, could pardon rebels and traitors just as he might pardon other criminals. Third, Lincoln's 1863 Proclamation of Amnesty and Reconstruction included within its reach not only southern rebels but also northern aiders and abettors.[46] As such, Lincoln's blanket amnesty might bring healing to the North while also drawing southerners back into the fold.

Within days of Lincoln's March 1864 proclamation, Josiah Grindall, a Baltimore rioter who had been indicted for treason in both 1861 and 1863, sought Lincoln's pardon under the president's December 1863 and March 1864 proclamations. U.S. attorney William Price endorsed the petition: "Grindall since the 19th of April 1861, in the outrages of which day he participated, has behaved himself in a peaceable & orderly manner, & I have reason to believe is now sorry for what he did on that occasion, and think his case a fair one for the exercise of the executive clemency."

Lincoln agreed, writing on April 2, 1864: "In this case, not as a precedent for any other cases, the District Attorney will be justified by me, if in his discretion, he shall enter a *Nolle Prosequi*."[47] Lincoln, at this stage in the conflict, was willing to pardon—or at least not prosecute—traitors who had turned from their wicked ways. But he did not wish Grindall's case to be a precedent for others. He would still hold charges—and the possibility of trials and convictions—over the heads of unrepentant traitors. Unless they returned to their full allegiance, Lincoln would not simply bestow a blanket amnesty on those still harboring enmity toward the Union.

Lincoln's strategic use of treason charges in places like Maryland—even when those cases were not brought to trial—signifies a usefulness for the law of treason that has been previously overlooked. The leading scholar of the Civil War and the Constitution, James G. Randall, argued that treason law "was of slight importance during the war" because of its impracticality as a legal weapon to suppress disloyalty during such a gigantic rebellion. Instead, according to Randall, Congress and the Lincoln administration relied on emergency legislation aimed at "offenses involving defiance of the Government . . . which needed punishment, but for which the treason law would have been unsuitable."[48]

While it is true that Congress and the president relied on the prosecution of lesser crimes than treason (such as discouraging enlistments, encouraging desertion, or corresponding with the rebels) to punish disloyal behavior during the Civil War, the Lincoln administration still successfully wielded the law of treason to its benefit in places like Maryland. The perpetual threat of a trial caused alleged traitors and their families enormous amounts of stress and financial burdens. In addition to hiring counsel, those accused of treason had to post bond for good behavior.[49] Many asked the government either to try or to dismiss their cases. Alleged rioter Samuel Mactier appealed to Secretary of War Edwin M. Stanton, whom he had met once at the spa at Capon Springs, for executive clemency: "I have been indicted for Treason," he told Stanton, "& have rested under this heavy charge for near three years. God knows, I am not guilty of any intent to do wrong, & the punishment which I have suffered in mind & body for near 3 years is only known to Him." Unlike with Josiah Grindall, however, Lincoln chose not to end the prosecution against Mactier.[50]

In October 1864, Chief Justice Roger B. Taney finally breathed his last.

Lincoln replaced one old nemesis with another, appointing his political rival and former secretary of the treasury, Salmon P. Chase, to sit in the Supreme Court's center chair. Because of Taney's perpetual illness during the previous three years and because of his refusal to allow Judge Giles to hear any capital cases without him, the Baltimore treason cases were still pending on the federal docket in Maryland when Chase began riding circuit. As the war came to a close, federal officials had to decide whether to pursue these cases or allow reunion come as quickly and peacefully as possible. Expecting Lincoln to issue a "general amnesty" in the spring or summer of 1865, Chief Justice Chase hesitated to hear any of the Maryland treason cases remaining on the docket. There was no need to exacerbate local political tensions if all would be forgiven soon anyway.[51] As a consequence, the Baltimore treason cases were postponed from term to term under Chief Justice Chase just as they had been under Taney. Despite Chase's public reluctance to preside over treason trials, federal grand jurors in Maryland returned indictments against several Confederate military leaders, including Bradley T. Johnson, Harry Gilmor, and George H. Steuart, as they returned home from the war.[52]

In March 1867, President Andrew Johnson appointed Andrew S. Ridgely U.S. attorney for the District of Maryland. Ridgely, it will be recalled, was the hotheaded bystander at the *Ex parte Merryman* proceedings who had proposed forming a posse comitatus to free John Merryman from his captivity at Fort McHenry. In 1866, Ridgely had been hired as an attorney for Dr. Samuel A. Mudd, the physician accused of assisting John Wilkes Booth's escape from Washington, D.C. Now, clothed with official power, Ridgely could influence the government's decision whether to prosecute or dismiss the Maryland treason cases.

In April 1867, Ridgely asked Attorney General Henry Stanbery what should be done about the remaining treason cases in Maryland. The attorney general replied that the government should "dismiss all indictments for treason based on acts committed by parties in a military capacity during the war." In other words, rebels who had served in the army or navy of the Confederacy and were indicted after the war would not be tried for treason. This decision was in keeping with the lenient terms of surrender that General Ulysses S. Grant had designated at Appomattox as well as Grant's desire that paroled Confederate soldiers not be tried for treason.

Of the fifteen treason cases on the docket, Stanbery's order covered only three. Most of the remaining twelve cases, Ridgely reminded Stanbery, "grew out of obstructing the Rail-ways and the passage of troops at Washington on and about the 19th Apl. 1861." While some of the defendants had acted in a "pseudo military capacity," Ridgely did not think the cases could be dismissed according to Stanbery's instructions. "Many, or most of them seem to me to have been the result of mere riotous excitement; highly discreditable, considering the character and position of those offending yet scarcely, at this late day, I think, demanding to be regarded or punished as treason."[53]

Dismissing the case against John Merryman seemed to be a priority for Ridgely. On April 15, 1867, Ridgely sent Attorney General Stanbery a full account of Merryman's 1861 escapades and suggested that the case "be disposed of under a *nolle prosequi.*" The Attorney General's Office answered in the affirmative on April 22. The following day—April 23, 1867—Merryman's case was finally dismissed, six years to the day after he had burned the bridges of the Northern Central Railroad.[54]

By the spring of 1868, only nine treason cases remained on the docket in Maryland.[55] Chief Justice Chase continued to doubt the wisdom or utility of trying these cases. "I can see no good to come, at this late day, from trials for treason," he wrote from Richmond, where he was set to preside over the treason trial of Jefferson Davis. "I would rather engage in trials of mutual good will and good help." U.S. attorney Ridgely again pressed Attorney General Stanbery that "some disposition should be made of these cases. The parties are entitled to be tried or to be released from their Bonds." Like Salmon Chase, Ridgely did "not see how the Publick good can be promoted by further prosecution of the parties," and he respectfully asked Stanbery for permission to dismiss the cases. But the Johnson administration was not yet ready to take that step. When, on July 4, 1868, President Johnson issued his proclamation granting "a full pardon and amnesty for the offence of treason against the United States" to all rebels, he excluded all "persons as may be under presentment or indictment in any court of the United States . . . upon a charge of treason or other felony." It would not be until November 4, 1868—the day after Ulysses S. Grant won election to the presidency—that the Baltimore rioters were finally released from their bond. Seven weeks later, on Christmas Day 1868, Johnson issued his final presidential proclamation, granting full pardon and amnesty to all former rebels. By this point, Jefferson Davis—the archtraitor himself—was the only former rebel with a treason indictment still pending against him.[56]

∿

Even if federal prosecutors could have proved that the Baltimore rioters and bridge burners had committed acts that were treasonable, the government would still have had to convince a jury that the defendants had acted with traitorous *intent*. Proving the defendants' intention would, in many ways, have been the most difficult aspect of these cases.

The events of April 1861 had occurred prior to any major battle of the war. As such, some northerners claimed that it was unclear at that point whether armed conflict was inevitable.[57] If war was not being levied against the United States in April 1861, could John Merryman and the rioters be accused of committing treason according to the constitutional definition? U.S. attorney William Price admitted his doubts to the attorney general. The Baltimoreans had committed their crimes "in the opening of the rebellion," he wrote—before Americans had come to comprehend "the realities of this terrible war, or understood exactly what it meant."[58] In other words, the Baltimore rioters and bridge burners might not have seen themselves as levying war against the United States because in April 1861 civil war had not yet begun.

The rioters' and bridge burners' actions and intentions could be interpreted in various ways. "Now you will perceive that to constitute the crime of treason," Price told the attorney general, "the intent must have been to aid the rebels by keeping back the soldiers who were on their way to oppose them." But proving *this* intention would be difficult, especially if the defendants had good lawyers. Certainly, they may have burned the bridges to aid the rebels; "or it may have been to prevent collision in this city, which was then in a highly excited and inflammable state, by which the town would have been reduced to ashes." From this perspective, the bridge burners were doing a public service—acting under the authority of the governor, after all—to save their city from greater disturbance and ruin. Price's successor, U.S. attorney Andrew S. Ridgely, took the argument one step further by claiming that Merryman's actions had likely prevented another mob attack on "ill equipped and comparatively defenceless" soldiers.[59]

If Merryman's defense team followed this line of reasoning and argued that Merryman had acted to protect the city, it would be difficult to prove that he had been actuated by a treasonable intent. The Maryland leaders who ordered the burning of the railroad bridges ostensibly did so because they believed that stopping further troop movements through Baltimore was essential to the safety, security, and peace of the city. If Merryman obeyed these orders with the same view in mind it would be difficult to convict him of a treasonable offense, his widely known southern sympathies notwithstanding. An 1815 precedent in the U.S. Circuit Court for the District of Maryland set a high standard for convictions of treason—one that would be difficult to meet in Merryman's case.

During the War of 1812, a Maryland lawyer named John Hodges returned several captured British stragglers to the British army when the British threatened to burn the town of Upper Marlborough if the stragglers were not returned. Hodges was charged with treason for adhering to the enemy by returning the captured men. The prosecution argued that only the fear of imminent death could justify Hodges's actions. The defense, by contrast, countered that Hodges had acted upon good motives because his concern was for the safety and protection of the community. "If the heart be uncontaminated by corrupt intentions, the man is innocent, for it is motive that qualifies actions," argued Hodges's attorney. If Hodges was accused of acting "wickedly, maliciously, and traitorously," the prosecution must prove his intentions. Without any hesitation the jury voted to acquit.[60] The context mattered in this case. Under certain circumstances, Hodges might have been found guilty of treason for returning stragglers to the British army. But with the threat of destruction to a Maryland town, the jury deemed his actions prudent and honorable. With *Hodges* as a precedent, Merryman could argue that his actions were intended to prevent greater harm to his community. As we will see in chapter 5, that is precisely the motivation that Merryman claimed.

The cases of the Baltimore rioters were more complex. On the one hand, the Whiskey and Fries Rebellion cases from the 1790s set strong precedents for trying rioters for treason. In those cases, two distinct groups of Pennsylvanians had been convicted of treason by levying war for rioting in opposition to federal taxes in the hopes that the laws would be unenforceable and that Congress would repeal them. On the other hand, the federal courts had consistently narrowed the definition of treason between 1807 and 1851 to exclude riots unless they were part of a larger treasonable conspiracy "for the purpose of overturning the government by force and arms."[61] One might be able to prove that many of the Baltimore rioters were disloyal sympathizers with secession, but it would be more difficult to prove that they were part of an organized conspiracy that sought to overthrow the government. Many rioters simply claimed to have been in the wrong place at the wrong time or to have foolishly allowed themselves to be swept up in the heat and excitement of the moment. "In reference to the passage of troops," wrote one of them remorsefully, "I confess, I am impulsive, & with my feelings outraged at seeing such a sight, I may have said or done something, which upon calm reflection I would not have done. . . . That I did any thing which I supposed transgressed the laws of my Country, I solemnly affirm was farthest from my intentions. I have ever been an upholder of the laws, as is known to every one who knows me."[62]

By 1861, the precedents of the 1790s held little value in American jurisprudence; the standards for conviction were much higher. In order to convict John Merryman, federal prosecutors would have had to prove not only that he had burned the railroad bridges but also that his intent had been to commit treason against the United States. Under the *Hodges* precedent, Merryman could simply claim that he sought to protect Baltimore from the further destruction that most assuredly would have occurred had more Union troops passed through the city. In order to convict the Baltimore rioters, they would have had to be shown to have been part of a large, organized, treasonable conspiracy. With judges William Fell Giles and Roger B. Taney sitting on the bench—both Marylanders and both Democratic appointees—Lincoln's prosecutors believed they had little chance of winning these cases. Instead, the administration allowed the treason charges to hang over the heads of the defendants for more than half a decade. In the meantime, Lincoln continued to permit the military to arrest and indefinitely detain Maryland civilians who were suspected of acting disloyally or harboring sentiments against the Union.

4

"NECESSITY IS THE TYRANT'S PLEA"

The Habeas Corpus Act, Part I: Congressional Reaction to Military Arrests and Tribunals

*T*he habeas corpus issue plagued Congress for the duration of the war. While John Merryman still sat imprisoned at Fort McHenry, congressmen on both sides of the aisle debated the legitimacy of Lincoln's suspensions of the writ. Democrats in both chambers berated Lincoln for his actions and his July 4, 1861, message to Congress. Senator James A. Bayard of Delaware argued that whether Merryman's incarceration "was a month, or three months, or a week, the imprisonment was none the less an utter violation of the Constitution." Senator Trusten Polk of Missouri jabbed the president for basing his actions on necessity. "I have already said that I do not believe any such necessity has an existence," he argued. "Has any person undertaken to show that it was in any way necessary for the public safety that Merryman should be arrested and incarcerated in Fort McHenry in the way that he was? No such case has been made out; no such case can be made out. This plea of necessity is the tyrant's plea for the prostration of civil liberty, and it will continue to be so."[1] While Polk's claim—that there was no necessity for Lincoln to act quickly and decisively in the spring of 1861—might ring hollow today, his prediction that "necessity" would lead to further arrests could not have been more prescient. Merryman's arrest was but one of the first.

Even after Merryman was released from Fort McHenry in July 1861, Maryland civilians—particularly those of the pro-secession bent—continued to fear the possibility of military arrest. "John Merryman is released on bail," reported one man to his sweetheart, "but Capt's Jarrett & Stump, and Henry Farnandis are taken in Belair. The Federals have their spies out in every direction, now, and it is hardly safe to talk."[2] In 1861, the Union military arrested and detained at least 166 Maryland civilians.[3] As prisoners continued to be brought to Fort McHenry during the summer of 1861, General Nathaniel P. Banks—who had replaced General Cadwalader on June 10—informed the Attorney General's Office that there were "insufficient accommodations at Fort McHenry for the safe keeping of prisoners."[4]

In July 1861, Maryland congressman Henry May, a Unionist, placed a national spotlight on the civil liberties issue in his state. May traveled to Richmond to meet with Jefferson Davis and other Confederate leaders, ostensibly to discuss a peaceful path toward sectional reconciliation, but no one in Washington was quite sure of the specific purpose of his visit. The press reported that while in Richmond May had denounced the Lincoln administration for arresting Maryland civilians. Moreover, he allegedly announced that thirty thousand citizens of Baltimore were in arms and ready to strike against "the heel of the tyrant" in their city.[5]

On July 15, Congressman John Fox Potter of Wisconsin introduced a resolution inquiring into May's conduct. The resolution called for an investigation as to whether May had been "holding criminal intercourse and correspondence with persons in armed rebellion against the Government of the United States." At the time that Potter offered the resolution, May had not yet taken his seat in the House because he was sick, although Republicans claimed that he was faking illness to avoid the consequences of his trip. "His recent visit to Richmond and his subsequent *illness,* were mere dodges to escape from his pledge [to support the Union]," intimated the *Chicago Tribune.* "May is undoubtedly a rebel at heart, although his necessities compel him to seem to be for the Union."[6]

The debate in the House became "a great rumpus." Clement Vallandigham of Ohio and other leading Democrats claimed that May had traveled to Richmond with a pass issued by General Winfield Scott and with the approval of President Lincoln (with whom May had met twice before departing). They chastised the Republicans for basing a resolution "of this kind on a mere newspaper report." May had gotten the permission of the president to go to Richmond "as a private individual," not on any official government business. But that was permission nonetheless. Despite these protestations, the House adopted the resolution to inquire into May's actions.[7]

After conducting its investigation, the House Judiciary Committee reported against the resolution on July 18, citing that its author was "unable to produce any evidence tending to prove any of the matters referred to in the resolution, but that they were grounded upon newspaper articles only." May then rose before the House and asked to make an explanation. He expressed his "indignation and disgust" at the attempt to strip him of his right to represent his constituents based only on the "idle gossip of the hour." He expressed his opposition to secession and said he went to Richmond to converse with the southern leaders to do anything he could to avert the impending civil war. "Sir, it was a private mission that I undertook; but it was a blessed one."[8]

May spent the bulk of his "explanation" chastising the president and the military for suspending the writ of habeas corpus and for using the military to arrest civilians in Baltimore. His constituents, he said, were facing unimaginable humiliation, degradation, and injustice, and he called on the House "to emancipate the down-trodden people of Baltimore from the military tyranny under which they are now groaning, and which has so utterly prostrated their constitutional liberties."[9]

Republicans began to assert that the newspaper rumors about May must be accurate. His anti-Lincoln statements in the House sounded remarkably similar to what he was reported to have said in Richmond. Still, May denied the reports. "It is absolutely untrue that I communicated any such information to any one; and it is equally untrue, in point of fact, that such a state of things exists." But May continued: "That there are thirty thousand men—ay, and more—who, unless the heel of oppression is lifted from them, will, if they can get the opportunity, vindicate their constitutional rights and liberties, is absolutely true."[10]

Such sentiments were precisely why the Republicans had doubted his loyalty. "I should not be surprised if that rebel government should have regarded him more as a sympathizer than as a mediator," ridiculed Schuyler Colfax of Indiana. But May insisted that oppression and tyranny must be opposed everywhere and at all times. The "courts and a jury of the land" ought to judge cases of disloyalty, he argued. "Not in time of war," replied a Maryland Republican.[11]

The issue of May's trip to Richmond was not pursued any further, but May would not drop the matter of arbitrary arrests. On July 31 he introduced a long resolution condemning the military for violating the Constitution by arresting civilians. Again on August 5 May offered another lengthy resolution blaming the Republican Party for being sectional and uncompromising in nature and for thus bringing about the war. The resolution further called for Congress to appoint peace commissioners "to procure an armistice between the contending armies, and restore peace at all events; and . . . to arrange a compromise to preserve the Union, if possible; but if not, then a peaceful separation of the respective States."[12]

By now the Republicans had had enough. Thaddeus Stevens of Pennsylvania called May to order, saying that the first resolution was "nothing but a speech." Alexander Diven of New York introduced his own resolution condemning "treasonable resolutions":

> *Resolved,* That at a time when an armed rebellion is threatening the integrity of the Union and the overthrow of the Government, any and all resolutions or recommendations designed to make terms with armed rebels, are either cowardly or treasonable.

But Clement Vallandigham retorted, "It is neither cowardly nor treasonable for the stronger to propose terms of peace to the weaker." He called Diven's resolution "unjust, unfounded, and offensive." Vallandigham's fellow Ohio Democrat Samuel S. Cox offered a resolution to censure Diven for proposing an unparliamentary resolution. But on August 6, the final day of the session, Diven and Cox offered explanations and withdrew their resolutions. The matter of May's loyalty, for the moment, appeared to be laid to rest.[13]

In truth, May's troubles were far from over. On September 13, during the autumn recess, he was arrested at his home by the order of Secretary of War Simon Cameron. May was first imprisoned at Fort McHenry, in Baltimore harbor, but then was transferred to Fort Monroe, in Virginia, and finally to Fort Lafayette, in New York. As we saw in chapter 3, May's arrest was tied to larger issues in Maryland politics at the time. It was widely believed that the Maryland legislature was preparing to vote the state out of the Union. In order to prevent this occurrence, Cameron issued orders to arrest several members of the legislature, pro-secession newspaper editors, the mayor and several policemen of Baltimore, and Congressman Henry

May. The prisoners were to be held "in close custody" and to be kept from any outside communication. "The exigencies of the Government demand a prompt and successful execution of this order," stated Cameron.[14]

May's defenders charged that he was arrested for political reasons. His "only crime," according to his brother, "is that while endeavoring to keep the peace in his own State at all times and on all occasions he has been opposed to the policy of your Administration in regard to the unhappy difficulties in which our country is now involved." May's health quickly began to fail because of the cramped quarters and "foul atmosphere" of the prison—"a treatment more suitable to a felon than to a gentleman whose honor is as pure as any man's in this land." After the death of one of his brothers in mid-October, the military released May on parole so that he could attend the funeral.[15]

May's views of the war and how it ought to be prosecuted were the cause of his troubles in Congress and of his arrest two months later. After shots had been fired, many northerners believed it was treasonable to oppose the war or to advocate for peaceable secession. As a constitutional possibility, peaceable separation made some sense in December 1860 or January 1861, but the concept had become illogical by August 5, when May offered his second lengthy resolution. War had begun in earnest. The rebels had fired on Fort Sumter in April, and on July 21 a momentous battle had been fought within earshot of Washington, D.C. The Union had been defeated at Bull Run, and confusion and disarray pervaded the national capital. Peaceable separation was no longer a viable option.

The Washington correspondent for the *Philadelphia Inquirer* chastised May for his views, and the article was carried in papers throughout the country. "So far as Mr. May himself is concerned, I am positive in saying that he is ardently and sincerely attached to the Union, and wishes it reconstructed. But he is opposed to the war, which he believes to be unjust and unnecessary." May believed that war could not reconstruct the Union and that the longer it was waged the less likely reconciliation of the states would be. The correspondent noted that May's mission to Richmond, "if it was a mission for peace, has been fruitless. War is now the word—a sharp and decisive war."[16]

This last sentence captured why May was being targeted for disloyalty and why Cameron believed his arrest was justified. May had campaigned as a Unionist, but now that war had come he appeared to oppose any attempt to coerce the South back into the Union. Moreover, May had become the most vocal critic in Congress of Lincoln's policies for keeping Maryland from seceding. "His speeches and his action in Congress are at war with his professions of patriotism during the canvass," reported the *New York Times*. "While professing a love for the Union, he goes even beyond Breckinridge or Burnett in denouncing its defenders." It was a "National misfortune" to have such men in Congress. "They mar the harmony of that body, though, thanks to its patriotism, they cannot influence its action. They give courage and hope to the rebels, by fostering the delusion that there is a party even in the loyal States who sympathize with their treason, and are ready to consent that this Union shall be dissolved." Such men as May, the *Times* believed, would lose at the next election and descend into "political graves from which there will be no resurrection."[17]

The *Times*'s analysis was wrong in one very significant respect. Congressman May, somehow, had much more influence on national policy than the *Times*'s editors ever could have imagined. May used his remaining time in Congress to confront the White House and congressional Republicans with the formidable habeas corpus issue, which he approached both as a congressman and as a former political prisoner. In March 1862, May introduced a bill in the House of Representatives that would require the secretaries of state and war to send lists of "political prisoners" to the federal courts; if those persons were not indicted by a grand jury they were to be released.[18] After a significant period of dithering, Congress eventually enacted these provisions as part of the Habeas Corpus Act of March 3, 1863.

~

For the first year and a half of the war, Republicans in Congress were hesitant to take any real action on the habeas corpus issue.[19] Democrats and Conditional Unionists, like Henry May and Clement Vallandigham, hoped that Congress would act to rebuke the Lincoln administration, but with Republican majorities in both chambers there was little chance of that. In July 1862 the House passed an amended version of May's March 1862 bill. The legislation still provided for the release of political prisoners who were not indicted in the federal courts but it now also permitted the president to suspend the writ of habeas corpus.[20] In many ways it is amazing that the Republican-controlled House passed the measure. To be sure, the provision authorizing the president to suspend the writ satisfied Republicans, but those sections that required indictments for suspected traitors seemed an almost inexplicable sop to the minority party.

Indeed, some Radical Republicans opposed the amended version of May's bill, believing it was "an ingenious contrivance to free Maryland traitors, whom they *know* could be convicted." Henry Winter Davis, who was out of Congress when the bill was being debated (because he had been defeated by Henry May in 1861), pleaded with Senate Judiciary Committee chairman Lyman Trumbull not to pass the bill. "I beg you in the name of all loyal men in Md. not to pass House Bill no 362," Davis wrote to Trumbull. "It is a secession contrivance to turn loose all the mischievous men now held by the Govt." Davis conceded that the bill's provisions authorizing the suspension of habeas corpus were necessary, but he believed that the rest of the bill (the portion first introduced by May) was "the work of J. Mason Campbell a notorious secessionist," who also happened to be the son-in-law of Chief Justice Taney. If the bill became law, Davis warned, it would place suspected traitors back into the hands of the "disloyal" federal judges in Baltimore. Accordingly, the situation in Maryland would become intolerable for Union authorities who were charged with maintaining control of the state.[21] When H.R. 362 arrived in the upper chamber, the Senate took no immediate action on it.

In December 1862, Pennsylvania Radical Thaddeus Stevens introduced a second bill in the House empowering the president to suspend the writ of habeas corpus during the rebellion. More importantly, Stevens's bill also voided any current or future civil or criminal prosecutions against the president or any of his subordinates for any actions they took in accordance with the president's orders. In an unusual—and perhaps unprecedented —turn of events, Democratic attempts to block the bill enabled Republicans to adopt it within minutes of its introduction, before it was even printed, and without any substantive debate. Thirty-six House Democrats later issued a protest against the proceedings by which the bill had been passed, but the Republican majority tabled the protest.[22]

These two House bills met fervent opposition in the Senate. Democrats objected to any measure that would authorize the president to suspend the writ of habeas corpus. Senator Lazarus Powell of Kentucky argued that the legislative branch could not delegate such authority to the executive branch. "It was decided by the supreme court of the United States, by Chief Justice Marshall, that it is a legislative power," Powell declared. "It has been so held by the commentators upon the Constitution, Judge Story and others. It has been so held since this rebellion commenced, in a most exhaustive decision by the venerable Chief Justice of the United States, a gentleman eminent for his learning and for his private worth, who gave an opinion on that subject in the case of Merryman, that has not been and cannot be successfully answered."[23]

Senate Democrats strongly denounced Thaddeus Stevens's proposal to void all civil and criminal proceedings against military officers. One of the bill's most outspoken critics was Senator Willard Saulsbury, a slave-owning Democrat from Delaware. On January 27, 1863, Saulsbury argued that military arrests in the North did "more to render" disunion "permanent and eternal, than anything else" because these arrests demonstrated to the South the North's utter disregard for constitutional liberty. Furthermore, Saulsbury contended that by granting total immunity to Union officials, Stevens's Indemnity Bill would only legalize an illegal act. If Americans continued to submit to such despotism "for the sake of Union," Saulsbury exclaimed, the people would lose their liberty to "a consolidated Government, to be governed by the will, [and] the personal and partisan feelings of one man."[24]

Senator Jacob Howard, a Michigan Republican, replied that Saulsbury's speeches in the Senate were harmful to the Union war effort: "The effect of these speeches has already, in my judgment, produced the most unhappy effects in the Army. Yes, sir, even in the Army it has produced, and is to-day producing, a spirit of insubordination and even of mutiny, which, if not checked by the strong and honest arm of power, may bring about results most disastrous to us and to the nation itself." Saulsbury shot back that he had a right to represent the people of Delaware as he best saw fit, that secession was illegal, and that the South was wrong to secede, but that he was a southern slaveholder who believed the peculiar institution should be forever preserved on his native soil. These were the nation's founding principles, he argued, and he would continue to live by them. Moreover, Saulsbury insinuated that Delaware would never submit to a centralized authority that ordered her to free all of her slaves. "If that be treason, everybody who chooses so to consider it may make the most of it," the senator declared, paraphrasing Patrick Henry's 1765 speech before the Virginia House of Burgesses.[25]

Turning the bill on its head, Saulsbury argued that, rather than indemnify the president, Congress ought to appropriate money to compensate those who had been wrongfully arrested. He did not believe the president should be personally responsible for the damages, but this was more from his low view of Lincoln's abilities than a belief that the president was actually innocent of wrongdoing. Saulsbury called Lincoln "a weak and imbecile man; the weakest man that I ever knew in a high place." He was called to order but was allowed to continue. "Sir, it is out of order, I am told, so to characterize the act of an Administration; but if I wanted to paint a tyranny; if I wanted to paint a despot, a man perfectly regardless of every constitutional right of the people, whose sworn servant, not a ruler, he is, I would paint the hideous form of Abraham Lincoln. If that be treason . . ." Again the senator was called to order. He thundered back: "The voice of freedom is out of order in the councils of the nation!" Vice President Hannibal Hamlin, then presiding over the Senate, ordered the sergeant-at-arms to escort Saulsbury from the Senate chamber.[26]

Debate on the bill continued, and Saulsbury made his way back into the room. One soldier in the gallery observed that "he was so Drunk that he could not finde his Chair." When he again began to speak, Senator Charles Sumner, a Massachusetts Radical, called him to order, but Saulsbury would not be quiet. "I am not a slave to power," he proclaimed without any apparent sense of irony. Again the sergeant-at-arms approached the Delawarean, but this time he would not submit. When the presiding officer ordered the sergeant to apprehend Saulsbury, the defiant senator replied, "Let him do so at his expense." With that, he drew a pistol from his coat and pointed it at the sergeant. It was some time before he could be escorted peacefully from the floor.[27]

Senator Daniel Clark of New Hampshire introduced a resolution to expel Saulsbury from the Senate, but after he publicly apologized, the matter was dropped. Word spread quickly throughout the nation of what had happened. Sidney George Fisher of Philadelphia lamented the "disgraceful scene" that had occurred at the Capitol, while Saulsbury's colleague, James A.

Bayard, Jr., himself an outspoken Peace Democrat, believed Saulsbury would be calm for the remainder of the session: "He was cowed, & I trust will remain so, & was far more fearful of expulsion than sensitive about the degradation. His nature is unrefined and it would be impossible to make a gentleman out of him—nor has his early training benefited him— His worst feature is that when drunk he is rashly defiant . . . but when sober he is an arrant coward—We must do the best we can with him, but such conduct injures our cause & State—It will not be repeated, as timidity will restrain him." Indeed, Bayard had feared a collision between Sauls- bury and the Republicans for some time. Saulsbury had gone into the Sen- ate drunk on several other occasions, and on January 10, 1863—just two and a half weeks before the pistol incident—Bayard wrote that "Saulsbury made a good speech the other day, but in some respects imprudent for it excites party passion—He has I fear just rashness enough to get himself in a scrape without determination enough to abide the issue."[28]

Perhaps it was exasperation that caused Saulsbury to enter the Senate chamber intoxicated and with a concealed weapon. Perhaps he could no longer bear to see the citizens of his and other states arrested by the mili- tary without ever being charged with a crime. Perhaps he could no longer watch in silence what he viewed as acts of tyranny, and the prospect of the president and his subordinates being indemnified was more than he could endure. But Saulsbury and the Democrats were in a hopeless minority, and there was little they could do to stop the bill's passage.[29]

The Senate amended Stevens's bill by striking out the language that voided damages suits against government officials and replacing it with certain protections for civil and military officers should such suits arise. A conference committee then assembled a report that included the Sen- ate's amendments to Stevens's bill, a clause authorizing the president to suspend the writ of habeas corpus, and the provisions from Henry May's 1862 bill that offered protection to political prisoners. In the final days of the session, both houses adopted the conference committee's report (al- though Senate Democrats claimed that it was never put before the Senate for a vote),[30] and on March 3, 1863, Abraham Lincoln signed it into law.[31] Nearly two years after the executive branch had first suspended the privi- lege of the writ of habeas corpus, the legislative branch finally stepped in to authorize and regulate the president's actions.

The Habeas Corpus Act of 1863 set out to accomplish three things. Most importantly, the act authorized the president to suspend the privilege of the writ of habeas corpus in cases of rebellion and it implicitly recognized Lincoln's previous suspensions as legal.[32] Second, the law provided that Union authorities who were being sued for wrongful arrest by northern traitors could have their cases removed from the state courts to the federal courts. In these suits, Union officials could use orders from the president as a defense against charges of official misconduct. Third, the act sought to stop the use of military tribunals in the North. Congress required the secretaries of state and war to submit to the federal courts lists of "all persons, citizens of states in which the administration of the laws has continued unimpaired in the said Federal courts, who are now, or may hereafter be, held as prisoners of the United States . . . in any fort, arsenal, or other place, as state or political prisoners, or otherwise as prisoners of war." If a grand jury did not indict any of the prisoners on these lists by the end of the next session of the local federal court, they were to be freed upon taking an oath of allegiance.[33]

Ironically, the Habeas Corpus Act deprived Lincoln of the ability to suspend the writ in any meaningful way. In his famous letter to Erastus Corning, Lincoln argued that the purpose of suspending the writ was to arrest civilians "not so much for what has been done, as for what probably would be done." As such, Lincoln might arrest people who had not yet committed any "defined crimes" but who, "if not hindered," were "sure to help the enemy." Lincoln, in short, claimed the power to arrest and indefinitely detain Americans who *might* be plotting against the government but who had not yet committed a federal offence. And he believed that he must be able to hold them until the time of public danger had passed. The terms of the Habeas Corpus Act, however, implied that the targets of military detention should be persons who were suspected of having committed an actual, defined crime (that is, something for which they could be indicted in the federal courts). The act thus placed the fate of disloyal civilians back into the hands of the federal judiciary—the very branch of the government that Lincoln had hoped to bypass by suspending the writ in the first place.[34]

Thus, while on the surface the Habeas Corpus Act seemed to give Lincoln what he needed by granting him the power to suspend the writ of habeas corpus, in actuality it denied him the authority that he had been claiming for the previous two years. Under the act, Lincoln could no longer hold civilians indefinitely—his administration was now required to supply lists of prisoners to the federal courts, and if those prisoners were not indicted, they were to be released. Furthermore, the requirement that detainees either be indicted or discharged demonstrates that Congress was not authorizing Lincoln to make the types of arrests that he believed he needed to be able to make (that is, preventive arrests of persons who were suspected of disloyalty but who had not yet committed a "defined crime"). The Habeas Corpus Act, in reality, granted Lincoln only a limited power to make emergency arrests, most of which would have to be of persons who could have been arrested for committing a federal offense anyway. The act, in short, made suspension of the privilege of the writ of habeas corpus practically worthless.[35] It is little wonder, then, that Lincoln disregarded it. In fact, Lincoln treated the Habeas Corpus Act in the same way that he responded to Chief Justice Taney's opinion in *Merryman*: he ignored it. Lincoln had a war to fight and a nation to save and he would not allow himself or his administration to be hamstrung by another branch's interpretation of the suspension clause.

~

Henry May could have claimed something of a victory with the passage of the Habeas Corpus Act of 1863.[36] In fact, in a perverse sort of way, even Roger B. Taney should have found some satisfaction in its adoption. The act seemed to tacitly recognize the chief justice's view that only Congress could suspend the writ of habeas corpus (although Taney denied that Congress could delegate that authority to another branch of the government). Even more importantly, the sections that offered protections to "political prisoners" were drawn directly from the bill that May had introduced in the House of Representatives in March 1862. In what might be one of the most significant ironies in American history, some evidence suggests that Taney may have had a hand in writing those provisions. Henry Winter Davis, a leading Baltimore politician, believed that May's bill had been written by Taney's son-in-law, J. Mason Campbell, and then "submitted to Taney . . . for revisal."[37] Such a proposition was certainly plausible considering that May's bill sought to place military prisoners back into the jurisdiction of the federal courts, just as Taney had attempted to do in his *Merryman* decision. It is thus quite possible that Lincoln and the Republican majority in Congress gave their stamp of approval to a measure that had the approbation—if not the intellectual imprint—of the infamous author of *Dred Scott* and *Ex parte Merryman*.[38]

At most, however, the Habeas Corpus Act was a Pyrrhic victory for the Democrats. In truth, it was no victory at all. Despite the statutory language that required civilian prisoners to either be indicted in a federal court or released, the military continued to use its own tribunals to try civilians suspected of aiding the rebellion or committing acts of disloyalty. May and his Democratic colleagues would thus still be faced with the military trial of American citizens, which they believed violated several express provisions of the Constitution.

The Constitution requires that treason trials, like all criminal trials, must be civil proceedings.[39] "The trial of all crimes, except in cases of impeachment, shall be by jury," states Article III, "and such trial shall be held in the state where the said crimes shall have been committed." Conviction for treason requires an even higher standard of proof: "the Testimony of two Witnesses to the same overt Act, or . . . Confession in open Court." This provision was included in the Constitution, according to Benjamin Franklin, because "prosecutions for treason were generally virulent; and perjury too easily made use of against innocence." The Fifth Amendment further requires: "No person shall be held to answer for a capital, or otherwise infamous crime, unless on a presentment or indictment of a Grand Jury, except in cases arising in the land or naval forces, or in the Militia, when in actual service in time of War or public danger." Accordingly, members of the military—and perhaps enemy combatants—may be tried by courts-martial or military commission (subject to congressional legislation), but American civilians residing on the home front must be tried in civil courts. Finally, the Sixth Amendment states: "In all criminal prosecutions, the accused shall enjoy the right to a speedy and public trial, by an impartial jury of the State and district wherein the crime shall have been committed."[40] Lincoln's suspension of the writ of habeas corpus ought not to have been construed as also suspending these other constitutional protections.[41] But during the Civil War that is precisely what happened.

The military had been arresting civilians in the loyal states since the spring of 1861. In September of that year, General John C. Fremont began bringing civilians in Missouri before military tribunals. The practice of trying civilians in military courts soon spread throughout the border regions and into the North and South. President Lincoln codified the use of military commission trials for civilians who inhibited the draft or were "guilty of any disloyal practice" in a proclamation suspending the writ in September 1862.[42] As a consequence, military commissions, which were a creation of the executive branch, were inextricably linked to the suspension of habeas corpus and gained wide usage in all sections of the nation during the war. Congress never "established" these courts, as articles I and III of the Constitution would seem to require.[43] Once they were in use, however, Congress authorized military courts to try civilians in certain instances.[44] When Congress intended for civilians to be tried by military commissions, it explicitly said so, such as for "persons who shall be found lurking as spies" or for military contractors who defrauded the government. Most congressional legislation, however, required civilians who committed war-related crimes to be tried in the federal courts.[45] The Habeas Corpus Act of 1863 confirmed Congress's intention that most civilians should be tried in civil, not military courts. In border states like Maryland, and in other places throughout the nation, however, civilians continued to be brought before military tribunals.

In Maryland, civilians faced military trials and punishments for actions that were often not directly related to the war effort. In 1864, for example, two Baltimore women were tried and convicted by military commissions for disloyal speech and conduct. Sarah Hutchins was charged with holding intercourse with the enemy, with violating the laws of war, and with "treason under the laws of war" for procuring a ceremonial sword for rebel cavalryman (and former member of the Baltimore County Horse Guards) Harry Gilmor, and for attempting to send him a letter. Hutchins was found guilty and sentenced to imprisonment for five years at labor and fined $5,000. General Lew Wallace approved the sentence and sent her to Fitchburg Prison in Massachusetts.[46] Ann Kilbaugh, a washerwoman in Baltimore, was charged with "conduct and the use of language tending to promote sedition and encourage rebellion" for verbally disparaging Union soldiers, the federal government, and loyal women who carried "their damned old Union flag." She was found guilty and was sentenced to six months of hard labor; however, General Wallace commuted her sentence to thirty days' imprisonment.[47]

Many border state civilians renounced their allegiance to the United States and moved south to join the rebel army or serve the Confederate war effort in other capacities. When three citizens of Baltimore—John W. Scott, Simon I. Kemp, and Pierre C. Dugan—who had moved to Richmond to work for the rebel government were captured by Union military authorities, they were brought before a military commission on charges of treason for taking an oath of allegiance to the Confederacy. The defendants pled guilty to the specification (taking the oath) but not guilty to the charge (treason), saying that they had renounced their residence in Maryland and their United States citizenship. All three were found guilty of treason and sentenced to hang. Judge Advocate General Joseph Holt approved of the sentences, but Lincoln commuted them to imprisonment for the duration of the war, essentially deciding that the three men had to be treated as prisoners of war.[48]

John Merryman's friend and fellow Baltimore County horse guard Charles Cockey was arrested at his home on the night of July 14, 1864, for assisting Confederate general Jubal A. Early's troops during the rebel raid into Maryland.[49] A military commission found him guilty and sentenced him to five years imprisonment and a $1,000 fine. Lincoln received letters seeking clemency from a member of the Maryland state senate and from Cockey's attorney. Even more interesting was a letter signed by the members of the military commission that had convicted and sentenced Cockey:

Thoug[h] the sentence which this Court pronounced upon the accused is perfectly accordant with the testimony adduced—as it appears in the record and was uttered on the stand—yet the accompanying documents, signed by four (4) witnesses upon whose statements the prosecution of the case entirely depended, containing retractions, and we believe facts, which overshadow the validity of their previous evidence and dispose us to give, even at this late hour, to the prisoner, the benefit of those doubts which a humane principle of the law always allows as his right.

The witnesses now claimed that Cockey had "only committed an act of great indiscretion, which is nothing new for him to do. He is a playful, frolicksome man, disposed to be in every crowd, his object being fun and frolic, never known to do any intentional harm." As further evidence, the military judges pointed out that during a previous rebel raid into the state Cockey had helped Maryland Unionists protect their livestock from the invading forces. Cockey's actions, the commission now believed, were "occasioned by no more serious motive than mere curiosity."[50]

Lincoln heard these new facts and requested the War Department to "please report on this case." Secretary of War Edwin M. Stanton determined, however, that these new facts were "no[t] sufficient grounds for interference" with Cockey's sentence. Cockey remained imprisoned at Fort Warren, in Boston, until Andrew Johnson remitted his sentence on June 7, 1865.[51] Cockey's conviction highlighted two problems that Lincoln's critics frequently pointed out during the war: 1) that military courts were not bound by the same rules of evidence as civil courts and therefore were not fit venues for the trial of civilians, and 2) that military officers often lacked the legal training necessary to sit as judges. But in time of war such arguments did not hold sway. When lawyers protested that military courts did not have jurisdiction to try civilians for these and other reasons—and they did so at the opening of many military commission trials—the military judges simply dismissed the arguments and moved forward with the proceedings.

Beyond question, most military arrests and trials occurred in the border states of Maryland, Kentucky, and Missouri, where "civil disorder" often reigned and the terrors of guerrilla warfare sometimes blurred the lines between soldiers and civilians.[52] Nevertheless, military commission trials of civilians also occurred in the District of Columbia and the northern states. At least three men were found guilty by military commissions in Washington in August 1864 for "the utterance of disloyal sentiments," even though some of the language had been overheard from an upstairs room in a private residence.[53] During the presidential election of 1864, several state agents from New York were brought before military commissions in Baltimore and Washington for attempting to cast fraudulent ballots among the soldiers' votes of their state. These New Yorkers should have been tried in New York civil courts for violating their state's election law, but the military insisted that it had jurisdiction in their cases.[54]

Following passage of the Conscription Act in March 1863, more than two dozen Pennsylvanians faced trials by military commission.[55] The Union army arrested between seventy and one hundred civilians in central Pennsylvania in August 1864 based on the belief that they were part of a secret, organized, traitorous conspiracy bent on violently resisting the draft (the so-called "Fishing Creek Confederacy" in Columbia County). The military commander questioned the detainees from the pulpit of a local church and selected forty-four to be incarcerated at Fort Mifflin in Philadelphia. Of the forty-four, twelve were tried by a military commission in Harrisburg and seven were convicted of various charges related to draft resistance. The prisoners claimed not to have resisted the draft but only to have politically opposed the Conscription Act as an unconstitutional centralization of federal power.[56] In such cases, military authorities were unable to delineate the line between political opposition to the draft and violation of the law. Dozens of Pennsylvanians from other parts of the state were similarly arrested and tried before military commissions.[57]

Military arrests and trials were also prevalent in the Old Northwest, where federal authorities feared rampant draft resistance and rumors of a conspiracy to further sunder the Union through the creation of a Northwest Confederacy. The most famous instance of a civilian being tried before a military commission during the Civil War is the case of former Ohio congressman Clement L. Vallandigham. On April 13, 1863, General Ambrose Burnside, headquartered in Cincinnati, issued his infamous General Orders No. 38. This military order informed civilians of the Old Northwest that they would be arrested by the military and "tried as spies or traitors" if they committed any acts that would benefit the rebels. In its broadest language, the order stated that "the habit of declaring sympathies for the enemy will not be allowed in this department" and that those who violated this order would be sent "into the lines of their [Confederate] friends." Burnside wanted all to know that "treason *expressed* or *implied*" would face swift and condign punishment.[58]

Two days later, Burnside's subordinate in Indianapolis, General Milo S. Hascall, issued General Orders No. 9. Intending to carry into effect Burnside's order, Hascall declared that the country would "be saved or lost" during Lincoln's time in office. Therefore, any newspaper editor or public speaker who counseled or encouraged resistance to the war measures adopted by Congress, particularly conscription, would be "treated accordingly." Equating the Lincoln administration with the government , Hascall declared that "he who is factiously and actively opposed to the war policy of the Administration is as much opposed to his Government."[59] Opposition to Lincoln and the Republican majority in Congress, in Hascall's view, was treason.

Democrats protested the vagueness of these orders. "We are unable to say exactly what this language means," wrote the editors of one Indiana newspaper, while another pointed out that "there is no such crime as 'implied treason.'" But Hascall's policy effectively squelched the midwestern Democratic press. Several editors were arrested and their newspapers were shut down; others toned down their opposition rhetoric in order to stay in business. "However galling this may be," stated the *Sullivan Democrat,* "we have no alternative but to quietly submit."[60]

Not all passively acquiesced, however. Ohio Peace Democrat George Pugh was infuriated by the military's defining of treason in General Orders No. 38: "I spurn, I execrate, I trample under foot the order of any military officer *defining treason* and prescribing liberty," he declared. "Come what will, come imprisonment, exile, stripes, hard labor, death, I defy Order Number 38." After Vallandigham denounced these orders in a public speech he was arrested by the military at his home at 2:00 a.m., on the morning of May 5, 1863. Vallandigham was tried by a military commission and sentenced to imprisonment for the duration of the war, but Lincoln commuted the sentence to banishment to the Confederacy.[61]

Vallandigham appealed the tribunal's decision to a federal judge in Ohio, but the judge replied: "The Court can not shut its eyes to the grave fact that war exists, involving the most imminent public danger, and threatening the subversion and destruction of the Constitution itself. In my judgment, when the life of the republic is imperiled, he mistakes his duty and obligation as a patriot who is not willing to concede to the Constitution such a capacity of adaption to circumstances as may be necessary to meet a great emergency, and save the nation from hopeless ruin. Self-preservation is a paramount law, which a nation, as well as an individual, may find it necessary to invoke." The Supreme Court also refused

Vallandigham's appeal, claiming that it did not have jurisdiction over the decision of a military court.[62]

Clement Vallandigham was only one of several midwesterners to be tried by a military court for violation of General Orders No. 38. At least five other men—including a state senator from Indiana—were arrested and tried under Burnside's infamous edict. So was Meta Mason, a seventeen-year-old orphan in Kentucky, who was court-martialed for writing a letter full of personal, but war-related, news to her brother in the Confederate army. For this overt act she was charged with "giving comfort to the enemy" and "giving the position and conduct of Federal soldiers." Mason claimed that she did not know about General Orders No. 38, nor that military orders applied to "ladies." Despite her feigned ignorance, Mason was found guilty and sentenced to imprisonment at Johnson's Island in Sandusky, Ohio.[63] Even more severely, a Cincinnati man was sentenced to death by a military commission for sending an antiwar letter to a Union soldier in the spring of 1863.[64] Arrests in Ohio, Indiana, and Illinois gained nationwide attention in 1864 as the presidential election was approaching. The military arrested more than one hundred midwestern civilians for alleged membership in traitorous secret societies that were intent on freeing Confederate soldiers in northern prison camps and for plotting to form a Northwestern Confederacy. Of these, about a dozen were tried before military tribunals, several of whom were sentenced to be hanged for their allegedly disloyal actions.[65]

By 1864, the debate that had begun between Lincoln and Taney over the arrest of an unknown man in Maryland had mushroomed into an issue of national consequence.[66] Strangely enough, the aged chief justice had anticipated the establishment of military commission trials in his *Merryman* opinion. "Even if the privilege of the writ of habeas corpus were suspended by act of congress," Taney had written in his rebuke of Lincoln, a civilian "could not be detained in prison, or brought to trial before a military tribunal" because such a trial would still violate the Bill of Rights.[67] While Taney's argument went beyond the facts of the *Merryman* case, it had great relevance to the military commission trials that occurred in the later stages of the war. Lawyers representing civilians before military courts frequently borrowed language and legal argumentation from Taney's opinion in *Ex parte Merryman* to challenge the jurisdiction of the military courts, although they did not specifically cite the chief justice for the obvious reason that doing so would have undoubtedly earned the enmity of the military officers composing the courts.

The most thorough scholar of civil liberties during the Civil War, Mark E. Neely, Jr., has estimated that at least fourteen thousand civilians were arrested by Union military authorities during the Civil War; at least 4,271 civilians were tried by military courts.[68] Ironically, the Habeas Corpus Act that Clement Vallandigham had so strenuously opposed when he was in Congress *should* have saved him and these others from trials by military tribunals. The act was intended to do away with indefinite incarcerations and military trials of civilians, but as the cases of Vallandigham, Sarah Hutchins, Ann Kilbaugh, Meta Mason, the Fishing Creek Confederates, Charles Cockey, and many others demonstrate, military arrests, trials, convictions, and long imprisonments continued even after the passage of the act.

Lincoln claimed that civilian arrests by the military were more preventive than punitive. In his famous public letter to Erastus Corning of June 12, 1863, the president declared that these types of "arrests are made, not so much for what has been done, as for what probably would be done." As such, they were "more for the preventive, and less for the vindictive" than traditional judicial arrests in which someone was suspected of committing a crime. In another defense of his administration's policies, Lincoln wrote: "The military arrests and detentions, which have been made . . . have been for *prevention,* and not for *punishment*—as injunctions to stay injury, as proceedings to keep the peace." As a consequence, Lincoln suggested, these proceedings "have not been accompanied with indictments, or trials by juries, nor, in a single case by any punishment whatever, beyond what is purely incidental to the prevention."[69]

Lincoln's arguments were, at best, disingenuous. Thousands of courts-martial and military commission case files came across his desk throughout the war. He was tormented by the daily onslaught of letters and petitions claiming innocence or pleading for mercy. As Mark E. Neely astutely observes, "Such a statement at least stretched the truth in the case of Vallandigham and was altogether untrue in respect to many others. Since the president repeatedly reviewed the results of trials by military commission in his White House office, the statement did not stem from ignorance either.

Sentences to hard labor or prison terms fixed by years (and not the duration of the conflict) were punishments, pure and simple. Lincoln did not want to admit that the alternative military-justice system for some civilians had been set up. He must have hoped its disappearance at war's end would erase the military trials of civilians from national memory."[70]

In truth, the existence of this "alternative military-justice system" after March 1863 reveals that the Habeas Corpus Act was an impotent piece of legislation that offered no real protection to civilians accused of treason or disloyalty. The military continued to arrest and try civilians without supplying lists of prisoners to federal judges, and those arrested wallowed away in prison cells and military forts throughout the Union home front. The act failed, in large measure, because of the refusal of Judge Advocate General Joseph Holt to abide by the text of the law. When Secretary of War Edwin M. Stanton asked Holt to supply lists of civilian prisoners to be sent to the federal courts, Holt claimed to "strictly construe[ ]" the Habeas Corpus Act to exclude "those cases which are clearly triable by court-martial or military commission and which are being every day thus tried and readily and summarily disposed of." Guerrilla fighters, bushwhackers, spies, and those who sent intelligence to the enemy, according to Holt, would naturally be considered military prisoners and excluded from the lists.[71] Of course, Holt knew (because he personally reviewed the case files) that many other classes of cases were also being tried by military commissions, but he conveniently omitted the names of these prisoners from the lists he sent to the judges.[72]

In December 1864, Senator Lazarus Powell of Kentucky introduced a resolution in the Senate to inquire into the arrests of two former Union army officers, one of whom was now a Democratic presidential elector for the Commonwealth of Kentucky and the other of whom was lieutenant governor of the Bluegrass State. Senator Reverdy Johnson, a conservative Maryland Unionist who had once supported Lincoln's habeas corpus policy, spoke in favor of the resolution. In the process, he lamented the entire disregard that Union military officers had been paying to the Habeas Corpus Act of 1863:

"Congress passed, some two years ago, I think, an act which was intended to put an end, in a measure, to the principal injustice which was the result, and sure to be the result, of these military arrests," stated Johnson, and in all cases, as provided for by that act, where the parties were not liable to military control, the persons charged were to be handed over to the civil tribunal, and if an indictment was not found within a limited period they were to be discharged. I speak knowingly when I say to the Senate that that law has been altogether disregarded in Maryland, and that it has equally been disregarded within this District. Men without number have been arrested, and have been handed over, not to the civil tribunals for trial, but to military commissions, and have been convicted and sentenced to the penitentiary, and are now, some of them, suffering under those sentences.

Johnson was careful not to criticize Lincoln in his speech, but he pointed out that Lincoln's subordinates in the military "seem to think that they are under no obligation at all to observe the civil laws; not only not bound to observe the laws of the States where they happen to be located at the time, but not bound to observe the laws of Congress; and they not only assume jurisdiction, but I know, if I know anything of law, that they have from time to time, and indeed constantly, convicted upon evidence that would not be received in any court of civil justice in the country."[73]

In 1861, Johnson had been a warm supporter of Lincoln's policy to keep Maryland in the Union. Shortly after Taney issued his opinion in *Ex parte Merryman,* Johnson published an essay defending presidential suspension of habeas corpus in times of rebellion.[74] His experiences during the war, however, caused him to reconsider his views. Johnson became a prominent advocate for several Maryland civilians who were detained by the military, so much so that General Benjamin Butler later called him a "rank and bitter secessionist, and worse than others because he concealed it." By 1864, the military's disregard of congressional legislation and the constitutional rights of U.S. citizens had caused Johnson to utterly reject the Union military's policy in Maryland.[75]

In June 1865, Johnson elaborated his views on why military commissions did not possess the authority to try civilians in his defense of Mary Surratt at her trial for the assassination of Abraham Lincoln. In addition to their violating the provisions of Article III, the Fifth Amendment, and the Sixth Amendment, Johnson maintained, military commissions were unlawful because they were courts created by the executive branch rather than by Congress. "If the Executive can legally decide whether a citizen is to enjoy the guaranties of liberty afforded by the Constitution, what are we but slaves?" he asked the military judges rhetorically. Mary Surratt and the other alleged conspirators were citizens of Maryland and the District of Columbia—jurisdictions that had stayed loyal to the Union and places where the courts remained open and functioning. American citizens accused of crimes, according to Johnson, must be tried in civil courts in accordance with the provisions of the Constitution, the Bill of Rights, and relevant acts of Congress. If guilty, they must be punished. But citizens could not be tried by "illegal" courts and by judges who were "dependent" on the will of the president. "Never was there a more dangerous theory. The peril to the citizen from a prosecution so conducted, as illustrated in all history, the very elementary principles of constitutional liberty, the spirit and letter of the Constitution itself, repudiate it."[76]

Johnson lost his case. Mary Surratt and three of her coconspirators were hanged on July 7, 1865. The *Washington Evening Star* approved of the swift justice in this case: "Their deeds have been judged patiently and impartially. Seven weeks were devoted to their trial, witnesses have been summoned from remote locations, every point that in some manner suggested innocence was carefully weighed, and the sentence of death executed only because there was not one reasonable doubt of overwhelming guilt."[77] One Democratic observer was less sanguine. "I think the summary execution of the conspirators struck a deep chord in the public's bosom," he confidentially wrote to a friend. "There were few words uttered, but the shock was almost universal, as it became known that the condemned were to die upon twenty four hours notice."[78] Most Americans, however, seemed to approve of the proceedings. At a time when northern vengeance needed to be satisfied, historian Elizabeth D. Leonard has suggested that Mary Surratt's execution—notably the first woman to be executed by the federal government—served as "a symbol of all the other women of the Confederacy who throughout the war had engaged in treasonable behavior," yet who had gone largely unpunished. Mary, in short, was hanged as "the supreme representative" of all traitor women.[79]

In 1866, Reverdy Johnson's arguments were brought before the Supreme Court of the United States by an unlikely team of lawyers, including former Buchanan administration official Jeremiah S. Black, future

Republican president James A. Garfield, Indiana Democrat Joseph Ewing McDonald, and New York lawyer David Dudley Field. These nationally prominent attorneys appeared before the Court to represent accused Indiana traitor Lambdin P. Milligan. Milligan and several others had been arrested by the military during the 1864 presidential campaign for joining a secret society with intentions to overthrow the federal government. A military commission sentenced Milligan and two others to be hanged. Milligan appealed his conviction to the nation's highest court.[80] Arguing the case for the government (to uphold Milligan's conviction by a military court) was none other than Benjamin Butler, the Union commander who had forcibly occupied Baltimore in May 1861.

The Court accepted Reverdy Johnson's arguments in *Ex parte Milligan*. Writing for a five-member majority, Justice David Davis contended that trying civilians before military tribunals violated the Habeas Corpus Act of 1863, which explicitly required civilian prisoners either to be indicted in the federal courts or set free. Taking his argument a step further, Davis argued that the executive branch violated the Constitution itself by trying civilians in military tribunals. The rights for criminals guaranteed in the Bill of Rights, according to Davis, could not be taken away from American citizens, even in wartime. Military trials of civilians in locations where the civil courts were open, in short, were unconstitutional.[81]

A four-justice minority, led by Chief Justice Salmon P. Chase, argued that Congress *could* authorize military trials of civilians if Congress deemed such measures necessary to the nation's war effort. In other words, if Congress had decided that military tribunals were needed to win the war—even in areas where the civil courts remained open—it was within Congress's constitutional power to establish such tribunals. Chase's opinion was a concurrence rather than a dissent, however, because in the case of the Civil War, Congress had not authorized such tribunals. Rather than authorize such military courts, the Habeas Corpus Act had required civilian trials for accused criminals like Milligan. As such, the executive branch had blatantly ignored Congress's express intentions when it tried Milligan and others like him before military commissions.[82]

Both the majority opinion and the concurrence were strong rebukes of the Lincoln administration's wartime policy (an irony, since five of the nine justices had been appointed by Lincoln during the war), but the narrow division on the Court left open for the future whether Justice Davis's or Chief Justice Chase's view would carry the day. The timing of the *Milligan* decision was also significant. The judiciary had hinted in *Vallandigham* that it would not interfere with the president's wartime policy while the war was still being waged. But once the war was over, the courts would again weigh in on the constitutional issues of vital significance to the American people. "During the late wicked Rebellion, the temper of the times did not allow that calmness in deliberation and discussion so necessary to a correct conclusion of a purely judicial question," wrote Justice Davis in his *Milligan* opinion. "Then, considerations of safety were mingled with the exercise of power, and feelings and interests prevailed which are happily terminated. Now that the public safety is assured, this question, as well as all others, can be discussed and decided without passion or the admixture of any element not required to form a legal judgment. We approach the investigation of this case fully sensible of the magnitude of the inquiry and the necessity of full and cautious deliberation."[83]

Lincoln's response to the Habeas Corpus Act created the circumstances in which the Supreme Court would hear and hand down its *Milligan* decision, albeit after the war had ended. What has not been previously recognized is that Lincoln's response to the Habeas Corpus Act was almost identical to his response to Taney's decision in *Merryman*. In both instances, Lincoln ignored the dictates of another branch of the federal government. Lincoln masked his disregard of Congress by justifying his post-March 1863 suspensions on the Habeas Corpus Act—but this was a mere formality. In truth, Lincoln never doubted his ability to suspend the writ of habeas corpus when he needed to; he also continued to determine for himself just what that suspension meant. Unlike Chase in *Milligan*, Lincoln did not believe that he needed congressional authorization to use military tribunals. He would decide for himself if they were necessary for the Union war effort. He would decide for himself if suspension of habeas corpus meant that the procedural safeguards of the Bill of Rights would also be suspended. In short, Lincoln believed the president was a final arbiter on the meaning of the Constitution; as commander-in-chief, he would interpret that document as he best understood it and best saw fit.[84]

The lesson Lincoln had learned during the *Merryman* fiasco would serve him for the duration of the war. If he needed to do something to win the war, he would interpret the Constitution for himself and would, if necessary, bypass both Congress and the courts. In this light, it seems likely that Lincoln signed the Habeas Corpus Act into law only to secure protections for Union officials who were being sued by northern traitors for wrongful arrest. He did not see the act as somehow legalizing his earlier suspensions because he never doubted the legality of the actions he had taken. Nor was he concerned with the provisions of the act that protected suspected traitors. No, Lincoln signed the Habeas Corpus Act into law only to protect those below him in their efforts to wage the Union war effort effectively.

5

"THE GOVERNMENT MUST IN SOME WAY SUSTAIN YOU IN YOUR OFFICIAL ACTS"

The Habeas Corpus Act, Part II: The Failure of Congress to Protect Those Waging War

*T*he military arrest and trial of civilians was only one part of the habeas corpus problem that arose during the Civil War. Prior to the passage of the Habeas Corpus Act in March 1863, military officers and government officials who participated in the arrest of civilians were vulnerable to civil prosecution in civil courts for their actions in defense of the Union. These lawsuits struck fear in the hearts of Union commanders. Indeed, one Pennsylvania Supreme Court justice believed that "[i]ndemnity for the past is necessary to prevent many innocent men from being harassed and ruined."[1] Moreover, such suits allowed disloyal Americans to use the state and federal judiciaries to undermine the Union war effort. High Union officials understood the damage that these suits could cause. As a consequence, they pressed Congress to pass indemnifying legislation.[2] The result, however, was disappointing. The Habeas Corpus Act, or Indemnity Act, of 1863 did little to protect Union officials, and damages suits continued to plague Union authorities during the second half of the war. So threatening were suits of this nature, and so weak was the protection offered by Congress, that Union leaders were forced to take drastic measures to protect themselves against their "disloyal" adversaries. One powerful figure, for example, recommended re-arresting Maryland civilians who were suing him for wrongful arrest so that they could no longer prosecute their suits against him. In the absence of adequate congressional protection, those waging war on behalf of the Union had to devise their own methods for saving themselves from disloyal civilians within the loyal states.

Suspected traitors in the North began filing lawsuits against Union officials very early in the war. Baltimore police commissioner Charles Howard, for example, sued a military officer in August 1861 for illegal search and seizure. Other Baltimoreans sued General John E. Wool for damages from the time they were held in his custody at Fortress Monroe.[3] In April 1862, Philadelphia resident Pierce Butler sued former Secretary of War Simon Cameron for trespass, assault and battery, and false imprisonment. The matter, which originated in the Pennsylvania state court system, never went to trial, but Cameron was not taking any chances. Cameron sent word of the suit to the president. He also wrote to General George Cadwalader asking him to "disabus[e] the mind of your brother of prejudices against me." General Cadwalader's brother, John, was the U.S. district judge in Philadelphia. The general responded that the "Govt. must in some way sustain" Union authorities in their "Official acts." "I am myself vulnerable and liable to be harassed by Merryman & others in Baltimore," he continued. "I will no doubt be arrested the next time I go to Maryland which I should regret at this moment." Cadwalader's fears were not overstated. Indeed, Philadelphia lawyer Benjamin H. Brewster noted that Cadwalader "dreads the Merriman case."[4]

Cameron's legal troubles and the fears of military commanders like Cadwalader forced the Lincoln administration to deal with the issue of damages suits. Cameron warned Lincoln that suits of this nature were "intend[ed] to divide and conquer your administration, and thus bring [secession-sympathizing Democrats] into power." Indeed, Lincoln saw Pierce Butler's suit against Cameron as "a matter which deeply concerns the public welfare as well as the safety of the individual officers of the government." At a cabinet meeting on Friday, April 18, 1862, the issue of civil suits against government officials occupied the cabinet's attention. In addition to Butler's suit against Cameron, Secretary of the Navy Gideon Welles was being sued by several gamblers for confiscating money they had won from a Navy paymaster. According to Attorney General Edward Bates, the suits "created much talk and some excitement in the Cabinet." Lincoln, too, "was a good deal stirred up . . . and talked about arresting the attorneys." Bates "suggested the propriety of getting congress to pass an act to regulate such actions—and Mr. Seward proposed that I should draw a bill." Bates drafted a bill and gave it to Lincoln and several cabinet members for comment. On April 22, he gave a copy to Senator Benjamin F. Wade of Ohio.[5] But it would not be until March 3, 1863—nearly a year later—that Congress adopted such indemnifying legislation.[6]

General Cadwalader's fears of John Merryman were not unfounded. On February 20, 1863, Merryman instituted proceedings against the general in a Maryland state court claiming $50,000 in damages for wrongful arrest. The sheriff of Harford County "attached" $50,000 worth of Cadwalader's property in Maryland, meaning that he seized it so that it could be used to ensure the satisfaction of a judgment against the general. Solicitor of the War Department William Whiting immediately hired attorney William Schley to serve as Cadwalader's counsel. "The suit against Gen. Cadwalader is one of great interest," Schley informed Secretary of War Edwin M. Stanton, "involving grave questions; & is likely to become a leading case."[7]

The timing, however, could not have been better for Cadwalader. Less than two weeks later, on March 3, Congress enacted the Habeas Corpus Act of 1863, offering protection to military authorities who had arrested civilians in the course of carrying out their official duties. Section 5 of the act provided for the removal of suits of this nature from the state courts to the federal courts.[8] It also stipulated that "any order of the President, or under his authority, made at any time during the existence of the present rebellion, shall be a defence in all courts to any action or prosecution, civil or criminal, pending, or to be commenced, for any search, seizure, arrest, or imprisonment, made, done, or committed." Cadwalader and others like him now had the protection that they needed. On the very day that Congress enacted the Habeas Corpus Act, Cadwalader rejoiced to former Secretary of War Simon Cameron, "We may congratulate ourselves upon the passage of the indemnification law!"[9]

Because Cadwalader was a Pennsylvanian, *Merryman v. Cadwalader* was removed to the federal courts on August 5, 1863.[10] In March 1864, however, Merryman decided no longer to pursue the matter and the U.S. Circuit Court for the District of Maryland dismissed the case on April 2, 1864. Cadwalader's lawyer, William Schley, claimed credit for the dismissal. "I made the fullest and most ample preparations for the trial and meant to take all necessary defences," Schley informed the general. And when meeting with Merryman's lawyer, "I did not conceal my intention to assail him very fiercely." For these services, Schley believed he was entitled to a "moderate" $1,000 fee.[11]

The timing of Merryman's decision to withdraw the case is significant. On the surface, it might appear that Merryman simply believed that the Habeas Corpus Act now precluded him from winning his suit and that it was not worth pursuing any further. Or perhaps he and his lawyers were intimidated by Schley's "fierce" preparations for trial. But neither of these circumstances explains John Merryman's decision. Merryman, in fact, was after something much larger. Merryman likely believed that in dropping the prosecution against Cadwalader he would receive pardon and amnesty from President Lincoln. As we have already seen, on December 8, 1863, Lincoln issued a proclamation stating that he would grant amnesty to rebels who were willing to take an oath of loyalty to the Union. In March 1864, several Marylanders who were accused of being traitors approached U.S. attorney William Price about receiving this amnesty.[12] It is quite possible that Merryman sought pardon at this time as well.[13]

After Lincoln issued his Proclamation of Amnesty and Reconstruction in December 1863, Assistant Attorney General T. J. Coffey informed U.S. attorney Price that indicted persons willing to take the oath of allegiance "in good faith" were "entitled to the pardon and of course to the exemption from prosecution." But how might a person prove their "good faith" when taking the oath? Coffey's explanation was revealing: "If however, any of them, like Merriman, have such suits pending against U.S. Officers for arrest or imprisonment for their participation in the rebellion, the indictments against them ought not to be discontinued unless besides taking the oath they also discontinue those suits. For unless they agree to do so, you have a right to assume that they have not taken the oath *in good faith*."[14]

It was shortly after this exchange that Lincoln issued his second proclamation of amnesty on March 26, 1864, excluding persons under indictment for treason from his December 1863 proclamation.[15] John Merryman of Hayfields, in other words, was still on the president's mind well into the war years. And Merryman's suit against Cadwalader was forcing Lincoln to reconsider his policy of reconstruction. When it became apparent to the president that someone like Merryman might be eligible for pardon under the first proclamation of amnesty, Lincoln determined that he had to issue a second proclamation to clarify the first by restricting the types of persons eligible for pardon. A man like Merryman—who was suing an officer of the Union army for $50,000 in damages—was certainly not loyal and should not receive pardon. But the December proclamation had promised pardon to anyone who was willing to take the oath of allegiance. Lincoln now feared that other southern sympathizers in the North might learn from Merryman's example and attempt to attain a pardon while simultaneously undermining the Union war effort by suing federal officers. It was John Merryman, in short, who forced Lincoln to issue the second amnesty proclamation in March 1864. In a sense, Merryman's suit against George Cadwalader compelled Lincoln to revise one of the basic premises of his reconstruction policy for the South.[16]

When it became apparent that Lincoln would not grant Merryman pardon, Merryman decided to file another suit against Cadwalader. On May 31, 1864, Merryman sued the general in state court, again claiming $50,000 in damages. Like the first, the suit was removed to the federal circuit court in Baltimore. This suit remained on the docket until April 1865, when Merryman's lawyer—former Baltimore mayor George William Brown—requested the clerk of court to strike the case from the court's docket.[17] Perhaps by the spring of 1865, with former abolitionist Salmon P. Chase having replaced Roger Taney as the presiding circuit justice in Maryland, Merryman came to believe that he had little chance of winning his suit against Cadwalader.

While Merryman's first suit against Cadwalader was still pending in the state court system during the spring of 1863, the Northern Central Railway Company decided to file a suit of its own against Merryman. The superintendent of the railroad estimated that the April 1861 bridge burnings had caused $117,609.63 in damages. In 1861, the Northern Central had sought that amount in compensation from the state of Maryland, but in January 1862 the state's highest court ruled against the railroad. One of the state's lawyers in that case, Thomas S. Alexander, wrote to Simon Cameron on May 5, 1863, that he had "come to the conclusion that the Northern Central R. Co. may and ought to sue Merryman for burning its Bridges, and think likewise it is expedient that Mr. Campbell the regular attorney of the Co. shall be associated with me in the prosecution of the case. If you agree with me in these suggestions and will have the proper authority sent me I will bring suit forthwith."[18] Ironically, J. Mason Campbell, Chief Justice Taney's son-in-law, would now be prosecuting a case against the man the chief justice had risked so much to save.

Less than two weeks later, on May 16, 1863, the Northern Central

Railway Company filed a suit in the Baltimore County Circuit Court for $200,000 in damages against John Merryman, Samuel Worthington, and Charles Cockey.[19] Like Merryman, Cockey had been twice indicted for treason for participating in the bridge burning and telegraph wire cutting.[20] In September 1863, Merryman offered to pay the railroad "about $2600 in compromise of the claim" but the railroad determined that this amount was "not commensurate to the reasonable expectations of the Co."[21] The case was continued through several terms in the circuit court until January 1865, when it was removed to the Baltimore City Superior Court. The transfer of the case papers appears in the Superior Court's volume of "Cases Instituted" in 1865, but it does not appear in the docket, suggesting that the matter was dropped in 1865 or 1866.[22]

∼

A century and a half later, little is known about Merryman's motives in burning the bridges. Why did he obey these orders? What were his feelings, if any, toward the railroad companies? Did he have any attachment to the Union, or was he more devoted to his city and state? Might the Baltimore Riot of April 19, 1861, have been repeated on an even larger scale had the railroad bridges not been destroyed? The military and criminal court records are virtually silent on these issues. Other materials offer some clues.

Baltimore lawyer Andrew Sterrett Ridgely testified before a committee of the Maryland House of Delegates in February 1865 that Merryman had been the mastermind behind the bridge burnings. But Merryman's motives, according to Ridgely, had been admirable. "I remember in the midst of this excitement [the April 19 riot] meeting near the Bank of Baltimore, Mr. John Merryman, of Baltimore county. . . . He was talking to one or two gentlemen and I joined the circle." According to Ridgely, Merryman "turned to me and said a plan had occurred to him by which to prevent any more troops to come to the city of Baltimore." Ridgely inquired what it was. Merryman replied that "if twenty men would join him he would go and destroy some of the bridges leading to the city. I said: Merryman does your object partake of the character of a police movement and is for the purpose and sole purpose of preventing bloodshed, and suspending the movements of those troops temporarily until this excitement subsides. I really think it's the wisest proposition I have heard to-day." Merryman allegedly confirmed his good intentions and asked Ridgely if he would be willing to join the expedition, but Ridgely declined. "I did not know Merryman well enough to put myself under his guidance at a time like this," Ridgely explained. Ridgely also did not wish to do anything that might later be seen as having been hostile toward the government. Another member of the conversation then "suggested to Merryman, that he should go down to the Mayor's Office and make the suggestion there and act[,] if they acted at all, on authority and not take it on their own responsibility."[23]

If this story is true, then Merryman's motives may have been commendable in proposing to burn the bridges.[24] He may have simply been seeking to find a way to stop further bloodshed in Baltimore. Curiously, Mayor Brown never suggested that the idea had come from Merryman— at least not in his public statements in 1861 nor in his 1887 memoir. Until now, Merryman's voice has been silent in accounts of these affairs. But in 1863, Merryman sent a letter regarding the bridge burnings to Lincoln's first secretary of war, Simon Cameron, discussing why he burned the bridges. Merryman's account differs from Ridgely's in that he implies that the order came from Governor Hicks. Of course, Merryman may have omitted his going to Mayor Brown's office on April 19 to suggest the bridge burnings to protect himself—for reasons that will be obvious in a moment. The truth of the matter may never be known with certainty. Either way, because this is the only known writing that offers a glimpse into the mind of John Merryman regarding the events of April 1861, the letter is worth reproducing in full.[25]

Hayfields, near Cockeysville
May 21st 1863

My dear Gen'l.

I take the liberty of addressing you respecting the institution of a suit by the N.C. Railway Company, against me, for damages to [the] Road—

You are well aware of my connexion with the Militia of the State of Maryland, and that the Road was damaged to a certain extent, by a body of said Militia, under my command, in obedience to orders from my superiors, including Governor Hicks—

The claim made against the State, by the Railway Company, was the proper action, particularly as the Legislature at one of its sessions, in 1861, had recognized the State's obligation to the Company—[26]

My whole course since the N.C. Railway went into the hands of your friends in 1859, has been open, and decidedly friendly, and I would have as soon destroyed my own dwelling, as any part of its property—The object of those in authority, in ordering the destruction of its property, was the protection of the City of Baltimore, that, their anticipations were well founded, no one knows better, than your son,[27] the President of the N.C. Railway Co, he has more than once repeated, the determination expressed, by the Military at that time in Harrisburg, of marching through Balto. & destroying the City, if opposition was offered, that they would have been opposed, no *sane* person denies—To show, how united the citizens were, I refer to one act—on Saturday 20th April, Columbus O'Donnell,[28] Johns Hopkins[29] and John Clark[30] (*now* three of the most *loyal* men in the United States) representing the monied Institutions of Baltimore, called upon the Mayor, & Board of Police, and proffered to advance Five hundred thousand dolls, *expressly* providing, that it should be used for the *defence* of the City—[31] If the injuries threatened had been visited upon the City of Baltimore, would not the N.C. Railway have been injured, to a greater extent, than by stopping its opperations, for a few weeks? particularly as for all damages, the Company have now, a just claim against the State—

It is at least remarkable, that, at this late day, these proceedings, should have been commenced—I am also, taken by surprise, as some fifteen months since, in a friendly conversation that Mr J. D. Cameron & myself had, at Calvert Station, in [the] presence of Mr Colder,[32] Mr J. D. C. unhesitatingly declared, that he believed the order for the destruction of the Bridges, emanated from Govr. Hicks, and we concurred in declaring said Hicks to be among the *damndest* villians, on the face of the Earth—

Many of the malignant, dark lantern, Know Nothings,[33] are much disappointed at the result of my prosecution in the U.S. Circuit Court, some of them, I learn have encouraged, if not, induced the Railway Co. to institute this suit, perhaps, with all, to make a fee—I name, Ths. S. Alexander[34] & Archd Sterling Jr,[35] as two of these creatures—These two men are now in office, by depriving the true, law abiding & taxpaying citizens of Baltimore of their rights—Neither of them, could ever have reached the threshold of position without the practices, inaugurated by these hated Know Nothings, in their dark lantern assemblages—

Some two weeks since, I was subp[o]enaed to attend at the present term of [the] Circuit Court of Baltimore County as a witness, against the N.C. Railway Co, they having been indicted for stopping travel on the York turnpike, at Cockeysville, my name, was placed on the indictment, at the instigation of those, who made the complaint before the Grand Jury, and without my knowledge, or consent—I immediately called upon the Prosecutor for the County Mr R. J. Gittings[36] and had my name erased from the list of witnesses, and he further consented to stop all proceedings, against the Company, upon my representing, that they were preparing to make a watering place, south of the crossing, and thus obviate the necessity of leaving any cars in a position to obstruct travel on the Turnpike, & on Monday last, the first day of the term, he dismissed all the witnesses. I merely recite this circumstance, to show, that I have been a consistent friend of the Company—

I regret to have taxed you, with this long communication, but, believing it possible, that the Board of Directors have commenced these proceedings upon some false representation, I know of, no person, more competent than yourself to bring about an adjustment—

I would be glad to hear from, or see you here at any time—

Very truly

Yr ob't Ser't

John Merryman

Genl Cameron.

It is not clear whether Cameron ever responded to this letter, but it is likely that he did not.

When considering Merryman's letter in light of the surrounding legal circumstances, two final questions present themselves. First, what was the connection between John Merryman and Simon Cameron; and, second, why was Merryman singled out as the lead defendant in the civil suit instituted by the Northern Central Railway Company? The answers to these questions reveal a great deal about the problems that ordering and carrying out "arbitrary arrests" caused for Union leaders during the Civil War. They also reveal that, by 1863, John Merryman's significance was no longer as a symbol of civil liberty in wartime; rather, he had become a mere pawn in the hands of one of the leading power brokers of the nineteenth century.

Simon Cameron is justly remembered as one of the most ruthless politicians and businessmen in American history. Before there were the robber barons of the Gilded Age, there was Simon Cameron. Cameron was known as the "Great Winnebago Chieftain" for allegedly bilking Indians in the Wisconsin Territory in the 1830s. By the 1840s he had attained a seat in the U.S. Senate as a Democrat, where, in 1845 he singlehandedly thwarted a nomination to the Supreme Court by a president of his own party. Whether it was deserved or not, he had a national reputation for buying votes at elections. When Cameron, now a Republican, won election to the U.S. Senate in 1857, the Democrats accused him of bribery. In 1863 he was again suspected of bribing enough Democrats in the Pennsylvania legislature to secure his election to the Senate. This time, however, he was thwarted by a mob of angry Democrats who crowded the galleries of the state capitol ready to shoot any Democratic legislator who did not vote against Cameron.[37] This instance, however, was an exception to the rule. When Simon Cameron wanted something, he usually found a way to get it.

Cameron had been investing in railroads since the 1830s. He had been on the Northern Central Railway's board of directors since its formation in 1854 and he owned a large share of the company's stock. In 1860, the Pennsylvania Railroad and several prominent Pennsylvanians began purchasing significant amounts of the Northern Central's stock; Cameron was likely instrumental in convincing the Pennsylvania Railroad to buy these shares so that the Pennsylvanians could control the company. As secretary of war at the beginning of the Civil War, Cameron directed a large amount of government business to the N.C. Railway. As was seen in Merryman's letter, Cameron's son, James D. Cameron, held high office in the company.[38]

John Merryman also had a vested interest in the financial success of the Northern Central Railway. Merryman's property bordered parts of the railroad line. In 1855, he advertised 150 acres of his Hayfields estate for sale as "a desirable FARM . . . within one and a half miles of Menkton Station, upon the Northern Central Rail Road." The Railway's *Annual Report* for 1859 also listed him, along with Simon Cameron, as one of the directors on the part of the stockholders for the year 1860.[39] Merryman's financial interests in the company suggest that he was being truthful when he claimed that his "whole course" toward the railroad was "decidedly friendly." Other prewar letters to Cameron substantiate Merryman's claim.[40] Despite these feelings of affection for the railroad, Merryman's actions had caused his friends and fellow investors significant financial loss. He may have, as a consequence, burned more than just physical bridges in April 1861.

Merryman was correct in his assumption that Thomas Alexander was one of those "creatures" who had "induced the Railway Co. to institute this suit." Had Alexander's motive simply been "to make a fee," however, Merryman was appealing to the wrong person—for no one knew better than Simon Cameron how to make a profit at other people's expense. What Merryman did not know was that Alexander was working *for* Cameron, and this case was neither about a fee nor about damages for the railroad. Merryman's lawyer, who had previously been a president of the Northern Central Railroad, asked Cameron to use his influence to induce the railroad company to drop the case, but there was little chance Cameron would abandon *this* civil prosecution.[41]

Why was Cameron so intent on prosecuting this case against his old associate John Merryman? Because in 1863, Cameron—like Cadwalader—was being sued by Maryland civilians who had been arrested by the military while he was secretary of war. On December 20, 1862, the Baltimore police commissioners filed suit against Cameron and the Northern Central Railway Company (as Cameron's garnishee) in the Baltimore City Superior Court. Each commissioner sought $20,000 in damages. After passage of the Habeas Corpus Act, the suits were removed to the U.S. Circuit Court for the District of Maryland.[42]

Cameron and his lawyer believed that the railroad's suit against Merryman would produce evidence that they could later use to exonerate Cameron in the civil cases in which *he* was the defendant. It appears that Cameron may have briefly wavered over whether to prosecute the case against John Merryman, but Thomas Alexander compelled his client to proceed: "In Merrymans case the defence will introduce all the incidents of April 1861 and will thus play into our hands. The ground of defence to be that M acted under the orders of his superiors. If he maintains this proposition in law he will furnish you with a complete defence against the actions of the com[missione]rs[.] For in all you did or are supposed to have done you may shelter yourself . . . behind the orders of the President." Cameron's interests, according to Alexander, were "therefore in the continued prosecution of the suit."[43]

In this light, Cameron should have been able to sympathize with Merryman. Merryman had acted under the orders of Governor Hicks, while Cameron had acted under the authority of President Lincoln. Cameron wanted to shield himself from criminal prosecutions and civil suits in the same way that Merryman did. But Cameron knew that many civilians had been arrested during his brief tenure as secretary of war, and the Habeas Corpus Act of 1863 notwithstanding, he might still be held liable for those detentions. Pierce Butler had already sued him. Now the Baltimore police commissioners. There was no telling who else might join in the game.

Cameron deeply feared that suits like these "may involve all my fortune." Prior to the passage of the Habeas Corpus Act in 1863, he pleaded with Lincoln and the Republicans in Congress to offer Union officials some sort of protection from these proceedings. In fact, part of Cameron's motivation for running for the U.S. Senate in January 1863 may have been to help usher indemnifying legislation through that stubborn body. Cameron implored Lincoln to throw his official support behind Thaddeus Stevens's Indemnity Bill when it went before the Senate in December 1862. "The bill now before the Senate, from the House, could be passed within this week, if you and the gentlemen of the Cabinet will give it some personal attention," Cameron told the president. "I spoke with several Senators in relation to it—but I have already learned that a man out of office in Washington is greatly shorn of power. If the bill is not passed, some of the gentlemen whom I left behind me, will, also, learn this fact when, in the course of time they get into the ranks."[44] Perhaps if Cameron had been elected to the Senate he could have helped pass Stevens's stronger bill. The act that was finally adopted, however, did not prohibit suits for damages; it merely offered certain protections in the proceedings of those suits. As a consequence, Union officials like Simon Cameron still had to face their adversaries in court.

Cameron and his lawyer lived by the rule that the best defense was a good offense. In addition to orchestrating the railroad's suit against John Merryman, Alexander suggested that Cameron ask the federal government to pursue the treason cases against the Baltimore police commissioners. "Permit me to suggest that the Government can aid you in this matter by requiring its attorney to press on the trial of the Treason cases at the next Term," Alexander explained to Cameron.

> It has been imagined that those cases were not to be tried in short order that the Government was afraid to bring them on. Hence the civil action against you and others. If the order goes forth that they *shall* be tried and if the order is accompanied by an intimation to the attorney [William Price], that the government expects convictions the other side will be driven to consider whether their interests nay their personal security is to be promoted by trying conclusions with the government and if they are wise they will be perfectly inclined to suffer bye gones to sleep as bye gones.

In other words, the only reason the Baltimore police were suing Cameron was because their time was not being occupied by the treason cases pending against them. Cameron forwarded Alexander's request to Lincoln.[45] Chief Justice Taney and his delaying tactics be damned—the Maryland treason cases needed to move forward. Unfortunately for Cameron, the police commissioners had not been among those U.S. attorney Price had chosen to re-indict in July 1863 after he had the circuit court quash the original sixty treason indictments from 1861.[46]

Alexander employed a number of other strategies to defend his client. He attempted to obtain the personal papers of the police commissioners that had been seized by the military at the time of their arrest so that he could prove the commissioners' disloyalty, but the military was unable to locate them. He also hoped to find disloyal correspondence from April 1861 in the official police telegraph books, but he does not appear to have been successful. Finally, among the many witnesses Alexander intended to call, he also planned to subpoena the files of several Baltimore newspapers. Cameron was well pleased with his attorney's efforts. He told Secretary of State William H. Seward that Alexander exhibited "uncommon ability, with great zeal and industry, in his preparation . . . of these cases." Cameron therefore asked the State Department to supply Alexander with "liberal compensation" for his labor.[47]

On November 2, 1863, Judge Giles, presiding alone in the U.S. Circuit Court for the District of Maryland, postponed the commissioners' suit against Cameron because it had not been entered upon the court's trial docket. The commissioners were happy for the delay because they wanted to wait until the case could be heard by Chief Justice Taney as well. Impatient and unhappy about the delays, Cameron wrote to Lincoln suggesting that the president re-arrest the police commissioners and charge them anew with treason. "My attorney thinks they will be favorably affected by the arrest of all the parties for Treason," Cameron informed the president. "The suits need not be prosecuted, unless it is found necessary in the progress of my suits," he continued. "These of mine are the first suits of the kind and a decision would not only be injurious to the Govt, but would be injurious to me—and hence my anxiety." In short, the Baltimore police commissioners could not prosecute their cases against Cameron from a military Bastille somewhere far away from Baltimore. Ever the cutthroat politician, Cameron reminded Lincoln that important elections would be held in Maryland in a few days. "These arrests, at *this time* will have a very favorable effect on the coming election and for that alone would be proper." The following day Cameron sent Lincoln two missives recanting his suggestion to re-arrest the police.[48]

On November 16, 1863, the U.S. circuit court convened to hear the cases of the Baltimore police commissioners against Simon Cameron. Thomas Alexander insisted that Cameron had not ordered the arrest of the Baltimoreans. Severn Teackle Wallis, the lawyer for the commissioners, informed the court that if Alexander would state in open court that Cameron had not ordered the arrests then they would drop the suits. After a brief consultation with his client, Alexander declared that Cameron "had no part in the arrest or imprisonment of the defendants, or either of them." Wallis then directed the court "to strike off the cases, which was accordingly done."[49] Once these cases were concluded, Cameron likely saw no reason to further prosecute the Northern Central's case against Merryman, which may explain why that matter was dropped before it went to trial. It is also quite possible that Cameron brokered a deal between Merryman, George Cadwalader, and the Northern Central Railroad so that Merryman would drop his suit against Cadwalader in exchange for the railroad dropping its suit against Merryman. Since Cameron was intimate with all of the parties involved in the various suits, he could have arranged such a deal. The timing of this scenario fits the extant evidence. Merryman dropped his suit against Cadwalader in the spring of 1865, which is about the same time that the railroad's suit against Merryman disappears from the records.

~

Many Unionists believed it was absurd that suspected traitors could sue government officials for wrongful arrest. "It is true that if a head of a department steps outside of his authority and acts maliciously, he is, as he ought to be, responsible in damages," argued U.S. attorney William Price of Maryland. But the president, in Price's estimation, had the "constitutional powers, in a state of war or insurrection," to arrest and imprison men like the Baltimore police commissioners, if they were suspected of disloyalty. "And the rule regulating the exercise of these powers, is, that he is the judge of the time, the case, & the mode of their exercise. If asked why these men were imprisoned? He need give no other reason, than that such was his judgment." Price's views of the Constitution and presidential war powers were remarkably similar to Lincoln's. The courts, in his view, were not the only branch of the government that could interpret the Constitution. In time of war, the commander-in-chief would determine the limits and extent of his own authority. If he believed certain actions were necessary, no other branch of the government should be able to contradict him.[50]

Secretary of State William H. Seward seems to have believed that he was immune from civil action, with or without the Indemnity Act. Seward famously boasted to Lord Lyons that he could arrest citizens anywhere in the United States simply by ringing a bell on his desk. When former minister to Bogota George W. Jones filed suit in January 1863 against Seward for wrongful arrest, Jones's lawyer informed Seward so that he might secure a lawyer for himself. Seward replied that the matter was "public" and "official," not "personal"; in short, he would not recognize the legitimacy of the proceedings against him by acting in his own defense.[51] Seward's view was to win the war first and settle legal disputes later. "Let us save the country," he told a friend, "and then cast ourselves upon the judgment of the people, if we have in any case, acted without legal authority."[52] Most

Union leaders, however, did not feel at liberty to deal with these matters so cavalierly.

Anxious Union officials proactively took measures to protect themselves from civil suits. Prior to the passage of the Indemnity Act, officers at the Old Capitol Prison in Washington, D.C., required prisoners to take oaths "both of allegiance to the Government and an obligation not to prosecute the Federal or State officers concerned in the[ir] arrest and imprisonment" before they would be discharged from prison. Senators James A. McDougall of California and Willard Saulsbury of Delaware, both Democrats, protested the requirement of such oaths for depriving citizens of their rights under the Constitution. From the prisoners' perspective, however, "the imposition of such an obligation on us" would "be the best evidence that we have been here for three months the innocent and injured victims of Lincoln's despotism" and that "the tyrants" who subjected "us to this despotism know themselves to be guilty of an offense for which we have redress against them."[53] In short, the prisoners might still sue.

Republican and War Democrat judges tended to be sympathetic to Union officials, while Democrat judges were less likely to sympathize with the view that Lincoln and his subordinates could decide for themselves when northern civilians needed to be detained. Pennsylvania's chief justice, Walter H. Lowrie, heard a case of illegal seizure in January 1863 in which a Democratic newspaper editor sued a U.S. marshal for confiscating his printing press under the First Confiscation Act of 1861. Chief Justice Lowrie, a Democrat, delivered a jury charge in which he argued that the president was subordinate to the law and therefore could not order his subordinates to violate the law, even in the midst of a gigantic rebellion. The jury ruled in the editor's favor, granting him a verdict of $512. Under the Habeas Corpus Act, the marshal appealed the case to the U.S. Circuit Court for the Eastern District of Pennsylvania. A federal jury awarded a verdict of $504.33. Things could have been worse for the marshal. "The verdict is considered under the circumstances very moderate," he wrote to the secretary of the interior.[54]

Several other cases resulted in damages for persons who had been arrested, but, as in the Pennsylvania case, the awards were usually minimal. In 1867, a federal judge in San Francisco awarded $635 to a Californian who had exulted in the assassination of Abraham Lincoln. Under an order of General Irvin McDowell, the plaintiff had been imprisoned at Alcatraz Island for saying that "the damned old son of a bitch should have been shot long ago," among other vile things. The judge held that because Mc-Dowell had acted without direct orders from the president he was liable for damages; however, the judge factored McDowell's "good motives," the state of public feeling, and the "gross misconduct of the plaintiff" into his calculations. The state of Indiana actually passed a law limiting damages in these types of cases to five dollars. As a consequence, when Lambdin P. Milligan sought $500,000 from the various civil and military officers who had seen to his arrest, military trial, and death sentence (including the twelve members of his military commission), he won a paltry $5 (plus court costs of about $1,000).[55]

The issue at stake in these cases was the fear that the judicial process placed in the hearts of those waging the war for the Union. While Lincoln —and perhaps Seward—might have felt largely immune from the actions that could be taken against them in state and federal courts, lesser figures feared that the courts might hamstring their efforts in waging the war or cause them significant personal and financial loss. After the federal court in Washington handed down a decision in a case for wrongful arrest in December 1864, Secretary of State Seward worried that "no Cabinet officer was safe," while Secretary of War Stanton "said he would [be] imprisoned a thousand years at least."[56] These cases demonstrate that the significance of *Ex parte Merryman* was not simply that a man had been arrested without judicial process for obstructing passage of troops and telegrams through Baltimore. Cadwalader and Cameron's reactions to Merryman and the Baltimore police commissioners reveal that *Merryman*'s larger significance was that government officials, both in their official capacity and as private citizens, needed protection from civil suits for actions they had taken while in office or the military service. Without ample protection and immunity they felt vulnerable and incapable of effectively waging the war.

The Baltimore Riot of April 19, 1861.
(Prints and Photographs Division, Library of Congress)

Baltimore Mayor George William Brown.
(Baltimore: Past and Present with Biographical Sketches of the Representative Men.
Baltimore: Richardson & Bennett, 1871)

Baltimore Police Marshal George P. Kane.
(Biographical Cyclopedia of Representative Men of Maryland and [the] District of Columbia.
Baltimore: National Biographical Publishing, 1879)

Maryland Governor Thomas H. Hicks.
(Prints and Photographs Division, Library of Congress)

General George Cadwalader.
(Prints and Photographs Division, Library of Congress)

John Merryman.
(Courtesy of Frances Love Merryman)

Two Unidentified Members of the Baltimore County Horse Guards.
(Courtesy of the Baltimore County Public Library)

John Merryman's Letterhead, featuring Hayfields.
(Historic American Buildings Survey, Prints and Photographs Division, Library of Congress)

Fort McHenry.
(Prints and Photographs Division, Library of Congress)

The Arrest of Baltimore Police Marshal George P. Kane.
(Prints and Photographs Division, Library of Congress)

Cannons Aimed at Baltimore from Federal Hill.
(Courtesy of the Baltimore County Public Library)

Secretary of War Simon Cameron.
(Prints and Photographs Division, Library of Congress)

Senator Reverdy Johnson.
(Prints and Photographs Division, Library of Congress)

Epilogue

"HABEAS CORPUS JOHN"

*J*ohn Merryman's petition for a writ of habeas corpus became a *cause célèbre* in both the northern states and the Confederacy. In Maryland, his case became a flashpoint of controversy and heated exchanges. Between April and August 1861, the Maryland legislature adopted resolutions and enacted statutes rebuking the Lincoln administration for its usurpations in their state. From the legislators' vantage point, the state and its citizens needed to be vindicated against the federal government's encroachments on civil liberties. Lincoln's policies in Maryland also seemed to justify the South's course of action. As a consequence, the general assembly requested their representatives in Congress to "urge and vote for an immediate recognition of the independence of the government of the Confederate States of America." While it is true that the assembly never voted for Maryland to secede, resolutions such as these can hardly be considered loyal.[1]

The assembly adopted several resolutions decrying the military occupation of Baltimore and the arrest of Maryland civilians. In one such set of resolutions, the legislature declared itself for "peace . . . in favor of a recognition of the Southern Confederacy" and viewed "with utmost alarm and indignation the exercise of the despotic power, that has dared to suspend [the writ of habeas corpus] in the case of John Merryman now confined in Fort McHenry." The assembly also adopted legislation to protect leaders in Baltimore who might be accused of taking actions against the Union. In May 1861 the legislature enacted a law prohibiting the prosecution of the mayor or police of Baltimore, or any of their subordinates, for any actions they had taken "in their efforts to maintain peace and good order, and prevent further strife on and after the occurrences on the nineteenth day of April."[2] Just as Lincoln and Congress would come to realize about officers at the federal level, the state of Maryland believed it needed to protect those who acted in controversial ways on behalf of the state.

On June 18, 1861, the legislature reaffirmed Merryman's commission as first lieutenant of the Baltimore County Horse Guards "as if he had taken the oath of office," which he presumably was unable to take since he was still confined in Fort McHenry. In January 1862, however, after the state government had fallen into firm Unionist hands, the legislature stripped Merryman of his commission. Both of these laws were symbolic gestures since the Horse Guards had disbanded by May 1861.[3]

The Union military presence in Maryland generally ensured that state authorities remained loyal to the federal cause during the war. As a consequence, the legislature enacted several laws to punish treason and disloyalty within the state. In February 1862, perhaps in response to *Ex parte Merryman,* the Maryland legislature denied the privilege of the writ of habeas corpus to persons charged with treason. The following month the state passed a major piece of legislation that defined and punished "Treason and other kindred offences," such as displaying rebel flags "with a view and intent to excite seditious feelings." Later during the war, the state constitution disfranchised Maryland voters who could not take an oath of both past and future loyalty to the United States.[4] As odious as such legislation must have been to southern sympathizers like Chief Justice Taney and John Merryman, Maryland Democrats were powerless to stop their enactment and execution.

Roger B. Taney had gone to great lengths to have his opinion reach as many readers as possible. The chief justice saw to the publication of the opinion in pamphlet form, and Mark Neely suggests that *Ex parte Merryman* ought to be read like a nineteenth-century political stump speech. Taney's opinion reached the broad audience he desired. South of the Mason-Dixon Line, Confederate leaders applauded Taney's actions in the *Merryman* case. "The eminent and venerable Chief Justice Taney . . . whose purity of character and whose great legal ability are acknowledged by all, has in a recent decision clearly exposed the unconstitutionality of the proceedings," wrote Confederate secretary of state R. M. T. Hunter of the suspension of habeas corpus in Maryland. Both publicly and privately Confederate president Jefferson Davis echoed Taney's criticism of that "ignorant usurper" in the North who was "trampl[ing] upon all the prerogatives of citizenship" and "exercis[ing] power never delegated to him."[5]

In Louisiana, twenty-two-year-old Maryland native James Ryder Randall stayed awake one night composing "Maryland, My Maryland," a rousing battle hymn that became Maryland's official state song in 1939. Its opening stanza expressed the hatred of Maryland secessionists for their northern countrymen:

> The despot's heel is on thy shore,
>   Maryland!
> His touch is at thy temple door,[6]
>   Maryland!
> Avenge the patriotic gore
> That flecked the streets of Baltimore,
> And be the battle queen of yore,
>   Maryland! My Maryland!

Randall's poem caused an instant sensation throughout the South and became one of the Confederacy's favorite anthems. In the final stanza, to the tune of a Revolutionary "bugle, fife, and drum," Maryland "spurns the Northern scum!" When Robert E. Lee's army invaded Maryland in September 1862, his men sang Randall's hymn, hoping to win complacent or undecided Marylanders over to the rebel cause.[7]

In another composition, Randall specifically lamented the loss of liberty experienced by men like John Merryman and the Baltimore police commissioners. When the "tyrant's war-shout comes," Randall pledged,

> We hear it! we heed it, with vengeful thrills,
> And we shall not forgive or forget;

He continued:

> Bigots! ye quell not the valiant mind,
> With the clank of an iron chain,
> The spirit of freedom sings in the wind,
> O'er *Merryman, Thomas,* and *Kane;*
> And we, though we smite not, are not thralls,
> We are piling a gory debt;

While down by McHenry's dungeon walls,
There's life in the old land yet!

In each stanza, Randall delineated reasons for fear and for anger, but also reasons to maintain hope for life in his native land. Another amateur secession-sympathizing poet told the story of John Merryman to the minstrel tune of "Old Dan Tucker."[8]

The contemporary significance of the *Merryman* case is apparent not only in the newspaper coverage of the "collision" between Lincoln and Taney but also in the case's widespread mention in the literature and popular culture of the day. Perhaps these colorful expressions of antifederal rage are a testament to the effectiveness of Taney's efforts to publicize his opinion. While Taney was powerless to control the events or outcome of the war, his pen nevertheless animated opposition to Lincoln that took other effective popular and artistic forms.

The remainder of Taney's life is well known. The old chief justice lived out his final days a frustrated judge. Privately, Taney wished for a peaceful separation of the states. As death approached, he needed great assistance to continue his work on the bench. "The last time I saw him was after the final adjournment," remarked the reporter of the Supreme Court, "when somebody was administering whiskey & water to him in the Judges rooms to keep him 'up,' after his effort at presiding." Anticipating that certain types of war-related cases would come before his bench, Taney drafted opinions that never saw the light of day. They were only discovered after his death, which occurred on October 12, 1864. "The Hon. old Roger B. Taney has earned the gratitude of his country by dying at last," rejoiced George Templeton Strong of New York. "Better late than never." Similarly, historian Don E. Fehrenbacher noted that the chief justice's death "put an end to the anomaly of a nation's fighting a war with its highest judicial officer bound in sympathy to the enemy." Ironically, Taney's death came on the first day of a two-day referendum in which his home state ratified a new state constitution that permanently abolished slavery in Maryland. The long-time defender of slavery would die on the same day as his peculiar institution. "Two ancient abuses and evils were perishing together," concluded Strong.[9]

In February 1865 a bill was introduced in the House of Representatives to honor the late chief justice with a marble bust in the Supreme Court's room in the Capitol. The bill quickly passed in the House but was rejected by the Senate. Charles Sumner of Massachusetts argued that "an emancipated country" should not honor the author of the *Dred Scott* decision, while John P. Hale of New Hampshire pointed out "that when the slavemasters had raised the banners of civil war, Judge Taney, who had been swift for thirty years to utter their decrees, had no aid to give his struggling country. In its hour of humiliation, trial, and agony, he never gave one cheering word nor performed one act to protect or save. He sank into his grave without giving a cheering word or a helping hand to the country he had vainly sought to place forever by judicial authority under the iron rule of the slave-masters." In short, the chief justice was a traitor who had tried to use the courts to harm the Union. It would not be until 1874 that Congress passed a bill to honor Taney with a bust in the courtroom—and then, it was attached to a bill honoring the now-late Chief Justice Chase as well.[10]

Maryland's Civil War experience impacted the state's postwar lawmaking and constitutionalism. The state repealed much of its wartime legislation as well as the loyalty oaths required by the 1864 state constitution. In 1867, after Maryland had fallen back into solid Democratic hands, the state adopted a new constitution that would have made Roger B. Taney proud. One provision declared: "That the provisions of the Constitution of the United States, and of this State, apply, as well in time of war, as in time of peace; and any departure therefrom, or violation thereof, under the plea of necessity, or any other plea, is subversive of good Government, and tends to anarchy and despotism." In another provision that might have surprised the late chief justice, the new constitution prohibited even the state legislature from suspending the writ of habeas corpus.[11]

≈

John Merryman's arrest at 2:00 a.m. on May 25, 1861, was only the first of several encounters he would have with the Union military during the Civil War. Indeed, within two weeks of his arrest, another "party of Pennsylvania Volunteers" returned to Hayfields to search his home—"much to the alarm of my unprotected family." From his cell at Fort McHenry, Merryman pleaded with Secretary of War Simon Cameron to offer the "assurance of personal safety" to his family and "to prevent a like occurrence."[12] But with no other means of protection, Merryman's only hope was in the goodwill of an old business associate and politician who now wielded tremendous power in Washington.

John Merryman's time at Fort McHenry was only a minor part of his wartime experience. For most of the 1860s, Merryman had both criminal and civil actions pending against him. He never could have imagined such an outcome in April 1861, when he followed orders from superiors to burn railroad bridges. Nor was May 25, 1861, the only time that Merryman was arrested by the military.

Sometime in late August 1862 a Baltimore County Unionist named John H. Longnecker sent a letter to the military claiming that a gathering of pro-southern citizens would be "arming and drilling for some disloyal purpose" at the home of one John White, near Hayfields.[13] Union general John E. Wool ordered Provost Marshal William A. Van Nostrand to proceed to White's residence and arrest those present. As Van Nostrand approached the house at midnight on September 1, he found it well lit. It was not at all what he expected of a secretive, traitorous, warlike meeting. Van Nostrand ordered his men to surround the building so that "not a soul" could escape. Upon entering the house, he was perplexed by what he found—it was full of men, women, and children. "Some were dancing and some were sitting around," he said. "I entered the building and stood at the parlor door before a person about the house was aware of it." Of the many faces in the crowd, John Merryman's was the only one Van Nostrand recognized.[14]

The partygoers were thoroughly astonished by the intrusion. "It was a sort of surprise party and fruit supper for the little children," remembered one of the attendees. "We laughed, talked and danced until about 12 o'clock, when the police officers, armed with pistols rushed in and alarmed the women and children considerably, they looked around and everybody was very much confused." Believing that his orders left him no discretion, Van Nostrand rounded up the eighteen men at the party (ages fourteen and up) and proceeded to arrest them. He then provided soldiers as escorts for the women and children to return home. At 4:00 a.m., John Merryman and his friends—several of whom had been members of the Baltimore County Horse Guards—were taken to Baltimore. "We went to the Station House and stayed there very uncomfortably until 10 o'clock the next morning when we were marched up to General Wool," recalled one of those arrested. Without discovering anything of a "treasonable character" about them, Wool ordered their immediate release. "Gentlemen, I understand this thing is a mistake and you have been subject to some inconvenience," Wool told them. The men each signed an oath of allegiance, and Wool requested that they relay his sincerest apologies to the ladies.[15]

Wool's decision to release the men was based on two concerns. On the one hand, he doubted that they were guilty of any crime and believed that they had been arrested by an overzealous military officer. On the other hand, Wool did not want any more damages suits filed against him. Like other Union leaders, General Wool was already being sued by several Maryland civilians. He had no desire to add any other names to the list of plaintiffs stacked against him. "I am in no respect willing to become responsible for the arrests made by Provost Marshal McPhail or his deputies," Wool told General Henry Wager Halleck—especially since these arrests had been made solely "on mere suspicion" of "disloyalty." In other words, Wool would not take the fall for an irresponsible subordinate: "Whosoever orders the confinement of these men, will be subject to the penalty for false imprisonment," he declared. Wool informed Halleck that he released the men because he saw no basis for their arrest or detention. "I adopted the course mentioned in regard to these prisoners," Wool continued, "because I knew if I had ordered them in the Fort for confinement I should have been subject to the penalty of false imprisonment. It is such arrests that produce a great deal of trouble, whilst the result produced is nothing but disgust and the driving of people into the ranks of the Rebels."[16]

In this instance—which was a full six months prior to the passage of the Habeas Corpus Act of 1863—General Wool acted cautiously in light of the dangers involved in arresting civilians suspected of disloyalty.[17] Wool, in fact, had at least seven damages suits filed against him during the Civil War. Most of these suits were dismissed before Appomattox, but two persisted into the postwar years. Finally, on April 23, 1867—the same day that Merryman's treason indictment was dismissed—juries rendered verdicts in the two suits still pending against Wool. In each case the jury found Wool liable for damages in the amount of one cent![18] After five years of bearing the heavy burden of litigation, Wool escaped with a minimal penalty plus court costs.

John Merryman had at least three other encounters with the federal military during the war. About a month after his arrest at the neighborhood dance, Merryman was one of 978 men from Baltimore County to be conscripted as part of the militia draft of 1862. A man of considerable means, Merryman furnished a substitute—an Irishman named James Malone —to get out of fighting. In the aftermath of the Gettysburg campaign, in July 1863, Union soldiers passing through Baltimore County pressed some of Merryman's horses into the federal service. In the spring of 1864, Union soldiers stationed near Hayfields severely beat Merryman. Afterward, his assailants encircled him singing "rally around the bridge burners," presumably to the tune of "Battle Cry of Freedom."[19]

When Confederate general Jubal A. Early invaded Maryland and Washington, D.C., in July 1864, Merryman hosted the rebel invaders at Hayfields. On July 10, Merryman enjoyed "an agreeable lunch" with Confederate general Bradley T. Johnson of Maryland. Johnson recalled fifteen years later: "The charming society, the lovely girls, the balmy July air, and the luxuriant verdure of Hayfield[s], all combined to make the scene enchanting to soldiers who had been for months campaigning in the battle-scarred plains and valleys of Virginia." From Hayfields, Johnson moved through Baltimore County, where he burned the home of Maryland's Unionist governor, Augustus W. Bradford, in retaliation for the Union army's earlier burning of the Virginia governor's home. Merryman used his personal rapport with Johnson to convince the rebels not to destroy Ashland Furnace, an iron foundry owned by a Baltimore County neighbor and friend.[20]

On a personal level, 1864 was an eventful year for the Merryman household. On January 21, 1864, Merryman's father, Nicholas, died at the age of seventy-five. He passed away at Hereford Farm, the home where several generations of Merrymans—including John—had been born and raised. John Merryman's wife, Ann, became pregnant later that spring. When, on December 5, 1864, she delivered a son, the Merrymans named him Roger Brooke Taney Merryman in honor of the recently deceased chief justice. Of their eleven children, R. B. T. Merryman was the only one to die in infancy.[21]

Merryman, like all Maryland slave owners, lost his human property during the war. Some of Merryman's slaves fled Hayfields at the first opportunity. In April 1863, the *Baltimore Sun* reported that Merryman "lost a valuable man" during one of the "regular stampede[s] of slaves." Following another such occurrence, the *Baltimore County Advocate* remarked that "if this state of things continue, and it undoubtedly will, in a short time there will not be an able-bodied slave in that section of the country." To the consternation of Baltimore County slave owners, the paper continued, "A number of the men have turned up in the negro regiment, the second one, which is being recruited in Baltimore."[22] By November 1864, slavery in Maryland was no more.

Following the war Merryman remained a prominent figure in Maryland politics and agriculture. In 1865, he started a fertilizer business in Baltimore City called John Merryman & Co. Much of his business was with the Deep South. In 1870 the Maryland legislature elected him state treasurer, and in 1874 he was elected to the House of Delegates. Merryman, according to one contemporary observer, was not "a politician in the common meaning of that term, and he prefers the more satisfying and profitable life of the farmer and civilian." In 1876, Merryman won a bronze medal for his cattle at the Centennial Exposition in Philadelphia. By the end of his life, it was claimed that "over 100 bulls bred by him are at the head of herds of cattle in Indiana, Illinois, Iowa, Minnesota, Nebraska, Wyoming, Colorado, Kansas, and Texas." In the late 1870s he served as president of both the National Agricultural Association and the Maryland State Agricultural and Mechanical Association. "His very name," said the *Baltimore Sun* in 1881, "in his own State and over a wide area outside of it, was 'familiar as household words.'" Among his neighbors and friends, however, he was "quite famous for sometime as Habeas Corpus John."[23]

By 1868, Merryman and the Northern Central Railway Company appear to have buried the hatchet. When, on April 27, 1868, Merryman sent a letter to the railroad's board of directors asking for assistance with an upcoming agricultural fair, the railroad "agree[d] to provide platforms and sidings on the Northern Central Railway, carry free the police force needed to preserve order, and make liberal arrangements for transportation of parties and distinguished guests during exhibitions." Merryman and his fellow farmers "accept[ed] with much pleasure the very liberal offer made by the Northern Central Railway Company."[24]

Merryman's work with railroads may have led to his early death. In February 1881, while he was "examining the route of the new Arlington and Pimlico Railroad" near Baltimore, Merryman contracted a "severe cold" that stayed with him for two months. In May he went to Savannah, Georgia, to recover, but when he returned to Maryland he suffered from kidney disease, a "debility of the heart," dropsy, and a "catarrh of the lungs." When the autumn chill returned he was too weak to recover. In early November, his doctors concluded "that the case was hopeless, and that death was even then hovering over the sick man's couch." John Merryman died at Hayfields at 8:00 a.m. on November 15, 1881. His family gathered around him as "he peacefully and quietly expired." He was buried in the graveyard of Sherwood Episcopal Church, where he had served as a vestryman since 1846. He was only fifty-seven years old.[25]

Hayfields remained in the Merryman family until 1978.[26] In the late 1970s and early 1980s, the Baltimore County Board of Commissioners (Merryman had actually been president of the board in the 1850s) rejected several development proposals for Hayfields, including plans to turn the 474-acre estate into a 1,600-unit residential community, a hospital, and a landfill.[27] In 1986, the Mangione family purchased Hayfields. About a decade later they opened the Hayfields Country Club in Baltimore County. The club has preserved much of the beautiful landscape by creating an eighteen-hole golf course around the mansion. Now, instead of plows, cattle, sheep, and horses, golf carts cross the sprawling fields. Arnold Palmer, Tom Watson, and Lee Trevino have all walked the hills and fields where Union and Confederate soldiers once encamped. The club has renovated the mansion and outbuildings into dining rooms, a grill, meeting rooms, a pro shop, and a clubhouse. Members now relax and swap stories in the library, where a portrait of Colonel Nicholas Merryman Bosley still hangs over the fireplace.

On a slow day one can catch of glimpse of Hayfields as it once was under John Merryman's watchful eye. The club has done an admirable job of preserving Hayfields's elegance and history while meeting the needs of its twenty-first-century members. Still, the deeper story of what happened in this place has been largely misunderstood and forgotten for 150 years. At this old farmhouse, perched on a hillside next to I-83, lived a man who on several occasions played an integral role in the shaping of national policy during the Civil War. It is little wonder that the story of Abraham Lincoln, Roger B. Taney, and John Merryman still captures our attention today.

Indeed, historians, political scientists, lawyers, and judges continue to write volumes about *Ex parte Merryman* and the struggle that ensued between Lincoln and Taney in the spring and summer of 1861. Since September 11, 2001, there has been an outpouring of words about John Merryman's famous proceedings, including more than a dozen scholarly articles and book chapters, numerous websites, and an exemplary fifty-three-page teaching unit produced by the Federal Judicial History Office. In 2004, Supreme Court Justice Antonin Scalia cited *Merryman* in his *Hamdi v. Rumsfeld* dissent.[28] The principles debated in the *Merryman* proceedings have tremendous relevance for twenty-first-century Americans who are concerned about civil liberties in wartime, the unchecked expansion of executive power, the privacy of passengers during airport screenings, or the legality of detaining enemy combatants at Guantanamo Bay.

Unfortunately, our scholarship had reached a point in which it appeared that little new could be said about this very important case. Writers on wartime civil liberties have told and retold the story of *Ex parte Merryman* with their focus on Lincoln and Taney rather than on John Merryman himself. These accounts have generally limited their scope to the time that Merryman spent at Fort McHenry, and they often concluded with Lincoln's July 4 message to Congress. As a consequence, the main point has always been to explain the civil liberties issue from the top down—to debate whether the president can or should exercise extraconstitutional powers in time of national emergency, or to understand how policy makers and judges treated the constitutional rights of American citizens during the Civil War. Little attention has been given to the complex situation the federal government faced in dealing with disloyalty in the North; even less has been given to the myriad ways that civilian detainees responded to their arrests.

Shifting the focus to John Merryman reshapes the story and brings new questions to the fore. Close examination of the Baltimore treason trials gives us a better understanding of the inadequacies of the federal judiciary in wartime. Lincoln was correct when he noted in his April 15, 1861, proclamation that the southern rebellion was "too powerful to be suppressed by the ordinary course of judicial proceedings, or by the powers vested in the Marshals by law."[29] What the president did not yet realize—but would soon come to learn—was that the problem of treason in the North was also too powerful to be suppressed by ordinary judicial proceedings. It was impractical to believe that persons accused of treason could be dealt with by the civil courts in the midst of such a gigantic war.

In 1861, federal prosecutors were quick to indict northerners (and some southerners) for treason in the civil courts; by the midpoint of the war they had become much more selective.[30] Attorney General Edward Bates understood the uphill battle facing prosecutors. A conviction for treason might make a martyr of the accused, while an acquittal would embarrass the government. Moreover, a single juror could cause a hung jury, yet all twelve jurors were required to convict a traitor. In addition, the U.S. Constitution places a heavier burden on federal prosecutors in treason trials. And finally, federal prosecutors were powerless to force the hand of uncooperative judges. Chief Justices Taney and Chase were not the only federal judges who were wary of presiding over treason cases. When thirty-five crewmen from a Confederate privateer were tried in 1861 for high treason and piracy, Supreme Court justice Robert C. Grier, sitting as a circuit judge in Philadelphia, declared that he did "not intend to try any more of these cases." There was other pressing business to attend to, he continued, and he would not waste his time "trying charges against a few unfortunate men here out of half a million that are in arms against the government."[31]

Writing privately to Professor Francis Lieber of Columbia University, in 1863, Judge Advocate General Joseph Holt noted that "the government seems long since to have abandoned all idea of punishing" treason.[32] This was not exactly the case. Holt, like Lincoln, knew that it was much easier to use the military to arrest and temporarily detain civilians suspected of disloyalty than to go through the hassle and expense of a civil trial. Certainly civilians who were arrested without charges saw themselves as being punished. Nevertheless, in Lincoln's mind, such actions—which might not be constitutional in peacetime—"might become lawful" in wartime "by becoming indispensable to the preservation of the constitution, through the preservation of the Union."[33] The president, in other words, could take actions in his role as commander-in-chief that he could not take at other times.[34] After all, civil liberty would be protected in the long run only if the nation survived. What good would the Bill of Rights be if there was no nation left in which to enjoy those rights? And Lincoln, of course, claimed that his policies restricting civil liberties were temporary and would cease once the rebellion was over.[35] His concern was with preserving the Union, not the precedents that his wartime actions might be setting for the future.

Ultimately, the Lincoln administration decided to try some civilians in civil courts and to leave others in the hands of the military. The outcomes of the criminal prosecutions in Baltimore were in line with what happened in treason trials elsewhere in the North. Many persons were indicted for treason during the Civil War; few went to trial; fewer still were convicted.[36] At best, then, the state and federal judicial systems turned out to be ineffectual mechanisms for managing the problems of treason and disloyalty in the North. At worst, however, they became tools in the hands of potentially disloyal northerners to attack the federal government as it was striving to restore the Union. Suits for damages against federal officials became a clear and imminent danger to those who were waging war on behalf of the Union.

The suits instituted by John Merryman and the Baltimore police commissioners represented only a few of the thousands of suits filed against Union officers during and after the Civil War. In the postwar period, state judges in Kentucky ignored the provisions of the Habeas Corpus Act of 1863 and refused to remove damages suits to the federal courts. Kentucky judges also allowed for the criminal prosecution of Union officers for legitimate actions they had taken during the war. Some three thousand cases came before the Kentucky state courts in 1865 and 1866. Similar cases occurred elsewhere in the Union. New Jersey authorities arrested a federal marshal and charged him with kidnapping for having detained someone suspected of disloyalty. Postwar civil suits and criminal proceedings also appeared on court dockets in California, Indiana, Vermont, Massachusetts, New York, Wisconsin, and other states. In response, Congress amended the Habeas Corpus Act of 1863 on May 11, 1866, to punish state judges who refused to move such cases into the federal courts. Under the 1866 statute, federal officials and military officers could sue state judges who refused to remove the suits against them into the federal courts. In addition, the statute required the judges to pay "double costs" to the officers or officials.[37]

Examination of the life and trials of John Merryman, rather than of just the case of *Ex parte Merryman,* reveals several stark new realities about the habeas corpus issue that arose during the Civil War. We can now see that the "civil liberties" problem was only one side of the habeas corpus issue. On the other side were the fears of government officials and military officers who could be ruined—both financially and by criminal prosecution—for the actions that they took on behalf of the government. These concerns are evident in the correspondence of both soldiers and civilians. An officer in the Ninety-second Illinois Volunteers informed Senate Judiciary Committee chairman Lyman Trumbull that suits against him "involve an amount sufficient to sweep away all my property if I am not protected." But these cases were about more than just money. William Schley, the lawyer who represented Generals Cadwalader and Wool, argued that "these suits are of great importance, far beyond any question of pecuniary damage." If Congress did not protect civil and military officers in the performance of their official duties (excepting malicious actions), Schley continued, "a public servant has a very thankless preferment."[38] While scholars have overlooked the issue of damages suits for more than a generation, it is a subject that demands attention.

In a recent article in the *Journal of Supreme Court History,* law professor John Yoo, of "torture memo" fame, argues that *Ex parte Merryman* and *Ex parte Milligan* "did not assume the landmark importance" of other cases like *Marbury v. Madison* or *Brown v. Board of Education* because *Merryman* and *Milligan* had little practical influence in their own times and have had little impact on American jurisprudence. It is understandable that Yoo would downplay these cases' significance. As a strong proponent of increased executive power in wartime, and as one who actually served in the executive branch and was placed in the position of writing legal memorandums regarding detainment and interrogation policies for the War on Terror, Yoo has a vested interest in arguing that Lincoln's view of executive power was correct and that Taney's perspective lacked a proper understanding of the realities and necessities of war.

Ironically, Yoo minimizes the significance of two cases that, on a personal level, actually have quite a bit of relevance for him now that he is no longer with the Department of Justice. In 2008, convicted terrorist Jose Padilla filed a civil suit against Yoo seeking damages for Yoo's role in writing the so-called "torture memos."[39] In many respects, the case against Yoo is profoundly different than Merryman's case against General Cadwalader. Yoo was a mid-level attorney writing policy briefs for the Department of Justice, while Cadwalader was the military commander who actually oversaw the incarceration of a citizen prisoner. Nevertheless, in 2009, a federal judge in California—an appointee of President George W. Bush, no less—ruled that there were grounds for the case against Yoo to go forward. Yoo may find, as Simon Cameron did in December 1862, that "a man out of office in Washington is greatly shorn of power."[40]

For generations, scholars of the habeas corpus issue in American history have focused their attention almost exclusively on questions related to civil liberties and presidential war powers. To be sure, these questions are eminently important and deserve continued consideration. But moving beyond old questions adds new dimensions to our understanding of the difficulties that face presidential administrations in wartime. The many trials of John Merryman reveal how the courts were yet another front on which Lincoln had to fight the Civil War. On the one hand, Lincoln could use the courts to wage war against suspected traitors. Indeed, one Lincoln appointee in Virginia viewed his court as "an advanced judicial picket station in a hostile country."[41] But, on the other hand, prosecuting traitors in the courts was only part of the legal battle. Lincoln also had to defend his subordinates there. In these courtroom battles, hostile judges and juries could make decisions and render verdicts that might alter the trajectory of the war and reconstruction. In an era before the legal concept of qualified immunity had been developed, Lincoln and his allies in Congress had to pass wartime legislation that would protect Union officials from the enemy within.

Notes

ABBREVIATIONS

Archives II   National Archives at College Park, Md.

Court-Martial Case File   General Court-Martial Case Files, Record Group 153, Records of the Office of the Judge Advocate General (Army), National Archives and Records Administration, Washington, D.C. (Each case file includes an alpha-numeric case number.)

CWL   Roy P. Basler et al., eds., *The Collected Works of Abraham Lincoln.* 9 vols. New Brunswick, N.J.: Rutgers University Press, 1953–55.

Fed. Cases   *Federal Cases: Comprising Cases Argued and Determined in the Circuit and District Courts of the United States from the Earliest Times to the Beginning of the Federal Reporter, Arranged Alphabetically by the Titles of the Cases, and Numbered Consecutively.* 30 vols. St. Paul, Minn.: West Publishing Co., 1894–97. (Each citation is preceded by a volume number and followed by page numbers.)

Grason   Maryland House of Delegates. *Evidence of the Contested Election in the Case of Ridgely vs. Grason, to the General Assembly.* House of Delegates Document V. Annapolis: Richard P. Bayly, 1865.

HSDC   Historical Society of Dauphin County, Harrisburg, Pa.

HSP   Historical Society of Pennsylvania, Philadelphia, Pa.

LC   Manuscript Division, Library of Congress, Washington, D.C.

Lincoln Papers   Abraham Lincoln Papers, Manuscript Division, Library of Congress, Washington, D.C.

MDHS   Maryland Historical Society, Baltimore, Md.

MHI   U.S. Army Military History Institute, Carlisle, Pa.

MSA   Maryland State Archives, Annapolis, Md.

NARA   National Archives and Records Administration, Washington, D.C.

NARA-P National Archives at Philadelphia

O.R.   *War of the Rebellion: A Compilation of the Official Records of the Union and Confederate Armies.* 128 vols. Washington, D.C.: Government Printing Office, 1880–1901.

RG 60   Record Group 60, General Records of the Department of Justice, National Archives at College Park, Md.

RG 107 Record Group 107, Records of the Office of the Secretary of War, National Archives and Records Administration, Washington, D.C.

Stat.   *The Public Statutes at Large of the United States of America.* (Each citation is preceded by a volume number and followed by page numbers.)

U.S.   *United States Reports.* (Each citation is preceded by a volume number and followed by page numbers.)

INTRODUCTION

1. Arthur T. Downey claims, without citation, that Merryman's "accommodation at Fort McHenry was not a dank dungeon, but rather an airy room on the second floor." The park rangers at Fort McHenry have told me that it is not known for certain in which part of the fort Merryman was imprisoned, but they think that it might have been a ground-level room near the front entrance that was more "dank" than Downey describes. See Arthur T. Downey, "The Conflict between the Chief Justice and the Chief Executive: *Ex parte Merryman*," *Journal of Supreme Court History* 31 (2006): 271.

2. Mark E. Neely, Jr., "The Constitution and Civil Liberties under Lincoln," in *Our Lincoln: New Perspectives on Lincoln and His World,* ed. Eric Foner (New York: W. W. Norton, 2008), 37. I must point out that, other than my historiographical disagreement over Taney's jurisdiction in *Merryman,* I find Neely's essay to be a brilliant and penetrating analysis of Lincoln, civil liberties, and party politics during the Civil War.

3. "Landmark Cases Related to Understanding Terrorism Cases—U.S. Courts Educational Outreach," http://www.uscourts.gov/outreach/topics/habeascorpus_landmark.htm (accessed April 19, 2010).

4. James M. McPherson, *Tried by War: Abraham Lincoln as Commander in Chief* (New York: Penguin, 2008), 27; Geoffrey R. Stone, *Perilous Times: Free Speech in Wartime, From the Sedition Act of 1798 to the War on Terrorism* (New York: W. W. Norton, 2004), 85.

5. Frank J. Williams, *Judging Lincoln* (Carbondale: Southern Illinois University Press, 2002), 63. The drillmaster for Merryman's unit was actually Nelson Bowman Sweitzer, a cap-

tain in the U.S. Army who was stationed at Fort McHenry. See Thomas H. Taylor, "The Baltimore County Horse Guards," *Maryland Journal,* April 23, 1897, copy on file at Fort McHenry National Historic Site, Baltimore, Md. Testimony in *Grason* (p. 10) says that his name was Captain Switzer. Testimony in *Grason* (p. 100) also suggests that Merryman did on occasion drill the Horse Guards, as did Captain Charles H. Ridgely, Lieutenant Richard Grason, Lieutenant George Carman, and Corporal Harry Gilmor.

6. Paul M. Angle, ed., *By These Words: Great Documents of American Liberty* (New York: Rand McNally, 1954), 308; Michael Vorenberg, "The Chase Court, 1864–1873: Cautious Reconstruction," in *The United States Supreme Court: The Pursuit of Justice,* ed. Christopher Tomlin (Boston: Houghton Mifflin, 2005), 103; James F. Simon, *Lincoln and Chief Justice Taney: Slavery, Secession, and the President's War Powers* (New York: Simon & Schuster, 2006), 186; Peter Charles Hoffer, *The Treason Trials of Aaron Burr* (Lawrence: University Press of Kansas, 2008), 100.

7. In a practical sense, Lincoln laid a foundation for the use of military commission trials in his April 1861 proclamation calling for seventy-five thousand state militiamen. In that document, Lincoln declared that the rebellion was "too powerful to be suppressed by the ordinary course of judicial proceedings, or by the powers vested in the Marshals by law." See Lincoln, "Proclamation Calling Militia and Convening Congress," April 15, 1861, in *CWL,* 4:331–33.

8. Legal historians have overlooked this very consequential method by which northerners suspected of disloyalty were able to "fight back" against the Union. For example, Stephen C. Neff has a section called "The Dissenters Fight Back" in his chapter on civil liberties in the North in his legal history of the Civil War, but nowhere in the chapter does Neff address the problem of damages suits in the state and federal courts. In his chapter on postwar pardons, Neff offers a brief discussion of state and federal "impunity" laws, but he does not address the issue of wartime suits for damages. See Stephen C. Neff, *Justice in Blue and Gray: A Legal History of the Civil War* (Cambridge, Mass.: Harvard University Press, 2010), 159–66, 233–38.

9. Mark E. Neely, Jr., "'Seeking a Cause of Difficulty with the Government': Reconsidering Freedom of Speech and Judicial Conflict under Lincoln," in *Lincoln's Legacy: Ethics and Politics,* ed. Phillip Shaw Paludan (Urbana: University of Illinois Press, 2008), 48; Harold M. Hyman, *A More Perfect Union: The Impact of the Civil War and Reconstruction on the Constitution* (New York: Knopf, 1973), 88–89.

10. Law professor John Yoo writes that *Ex parte Merryman* "is probably the only unambiguous example of a President of the United States refusing to obey an order of the federal judiciary." See Yoo, "*Merryman* and *Milligan* (and *McCardle*)," *Journal of Supreme Court History* 34 (2009): 257.

CHAPTER 1

1. Michael Burlingame, *Abraham Lincoln: A Life,* 2 vols. (Baltimore: Johns Hopkins University Press, 2009), 2:132–33; Lincoln, "Proclamation Calling Militia and Convening Congress," April 15, 1861, in *CWL,* 4:331–33.

2. A Virginian quoted in William Blair, *Virginia's Private War: Feeding Body and Soul in the Confederacy, 1861–1865* (New York: Oxford University Press, 1998), 11; Lincoln to Orville H. Browning, September 22, 1861, in *CWL*, 4:532.

3. George L. P. Radcliffe, *Governor Thomas H. Hicks of Maryland and the Civil War* (Baltimore: Johns Hopkins University Press, 1901), 14–70; Neal A. Brooks and Eric G. Rockel, *A History of Baltimore County* (Towson, Md.: Friends of the Towson Library, Inc., 1979), 237; Hicks to Cameron, April 20, 1861, Lincoln Papers; reproduced with slightly altered text in *O.R.*, ser. 1, vol. 2, p. 581. For an account of some of the bold actions taken by Governor Hicks to keep Maryland in the Union, see Timothy R. Snyder, "'Making No Child's Play of the Question': Governor Hicks and the Secession Crisis Reconsidered," *Maryland Historical Magazine* 101 (Fall 2006): 304–31.

4. Charles W. Mitchell, ed., *Maryland Voices of the Civil War* (Baltimore: Johns Hopkins University Press, 2007), 49–50; Samuel P. Bates, *History of Pennsylvania Volunteers, 1861–5,* 5 vols. (Harrisburg, Pa.: B. Singerly, 1869–1871), 1:5–7; *Baltimore Sun,* April 19, 1861; George William Brown (with endorsement by Thomas H. Hicks) to Lincoln, April 18, 1861, Lincoln Papers.

5. Thomas H. Hicks and George William Brown to Lincoln, April 18, 1861, Lincoln Papers; John Hay, diary entry for April 19, 1861, in Michael Burlingame and John R. Turner Ettlinger, eds., *Inside Lincoln's White House: The Complete Civil War Diary of John Hay* (Carbondale: Southern Illinois University Press, 1997), 2–3; Burlingame, *Lincoln: A Life,* 2:141.

6. L. A. Whitely to Simon Cameron, April 19, 1861, and John S. Gittings to Cameron, April 19, 1861, both in *O.R.*, ser. 1, vol. 2, p. 580.

7. This order was written by Adjutant General Lorenzo Thomas, by order of Cameron. See Lorenzo Thomas to S. M. Felton, April 19, 1861, in *O.R.*, ser. 1, vol. 2, p. 578.

8. Stephen M. Klugewicz, "'The First Martyrs': The Sixth Massachusetts and the Baltimore Riot of 1861," *Southern Historian* 20 (Spring 1999): 6–8.

9. Ibid., 8–9; *O.R.*, ser. 1, vol. 2, pp. 7–8; *Baltimore Sun,* April 20, 1861; Frank Towers, ed., "Military Waif: A Sidelight on the Baltimore Riot of 19 April 1861," *Maryland Historical Magazine* 89 (Winter 1994): 429; Henry Stump to Mary Stump, April 20, 1861, in "An Eyewitness to the Baltimore Riot, 19th April, 1861," *Maryland Historical Magazine* 53 (December 1958): 403; Mitchell, *Maryland Voices,* 51; testimony of Thomas J. Mitchell, September 13, 1861, William H. Delano, September 14, 1861, Charles W. Weyl and James R. Claridge, September 16, 1861, all in RG 21 (Records of the U.S. Circuit Court for the District of Maryland), Baltimore Division, Records of the Clerk of Court, Grand Jury Proceedings, 1861, NARA-P (hereafter Grand Jury Proceedings).

10. Klugewicz, "First Martyrs," 8–10; Edward Ayrault Robinson, "Some Recollections of April 19, 1861," *Maryland Historical Magazine* 27 (December 1932): 275; George William Brown, *Baltimore and the Nineteenth of April, 1861: A Study of the War* (Baltimore: Johns Hopkins University Press, 1887), 53; Testimony of Henry S. Durkee, September 6, 1861, William Lynch, September 9, 1861, John Cooper, September 9, 1861, in Grand Jury Proceedings.

11. Brown, *Baltimore,* chap. 4; *O.R.*, ser. 1, vol. 2, pp. 7–8; see also Mitchell, *Maryland Voices,* 58, 72–73. When Brown was later arrested for disloyalty, several prominent New Englanders, and even some members of the Sixth Massachusetts, petitioned the federal government on Brown's behalf, claiming that he should be released from prison. See *O.R.*, ser. 2, vol. 1, pp. 645–66. Prominent Baltimore attorney Andrew S. Ridgely also credited Brown with

"act[ing] boldly and well in protecting those troops." See *Grason,* 199. Frank Towers, however, suggests that the actions of Mayor Brown, Police Marshal Kane, and the other city leaders "should not be taken as support for the Union" but rather as a desire "to avoid the consequences of federal casualties." See Frank Towers, *The Urban South and the Coming of the Civil War* (Charlottesville: University of Virginia Press, 2004), chap. 5 (quotation from p. 167).

12. Testimony of John Ehrman, September 18, 1861, John Cunningham and Andrew Schwartz, September 19, 1861, John Plummer, September 20, 1861, all in Grand Jury Proceedings. Numbers on hats served as a form of identification.

13. Testimony of Benjamin Upton, September 17, 1861, in Grand Jury Proceedings; Klugewicz, "First Martyrs," 8–10; Brown, *Baltimore,* 53. Some estimates give higher casualty rates. See, for example, Towers, *Urban South,* 166.

14. Jabez D. Pratt to John C. Pratt, April 20, 1861, in Bruce Catton, ed., "Brother *against* Brother," *American Heritage* 12 (April 1961): 5; newspaper quoted in *Grason,* 271; Kane quoted in Charles W. Mitchell, "'The Whirlwind Now Gathering': Baltimore's Pratt Street Riot and the End of Maryland Secession," *Maryland Historical Magazine* 97 (Summer 2002): 211.

15. Brown, *Baltimore,* 56; Radcliffe, *Governor Hicks,* 54–55; *Grason,* 199–202; William Wilkins Glenn, diary entry for April 19, 1861, in Bayly Ellen Marks and Mark Norton Schatz, eds., *Between North and South: A Maryland Journalist Views the Civil War* (Rutherford, N.J.: Fairleigh Dickinson University Press, 1976), 30; *Baltimore Sun,* April 20, 1861; second report of speech quoted in Mitchell, *Maryland Voices,* 64.

16. Hay, diary entry for April 19, 1861, in Burlingame and Ettlinger, *Diaries,* 2–3.

17. Radcliffe, *Governor Hicks,* 56–57; Mitchell, *Maryland Voices,* 62–66; Brown, *Baltimore,* 58; *Philadelphia Inquirer,* May 14 and June 11, 1861; Glenn, diary entry for April 19, 1861, in Marks and Schatz, *Between North and South,* 30. Brown's April 20 order to burn the bridges stated that it was "By the authority of the Governor of Maryland and for the protection of the City of Baltimore." See Brooks and Rockel, *History of Baltimore County,* 239. For the account of Mayor Brown's brother—who also contended that Hicks gave his consent—see *O.R.,* ser. 1, vol. 2, p. 14. Discussion of who conceived of the idea to destroy the bridges will be further complicated in chapter 5.

18. Testimony of Alex Wiley, September 17, 1861, John Seveline, September 20, 1861, and Jackson McComas, October 2, 1861, all in Grand Jury Proceedings; Robert L. Gunnarsson, *The Story of the Northern Central Railway: From Baltimore to Lake Ontario* (Sykesville, Md.: Greenberg, 1991), 56.

19. John Cadwalader to Mrs. Kerr, April 30, 1861, Cadwalader Collection, Series VI (Judge John Cadwalader), Box 268, HSP. One member of the Baltimore County Horse Guards later claimed that the members of his unit never discussed whether or not the federal government had the right to bring troops through Maryland when they served on picket duty on the York Turnpike and later burned the railroad bridges. See *Grason,* 181.

20. Nathaniel P. Tallmadge to Lincoln, April 22, 1861, Lincoln Papers; Baltimore newspaper quoted in Mitchell, "Whirlwind Now Gathering," 211. See also Alice to Pa and Ma, April 19, 1861, in Gertrude K. Johnston, ed., *Dear Pa—And So It Goes* (Harrisburg, Pa.: Business Service Co., 1971), 134.

21. Hay, diary entries for April 20–23, 1861, in Burlingame and Ettlinger, *Diaries,* 3–9; Benjamin Brown French, diary entry for April 21, 1861, in Donald B. Cole and John J. Mc-

Donough, eds., *Witness to the Young Republic: A Yankee's Journal, 1828–1870* (London: University Press of New England, 1989), 351; Lincoln quoted in Burlingame, *Lincoln: A Life,* 141–42.

22. See n. 21; Brown, *Baltimore,* 71–75; *Grason,* 20, 28. One Marylander referred to the troops as "a half armed undisciplined body of some fifteen hundred men." Andrew S. Ridgely to Henry Stanbery, April 15, 1867, RG 60, Entry 9 (Letters Received by the Attorney General, 1809–70), Maryland Box 2.

23. Hay, diary entry for April 22, 1861, in Burlingame and Ettlinger, *Diaries,* 6; Lincoln, "Reply to Baltimore Committee," April 22, 1861, in *CWL,* 4:341–42; other report quoted in Burlingame, *Lincoln: A Life,* 2:145.

24. Hay, diary entries for April 22–23, 1861, in Burlingame and Ettlinger, *Diaries,* 6–9; see also Orville H. Browning to Lincoln, April 22, 1861, Lincoln Papers.

25. Lincoln specifically ordered that the railroad bridges around Baltimore be protected as the troops retreated to Pennsylvania. The text of the order stated: "The President, with a desire to gratify the Mayor of Baltimore, who fears that bloodshed would unnecessarily result from the passage through that City of the troops from Pennsylvania at this moment on the way, directs that they shall return to York in Pennsylvania." The officer in charge of the troops was commanded to "take care to leave force sufficient along the road, to keep it safe from depredation, of every kind, and within his entire control." Cameron later amended the order to keep the railroad lines "open at all hazards, so as to give the U. States the power to send troops or munitions if the necessity for bringing them by that route shall occur by the failure or inability of the Mayor of Balto. to keep his faith with the president." See Simon Cameron, copy of War Department Order, April 21, 1861, in Nathaniel P. Banks Papers, LC. The Pennsylvania troops obviously did not fulfill these very important orders as they withdrew from Maryland.

26. *The Biographical Cyclopedia of Representative Men of Maryland and [the] District of Columbia* (Baltimore: National Biographical, 1879), 312; Andrew S. Ridgely to Henry Stanbery, April 15, 1867, RG 60, Entry 9, Maryland Box 2. In some sources, the order is reprinted without the language "and break up the road." See *Grason,* 61, 192, 198.

27. Erick F. Davis, "The Baltimore County Horse Guard," *History Trails* 10 (Winter 1975–1976): 7; Bates, *History of Pennsylvania Volunteers,* 1:13, 23, 32; *Grason,* 62. When asked if he considered himself "in armed hostility to the Government of the United States" for burning the bridges as a member of the Horse Guards, this militiaman responded: "No. I did not." When pressed about the reason for burning the bridges, he continued: "I understood they burned them to prevent bloodshed in Baltimore." *Grason,* 66.

28. David Creamer, "Notes of Evidence before the U.S. Grand Jury, June Term, 1861," LC (a typescript copy is also available at MDHS); Samuel Yohe to George Cadwalader, June 8, 1861, RG 107, microfilm M492 (Letters Received by the Secretary of War: Irregular Series, 1861–66), reel 34; John Merryman to Simon Cameron, May 21, 1863, in Simon Cameron Papers, HSDC.

29. Creamer, "Notes"; *Grason,* 62–63; Samuel Yohe to George Cadwalader, May 29, 1861, copies in RG 107, microfilm M492, reel 34, and Cadwalader Collection, Series VII (General George Cadwalader), Box 438, HSP.

30. Isaac R. Dunkelberger, "Reminiscences and Personal Experiences of the Great Rebellion," in the Michael Winey Collection, MHI.

31. Creamer, "Notes"; William Schley to William Whiting, March 21, 1863, enclosures "F" and "G," in RG 107, microfilm M492, reel 34. Lovell apparently hired a lawyer to sue Merryman for damages, but it is not clear whether the case went to trial. According to the *Baltimore Sun* (March 11, 1861), the Horse Guards' uniform consisted of "a blue frock coat and gray pantaloons, trimmed with buff."

32. John Weston to Mother, April 26, 1861, and John Weston to Amelia Weston, April 28, 1861, both in Robert W. Frost and Nancy D. Frost, eds., *Picket Pins and Sabers: The Civil War Letters of John Burden Weston* (Ashland, Ky.: Economy Printers, 1971), 20–21.

33. Radcliffe, *Governor Hicks*, 62–70; *Baltimore Sun*, April 25, 1861. See the Epilogue for a brief discussion of the actions taken by the legislature in 1861.

34. Lincoln to Scott, April 25 and 27, 1861, both in *CWL*, 4:344, 347. Union general Robert Patterson had asked General Scott for authority to declare martial law as early as April 21. See Patterson to Andrew G. Curtin, April 21, 1861, in Banks Papers, LC. Secretary of the Treasury Salmon P. Chase also urged Lincoln to give General Scott broad power in Maryland. See Chase to Lincoln, April 25, 1861, Lincoln Papers.

35. Throughout the Civil War, Lincoln maintained that the Constitution was silent as to who could suspend the writ of habeas corpus. In a time of rebellion—when swift action was needed—Lincoln claimed that that power could be exercised by the president. While the record of the debate at the Constitutional Convention does not settle the question conclusively, it does give some evidence in support of Lincoln's construction of the Constitution.

On August 20, 1787, Charles Pinckney of South Carolina proposed that the writ "shall not be suspended *by the Legislature* except upon the most urgent and pressing occasions, and for a limited time" (emphasis added). The Convention referred Pinckney's proposal to the Committee of Detail "without debate or consideration." A week later Pinckney again offered his proposal. This time Pinckney's suggestion elicited a response. John Rutledge of South Carolina argued that habeas corpus rights were "inviolable," while James Wilson of Pennsylvania claimed that a suspension clause was unnecessary because judges possessed "the discretion . . . in most important cases to keep in Gaol or admit to Bail." Despite this opposition, the Convention voted on August 28 to include a suspension clause in the Constitution: "The privilege of the writ of Habeas Corpus shall not be suspended, unless where in cases of Rebellion or invasion the public safety may require it." With one substantive revision—changing "where" to "when"—this language eventually found its way into the U.S. Constitution.

Two points are significant regarding Lincoln's assertion that the president could suspend the writ of habeas corpus since the Constitution did not specify which branch of the federal government possessed the suspending power. First, the Convention specifically omitted any mention of Congress from the clause authorizing suspension. In fact, the words "by the Legislature" appeared only in Charles Pinckney's initial proposal—not in any version of the clause that was ever adopted by the Committee of the Whole House. Second, the Convention initially placed the suspension clause in Article XI of the draft constitution—and Article XI pertained to the judiciary. It was the Committee of Style and Arrangement that placed the suspension clause in Article I, section 9, where it remains today. The record of the debate at the Convention is thus silent as to what branch of the government possessed the power to suspend the writ of habeas corpus.

The ratification debates are also ambiguous. While some—if not most—Federalists and

Anti-Federalists discussed the suspension of habeas corpus as a legislative power, others spoke of it simply as a power that was given to "the general government." Of course, it could be argued that most members of the founding generation simply assumed that suspension was a matter for Congress to decide, just as it had been given to the state legislatures in the Massachusetts and New Hampshire constitutions of 1780 and 1784, respectively. But unlike those state constitutions, the U.S. Constitution did not say so explicitly.

Thus, Lincoln made a plausible claim that the text of the Constitution was ambiguous and therefore open to interpretation. Even if Lincoln was simply offering a kneejerk attempt to cover over a set of hasty decisions he had made at the beginning of the war, he could have pointed out that, to borrow language from his First Inaugural Address, no "right plainly written in the Constitution has been denied."

For the debates at the Constitutional Convention, see Max Farrand, ed., *The Records of the Federal Convention of 1787*, 3 vols. (New Haven: Yale University Press, 1911), 2:341–42, 438, 565, 576, 596; 3:213, 290; Philip B. Kurland and Ralph Lerner, eds., *The Founders' Constitution*, 5 vols. (Indianapolis: Liberty Fund, 1987), 3:324–29. For an anti-Lincoln discussion of why "where" was changed to "when" in the suspension clause, see [James F. Johnston,] *Suspending Power and the Writ of Habeas Corpus* (Philadelphia: John Campbell, 1862), 8.

36. Mark Neely argues that the strangeness and severity of this order was the result of a bit of careless editing by Lincoln. See Mark E. Neely, Jr., *The Fate of Liberty: Abraham Lincoln and Civil Liberties* (New York: Oxford University Press, 1991), 7.

37. Bates, *History of Pennsylvania Volunteers*, 1:117; Daniel Carroll Toomey, *The Civil War in Maryland* (Baltimore: Toomey Press, 1983), 17–22; Butler to Major Morris, May 13, 1861, and Butler, "Proclamation to the Citizens of Baltimore," May 14, 1861, both in Jessie Ames Marshall, comp., *Private and Official Correspondence of Gen. Benjamin F. Butler: During the Period of the Civil War*, 5 vols. (Norwood, Mass.: Plimpton Press, 1917), 1:81, 83–85.

38. *O.R.*, ser. 1, vol. 2, pp. 29, 639–40; ser. 2, vol. 2, pp. 225–27, 794–95; Butler quoted in Marc Egnal, *Clash of Extremes: The Economic Origins of the Civil War* (New York: Hill & Wang, 2009), 304. Winans was again arrested with other members of the legislature in September 1861.

39. Winfield Scott to Butler, May 14, 1861, in Marshall, *Private and Official Correspondence*, 1:85.

40. E. D. Townsend to George Cadwalader, May 16, 1861, and Cadwalader to Townsend, May 16, 1861, both in *O.R.*, ser. 1, vol. 2, pp. 639–40.

41. Lincoln, "Memorandum," [May 17, 1861], in *CWL*, 4:372.

CHAPTER 2

1. Francis B. Culver, "Merryman Family," *Maryland Historical Magazine* 10 (June 1915): 176–85; Culver, "Merryman Family," *Maryland Historical Magazine* 10 (September 1915): 293. Carl Brent Swisher wrote, without citation, that Roger B. Taney and Nicholas Merryman, John Merryman's father, had attended Dickinson College at about the same time. See Swisher, *The Oliver Wendell Holmes Devise History of the Supreme Court of the United States*, vol. 5: *The Taney Period, 1836–64* (New York: Macmillan, 1974), 845. Dickinson College archivist

Jim Gerencser has been unable to find any record of Nicholas Merryman's matriculation at Dickinson.

2. Culver, "Merryman Family," 297; Historic American Buildings Survey, "Hayfields Farm Buildings, Worthington Valley, Cockeysville Vicinity, Baltimore County, MD," Survey Number HABS MD-15, Prints and Photographs Division, Library of Congress (hereafter HABS Report); *Baltimore Sun,* October 9, 1881; J. Thomas Scharf, *History of Baltimore City and County* (Philadelphia: Louis H. Everts, 1881), 885; HABS Report; J. Bennett Nolan, *Lafayette in America: Day by Day* (Baltimore: Johns Hopkins University Press, 1934), 245, 257–61, 292–303.

3. *Baltimore Sun,* June 21, 1861, quoting the editor of the *Pittsburg Dispatch.*

4. See *First Circular of the Maryland Agricultural College* (Baltimore: Samuel Sands Mills, 1859); *Second Circular of the Maryland Agricultural College* (Washington, D.C.: Henry Polkinhorn, 1860), 9; *Circular of the Maryland Agricultural College* (Baltimore: John Murphy, 1863), 3; *Circular of the Maryland Agricultural College* (Baltimore: John Murphy, 1864), 3; *Catalogue of the Maryland Agricultural College, Prince George's County, for the Years 1865-6* (Baltimore: John Murphy, 1865), 3.

5. Vivian Wiser, "Improving Maryland's Agriculture, 1840–1860," *Maryland Historical Magazine* 64 (Summer 1969): 115; Alvin H. Sanders, *The Story of the Herefords* (Chicago: Breeder's Gazette, 1914), 279–83, 324–37.

6. HABS Report; *Baltimore Sun,* October 28, 1962; Nicholas Bosley Merryman, "Hayfields History," *History Trails* 19 (Winter 1984–85): 5–8.

7. Neal A. Brooks and Eric G. Rockel, *A History of Baltimore County* (Towson, Md.: Friends of the Towson Library, Inc., 1979), 221–36; U.S. Eighth Census, 1860, *Maryland Slave Schedule* (Washington, D.C., 1864); Barbara Jeanne Fields, *Slavery and Freedom on the Middle Ground: Maryland during the Nineteenth Century* (New Haven, Conn.: Yale University Press, 1985), 24–25. George H. Callcott writes that Merryman owned more than one hundred slaves in 1860 but the census records and Brooks and Rockel's *History of Baltimore County* seem to indicate otherwise. George H. Callcott, *A History of the University of Maryland* (Baltimore: Maryland Historical Society, 1966), 158.

8. Culver, "Merryman Family," 297; Andrew S. Ridgely to Henry Stanbery, April 15, 1867, RG 60, Entry 9 (Letters Received by the Attorney General, 1809–70), Maryland Box 2; Erick F. Davis, "The Baltimore County Horse Guard," *History Trails* 10 (Winter 1975–76): 5. One witness in *Grason* testified that the Horse Guards organized in the fall of 1860, but this was probably a poor recollection. The constitution and by-laws of the Horse Guards forbid political discussion at any drill, dress parade, or meeting of the unit, "under a penalty of five dollars for each offence," which suggests that even if the company was made up of "states' rights gentlemen," that they may not have discussed political topics when they were together. Still, members of the unit appear to have made pro-secession statements. A few days after the Baltimore Riot, they moved their headquarters from the Odd Fellows Hall in Towsontown to Edward H. Ady's hotel. Outside the hotel, Harry and Howard Gilmor took down the U.S. flag and hung another banner in its place. Most witnesses claimed that they hoisted a Maryland state flag, but others claimed that it was either a Palmetto flag or a white flag. About a week later, on April 29, the Union ladies of Towsontown rehung the American flag. See *Grason,* 9–14, 35–46, 48, 76–77, 106, 131–35, 156, 175–76, 231–33, 258.

9. Davis, "Horse Guard," 5–8; *Grason*, 59–61, 63–64, 107–12, 178–79, 259, 261, 268; Andrew S. Ridgely to Henry Stanbery, April 15, 1867, RG 60, Entry 9, Maryland Box 2. It was widely reported that the Baltimore County Horse Guards had seized federal arms during this time; in fact, they had been supplied with fifty guns by the state government. See Maryland House of Delegates, *Report of the Adjutant General of Maryland, to the General Assembly, Special Session, 1861,* House of Delegates Document E (Frederick: E. S. Riley, 1861), 13.

10. See chapters 1, 3, and 5 for further details on Merryman's actions in April 1861.

11. General Orders No. 12, April 27, 1861, in *O.R.,* ser. 1, vol. 2, p. 607.

12. Samuel Yohe to Captain Heckman, May 21, 1861, in *O.R.,* ser. 2, vol. 1, p. 575. It should be noted that Yohe's First Pennsylvania militia was the very same regiment that had been encamped around Cockeysville in April 1861, and which Merryman followed back to Pennsylvania while burning bridges on April 23. See Samuel P. Bates, *History of Pennsylvania Volunteers, 1861–5,* 5 vols. (Harrisburg, Pa.: B. Singerly, 1869–71), 1:13–15.

13. Fitz-John Porter to Yohe, May 22, 1861, in *O.R.,* ser. 1, vol. 2, p. 645.

14. James McHenry Howard, "Ridgely Family History," unpublished memoir (ca. 1894), typescript by Helen West Ridgely, Ridgely Family Papers (MS 1001), FC1–2, Folder 165, HAMP 21686, Hampton National Historic Site, National Park Service, Towson, Md. I thank Jim Bailey of Fort McHenry for bringing this document to my attention. See also James C. Bailey, "American Bastille?: Fort McHenry and Civil Liberty, 1861–1862" (M.A. thesis, University of Maryland at Baltimore County, 2007), 31–32. According to testimony in *Grason* (pp. 54, 61–62), the Horse Guards ceased drilling "not long after the regiment of soldiers came to Cockeysville, from Pennsylvania."

15. O. Howard McHenry to J. G. Barnard, June 20, 1861, Nathaniel P. Banks Papers, Department of Special Collections, Duke University, Durham, N.C.; Yohe to Cadwalader, May 29, 1861, Cadwalader Collection, Series VII (General George Cadwalader), Box 438, HSP; a copy is also available in RG 107, microfilm M492 (Letters Received by the Secretary of War: Irregular Series, 1861–66), reel 34.

16. Quoted in *Detroit Free Press,* August 11, 1861.

17. Edward Spencer to Anne Catherine Bradford Harrison, May 16, 1861, in Anna Bradford Agle and Sidney Hovey Wanzer, eds., "Dearest Braddie: Love and War in Maryland, 1860–61: Part 1," *Maryland Historical Magazine* 88 (Spring 1993): 86.

18. Cadwalader had asked General Keim and Colonel Yohe to furnish "more specific charges and specifications . . . against the accused with the names of witnesses," and he regretted that such information was not supplied prior to the hearing before Chief Justice Taney. See Cadwalader to E. D. Townsend, May 27, 1861, in *O.R.,* ser. 2, vol. 1, p. 574.

19. Unless otherwise noted, all quotations from the *Ex parte Merryman* proceedings are taken from the manuscript documents that are held by the U.S. District Court for the District of Maryland, copies of which are available at MSA and NARA-P (hereafter Original Case Papers). George Cadwalader to Roger Taney, May 26, 1861, Original Case Papers; also in 17 Fed. Cases 146.

20. *Baltimore County Advocate,* June 8, 1861; *Brooklyn Daily Eagle,* May 25, 1861; *Baltimore Sun,* May 27, 31, 1861; *Ex parte Merryman,* 17 Fed. Cases 144–46 (1861).

21. George William Brown, *Baltimore and the Nineteenth of April, 1861: A Study of the War* (Baltimore: Johns Hopkins University Press, 1887), 89; *New York Daily Tribune,* June 6, 1861.

22. *Ex parte Merryman* (1861), 17 Fed. Cases 146.

23. Ibid., 147.

24. Ibid., 148–53.

25. William Wilkins Glenn, diary entry for June 2, 1861, in Bayly Ellen Marks and Mark Norton Schatz, eds., *Between North and South: A Maryland Journalist Views the Civil War* (Rutherford, N.J.: Fairleigh Dickinson University Press, 1976), 33; William A. McKellip to Edward Bates, August 17, 1861, RG 60, Entry 9, Maryland Box 1.

26. *New York Daily Tribune,* May 29, 30, June 1, 5, 1861.

27. *New York Times,* May 29, 1861.

28. *New York World,* May 29, June 7, 1861.

29. Quoted in Thomas F. Cotter, "The Merryman Affair," *History Trails* 24 (Winter 1989–1990): 7.

30. *Washington (D.C.) National Intelligencer,* June 4, 1861. In the second quote, the *Intelligencer* quoted the *Boston Advertiser,* a Republican paper.

31. *Columbus (Ohio) Crisis,* June 6, 20, 1861.

32. *New York Weekly Journal of Commerce,* June 6, 1861; *Brooklyn Daily Eagle,* July 8, 1861.

33. "Judge Cadwalader's Opinion in the Habeas Corpus Case at Baltimore Respecting George Cadwalader's Action Regarding a Prisoner," manuscript opinion in Cadwalader Collection, Series VI (Judge John Cadwalader), Box 264, HSP.

34. John Montgomery to George Cadwalader, May 29, 1861 (encloses a copy of the opinion in different handwriting than the judge's draft at HSP), RG 107, microfilm M492, reel 34; Cadwalader family lore quoted in Walker Lewis, *Without Fear or Favor: A Biography of Chief Justice Roger Brooke Taney* (Boston: Houghton Mifflin, 1965), 534.

35. Taney's hostility toward Lincoln and the Union war effort is discussed further in the Epilogue.

36. Taney to George W. Hughes, June 8, 1861, in Samuel Tyler, *Memoir of Roger Brooke Taney, LL.D., Chief Justice of the Supreme Court of the United States* (Baltimore: J. Murphy, 1872), 430–31; Roger B. Taney to Samuel Treat, June 5, 1861, quoted in Carl Brent Swisher, *Roger B. Taney* (New York: Macmillan, 1935), 554; Taney to Franklin Pierce, June 12, 1861, in "Some Papers of Franklin Pierce, 1852–1862," *American Historical Review* 10 (January 1905): 368.

37. Frederic Bernal to Lord John Russell, May 30, 1861, Records of the Foreign Office (FO 5/784), National Archives of the United Kingdom; Brown, *Baltimore,* 90.

38. Swisher, *Taney,* 551; *Columbus (Ohio) Crisis,* June 6, 1861; *New York Times,* May 31, 1861; *New York Daily Tribune,* June 2, 1861; *New York World,* June 5, 1861.

39. Edward Bates, "Suspension of the Privilege of the Writ of Habeas Corpus," July 5, 1861, in *Official Opinions of the Attorneys General of the United States,* 43 vols. (Washington, D.C.: W. H. and O. H. Morrison, 1852–1996), 10:74–92. For a learned defense of Lincoln's suspension of habeas corpus by a leading member of the Philadelphia bar, see Horace Binney, *The Privilege of the Writ of Habeas Corpus under the Constitution* (Philadelphia: C. Sherman and Son, 1862), reprinted in Frank Freidel, ed., *Union Pamphlets of the Civil War, 1861–1865,* 2 vols. (Cambridge, Mass: Harvard University Press, 1967), 1:199–252.

40. Lincoln, "Message to Congress in Special Session," July 4, 1861, in *CWL,* 4:426.

41. Ibid., 429–31.

42. Section 14 of the Judiciary Act of 1789 permitted "all the before-mentioned courts of

the United States"—that is, the district, circuit, and Supreme courts—to "have power to issue writs of . . . *habeas corpus*" but then also specified "that either of the justices of the supreme court, as well as judges of the district courts, shall have power to grant writs of *habeas corpus* for the purpose of an inquiry into the cause of commitment." See *An Act to Establish the Judicial Courts of the United States,* act of September 24, 1789, in 1 Stat. 81. Footnote "e" on page 81 states: "As the jurisdiction of the Supreme Court is appellate, it must be shown to the court that the court has power to award a habeas corpus, before one will be granted." Chief Justice John Marshall grappled with the seemingly redundant language of Section 14 in his opinion in *Ex parte Bollman* (1807). For a helpful discussion of Marshall's opinion in *Bollman,* see Peter Charles Hoffer, *The Treason Trials of Aaron Burr* (Lawrence: University Press of Kansas, 2008), chap. 5.

43. Craig R. Smith, *Silencing the Opposition: Government Strategies of Suppression* (Albany: State University of New York Press, 1996), 28; Melvin I. Urofsky, *A March of Liberty: A Constitutional History of the United States* (New York: Knopf, 1988), 488; Jeffrey Rosen, *The Most Democratic Branch: How the Courts Serve America* (New York: Oxford University Press, 2006), 171; Douglas L. Wilson, *Lincoln's Sword: The Presidency and Power of Words* (New York: Knopf, 2006), 82.

44. Brian McGinty, *Lincoln & the Court* (Cambridge, Mass.: Harvard University Press, 2008), 89.

45. *An Act to Amend the Judicial System of the United States,* act of April 29, 1802, in 2 Stat. 158; see also Bruce A. Ragsdale, *Ex parte Merryman and Debates on Civil Liberties during the Civil War* (Washington, D.C.: Federal Judicial Center, 2007), 11, 26. As part of his effort to thwart the Baltimore treason cases (discussed in chapter 3), Chief Justice Taney informed Judge Giles in October 1862 that a U.S. district judge could not preside alone in capital cases. The minutes of the circuit court reveal, however, that Giles had presided alone over a murder trial in 1858. There was precedent in the District of Maryland, therefore, for a single judge to preside over cases—including capital cases—in the U.S. circuit court. See William Calvin Chesnut, "Address by Judge W. Calvin Chesnut: History of the Federal Courts in Maryland," *Report of the Forty-First Annual Meeting of the Maryland State Bar Association* 41 (1936): 87–88.

46. Mark E. Neely, Jr., "The Constitution and Civil Liberties under Lincoln," in *Our Lincoln: New Perspectives on Lincoln and His World,* ed. Eric Foner (New York: W. W. Norton, 2008), 38; Daniel A. Farber, *Lincoln's Constitution* (Chicago: University of Chicago Press, 2003), 17; see also William M. Wiecek, *Liberty under Law: The Supreme Count in American Life* (Baltimore: Johns Hopkins University Press, 1988), 83.

47. James G. Randall, *Constitutional Problems under Lincoln,* revised ed. (Urbana: University of Illinois Press, 1964), 131.

48. 17 Fed. Cases 147; Opinion of Taney, in Original Case Papers.

49. Supreme Court justice Robert C. Grier also seemed equivocal as to whether *Ex parte Merryman* was a Supreme Court decision. In a letter to Judge John Cadwalader regarding the habeas corpus issue, Grier implicitly revealed the complicated nature of the case: "As a constitutional question it has never been *directly decided* by the Supreme Court, and on such questions, I never decide before hand, according to personal *prejudices* or political proclivities." See Grier to Cadwalader, January 25, 1862, Cadwalader Collection, Series VI (Judge John Cadwalader), Box 268, HSP.

50. Petition for writ of habeas corpus, in Original Case Papers; 17 Fed. Cases 145; Andrew S. Ridgely to Salmon P. Chase, December 28, 1866, Salmon P. Chase Papers, Box 25, LC; Harold M. Hyman, *A More Perfect Union: The Impact of the Civil War and Reconstruction on the Constitution* (New York: Knopf, 1973), 83.

51. Ragsdale, *Merryman*, 11, 3. Neely points out the jurisdictional conundrum in which Taney found himself—with Section 14 of the Judiciary Act of 1789 authorizing justices of the Supreme Court to issue writs of habeas corpus but with *Marbury v. Madison* making such an extension of original jurisdiction unconstitutional. Neely suggests that "Roger B. Taney never asked that question" (Neely, "Constitution," 39–45). It seems highly unlikely, however, that Taney did not think about this question. His manuscript opinion (discussed below) suggests that he thought carefully about the question of jurisdiction. As a young lawyer, Taney also had participated in *Burr*-related cases and was very likely aware of the precedent in *Bollman;* he certainly was aware of the precedent in *Marbury.* See Edward S. Delaplaine, "Chief Justice Roger B. Taney—His Career at the Frederick Bar," *Maryland Historical Magazine* 13 (September 1918): 133–36. And, as noted above, a footnote in the *U.S. Statutes at Large* noted that the Supreme Court could only issue writs of habeas corpus as part of its appellate jurisdiction.

52. Taney, "Notes on *Ex parte Merryman*," in Howard Family Papers (MS 469), Roger B. Taney Collection, Box 10, MDHS. The final pencil insertions appear to be in a hand other than Taney's—most likely Taney's son-in-law, J. Mason Campbell. It is possible that Campbell convinced the chief justice to make this final change. Taney also likely settled on this phrase because of the language in Section 14 of the Judiciary Act of 1789 (see n. 42 above).

53. 17 Fed. Cases 147; Memo Opinion of Chief Justice Taney, and Certificate of the Clerk, both in Original Case Papers.

54. The records of the Supreme Court contain materials from three habeas corpus cases heard by justices "in chambers" between 1861 and 1881. Two of these cases were heard by the justices as appeals from the lower federal courts; the third, from 1861, involved the petition of a Union soldier to Justice Wayne to be released from military service. In light of *Ex parte Bollman,* it appears that Justice Wayne should not have claimed jurisdiction to hear this case. RG 267 (Records of the Supreme Court of the United States), Entry 22 (Papers in Habeas Corpus Cases Heard at Chambers), NARA.

55. Case files for George E. Worthington, Alfred H. Matthews, and Harrison Scott, all in RG 21 (Records of the U.S. Circuit Court for the Eastern District of Pennsylvania), Habeas Corpus Cases (1848–62), Box 1, NARA-P; George A. Coffey to Edward Bates, June 3, 1861, RG 60, Entry 9 (Letters Received by the Attorney General, 1809–70), Pennsylvania Box 2.

56. *Philadelphia Press*, June 5 and 6, 1861; J. Thomas Scharf, *History of Philadelphia, 1609–1884,* 3 vols. (Philadelphia: L. H. Everts, 1884), 1:768.

CHAPTER 3

1. Edward Bates to Nathaniel P. Banks, June 16, 1861, RG 60, microfilm M699 (Letters Sent by the Department of Justice: General and Miscellaneous, 1818–1904), reel 6; Joseph Barlow to wife, July 6, 1861, Joseph Barlow Collection, MHI.

2. James G. Hollandsworth, Jr., *Pretense of Glory: The Life of General Nathaniel P. Banks*

(Baton Rouge: Louisiana State University Press, 1998), 47; Charles W. Mitchell, ed., *Maryland Voices of the Civil War* (Baltimore: Johns Hopkins University Press, 2007), 140; Mark E. Neely, Jr., *The Fate of Liberty: Abraham Lincoln and Civil Liberties* (New York: Oxford University Press, 1991), 14–18, 75, 234; *O.R.,* ser. 1, vol. 2, pp. 138–56, and ser. 2, vol. 1, pp. 563–748; Simon Cameron to Abraham Lincoln, November 1, 1863, and Worthington G. Snethen to Winfield Scott, June 29, 1861, both in Lincoln Papers; Thomas S. Alexander to Severn Teackle Wallis, November 1863, Simon Cameron Papers, HSDC. George P. Kane claimed to have committed no wrongdoing in the early months of the war. See *O.R.,* ser. 2, vol. 1, pp. 644–50, 666–67.

3. *Speeches of the Hon. Henry May, of Maryland, Delivered in the House of Representatives, at the Third Session of the Thirty-Seventh Congress* (Baltimore: Kelly, Hedian & Piet, 1863), 40; Lincoln, "To the House of Representatives," July 27, 1861, in *CWL,* 4:461–62.

4. Severn T. Wallis to James A. Pearce, July 18, 1861, James Alfred Pearce Papers (MS 1384), MDHS; Frank Key Howard, *Fourteen Months in American Bastiles* (Baltimore: Kelly, Hedian & Piet, 1863), 20; Charles Howard to Simon Cameron, August 1, 1861, in *O.R.,* ser. 2, vol. 1, p. 634.

5. Edward Bates to William Meade Addison, July 12, 1861, RG 60, microfilm M699, reel 6.

6. From 1789 to 1911, U.S. district courts and U.S. circuit courts were both trial courts, or courts of original jurisdiction. In some instances circuit courts could exercise appellate jurisdiction over the decisions of district courts, although circuit courts were not given appellate jurisdiction in criminal cases until 1879. In 1842, Congress gave the district courts concurrent jurisdiction over all noncapital crimes—thus, as a capital offense, treason cases had to be remitted to the circuit court. Sessions of a district court were presided over by a U.S. district judge. Prior to 1869, sessions of a circuit court were usually presided over by a district judge and a justice of the Supreme Court of the United States, sitting as a circuit justice. See Russell R. Wheeler and Cynthia Harrison, *Creating the Federal Judicial System,* 3rd ed. (Washington, D.C.: Federal Judicial Center, 2005).

7. Order of William F. Giles, July 13, 1861. Most of the case papers for *U.S. v. Merryman* are in RG 21 (Records of the U.S. District Court for the District of Maryland, and Records of the U.S. Circuit Court for the Eastern District of Pennsylvania), Merryman Box, NARA-P (hereafter NARA-MB); *Baltimore Sun,* November 7, 1861; William Meade Addison to Edward Bates, June 5, 1862, RG 60, Entry 9 (Letters Received by the Attorney General, 1809–70), Maryland Box 1. Some citizens of Baltimore were also indicted for rioting in the Maryland state court system. See Baltimore City Criminal Court Docket, vol. 17 (C1814), MSA.

8. *Baltimore American and Commercial Advertiser,* July 4, 12, 1861; *Baltimore Sun,* July 11, 1861.

9. Indictment of John Merryman, July 10, 1861, in NARA-MB; *Philadelphia Inquirer,* June 22, 1861.

10. Indictment of John Merryman, July 10, 1861, in NARA-MB. In 1867, U.S. Attorney Andrew S. Ridgely believed that Merryman had burned only one bridge. See Andrew S. Ridgely to Henry Stanbery, April 15, 1867, RG 60, Entry 9, Maryland Box 2.

11. See chapter 5.

12. William Meade Addison to Edward Bates, June 5, 1862, RG 60, Entry 9, Maryland Box 1; Charles F. Hobson, *The Aaron Burr Treason Trial* (Washington, D.C.: Federal Judicial Center, 2006), 1–8.

13. Recognizance, in NARA-MB.

14. Taney to Giles, October 7, 1862, quoted in William Calvin Chesnut, "Address by Judge W. Calvin Chesnut: History of the Federal Courts in Maryland," *Report of the Forty-First Annual Meeting of the Maryland State Bar Association* 41 (1936): 87–88. As noted previously, Giles had presided alone over a capital case in 1858.

Under the Crimes Act of 1790, treason was punishable only by death; under the Second Confiscation Act (what historian James G. Randall called the Treason Act of 1862), a person convicted of treason could either suffer death and have his slaves set free or, at the discretion of the court, be imprisoned, lose his slave property, and be fined. Because Merryman and the Baltimore rioters committed their alleged acts of treason prior to the passage of the Second Confiscation Act, they were indicted under the 1790 law, which made them liable to be hanged. See *An Act for the Punishment of Certain Crimes against the United States,* act of April 30, 1790, in 1 Stat. 112, and *An Act to Suppress Insurrection, To Punish Treason and Rebellion, To Seize and Confiscate the Property of Rebels, and for Other Purposes,* act of July 17, 1862, in 12 Stat. 589.

15. RG 21, Minutes of the U.S. Circuit Court for the District of Maryland (1790–1911), microfilm M931, reel 3, NARA-P; Carl Brent Swisher, *Roger B. Taney* (New York: Macmillan, 1935), 556–60; George William Brown, *Baltimore and the Nineteenth of April, 1861: A Study of the War* (Baltimore: Johns Hopkins University Press, 1887), 45; William Price to Edward Bates, October 15, 1862, and Nathaniel Thayer to Bates, November 3, 1863, both in RG 60, Entry 9, Maryland Boxes 1 and 2; Taney to J. Mason Campbell, March 18, 1863, October 23, 1863, and May 14, 1864, Howard Family Papers (MS 469), Taney Collection, Box 10, MDHS; Taney to David M. Perine, June 5 and July 12, 1862, August 6, 1863, April 5, May 28 and July 28, 1864, all in Perine Family Papers (MS 645), Box 2, MDHS. James F. Simon aptly notes the irony of Taney's not allowing the civil prosecution to move forward: "Taney had demanded throughout the habeas corpus proceedings that the Lincoln administration justify Merryman's incarceration before a judge in a civil courtroom. But once the administration had belatedly complied with Taney's judicial directive, the Chief Justice denied the government the opportunity to prove its case." James F. Simon, *Lincoln and Chief Justice Taney: Slavery, Secession, and the President's War Powers* (New York: Simon & Schuster, 2006), 198.

16. Lincoln, "Memorandum on Maryland Patronage" (ca. April 1861), Lincoln Papers; see the letters of William H. Collins, Hiram Barney, Richard B. Dorsey, and Reverdy Johnson in RG 60, Entry 350 (Records Relating to the Appointment of Federal Judges, Marshals, and Attorneys, 1853–1901), Box 348, "William Meade Addison, 1861–1865" folder.

17. Worthington G. Snethen to Winfield Scott, June 29, 1861, Lincoln Papers; see also R. H. Atwell to Frederick W. Seward, November 8, 1861, RG 60, Entry 9, Maryland Box 1.

18. John A. Dix to Lincoln, August 28, 1861, Lincoln Papers. Some Marylanders pushed the Lincoln administration to retain Addison in office. See A. Randall to Salmon P. Chase, August 23, 1861, RG 60, Entry 9, Maryland Box 1.

19. Nathaniel P. Banks to Sir, July 13, 1861, RG 60, Entry 9, Maryland Box 1.

20. Edward Bates to Lincoln, October 25, 1861, Lincoln Papers ; William Meade Addison to Edward Bates, March 17, 1862, RG 60, Entry 9, Maryland Box 1; *Baltimore County Advocate,* April 12, 1862.

Following his tenure as U.S. attorney, Addison defended at least one Baltimorean accused of aiding the Confederacy. See William Meade Addison, *United States vs. John W. Heard: A Citizen of Maryland. Defence of the Prisoner before a Military Commission, at Fort*

McHenry, Md. Charged with Recruiting Troops in the Federal Lines for the Confederate Army. September, 1863 (Baltimore: Murphy & Co., Printers and Stationers, 1863); Court-Martial Case File NN-223 (a copy is also held at MDHS in MS 2132).

21. William Price, *The Position of Maryland: Letter of William Price, Esq., of Baltimore* (Baltimore: John Murphy, [1861]), 1–8; Thomas J. C. Williams, *A History of Washington County Maryland,* 2 vols. (1906; reprint, Baltimore: Regional Publishing, 1968), 1:426; Augustus Bradford to Edward Bates, March 25, 1862, Bradford to William H. Seward, May 13, 1862, both in RG 60, Entry 350, Box 348, "William Price, 1861–1865" folder, and Bradford to Lincoln, April 3, 1865, in "William Price, 1865–1869" folder. Price's nomination faced some resistance in the Senate because of his age. See Lyman Trumbull to Edward Bates, May 20, 1862, RG 60, Entry 9, Senate Box.

22. William Price to Caleb B. Smith, June 16, 1862, RG 60, Entry 58 (Letters Received Relating to Judiciary Accounts, 1849–89), Box 338; William Price to Bates, July 26 and September 1, 1862, both in RG 60, Entry 9, Maryland Box 1.

23. If Price was not busy enough with his duties as U.S. attorney, he also played a role in the prosecution of traitors accused under Maryland's state treason law. A state judge in Frederick complained to Governor Augustus W. Bradford that the state's attorney in that city was "an uncompromising rebel." As a consequence, Bradford asked Price to help prosecute the seventy treason cases pending in the state court at Frederick. See Madison Nelson to Augustus W. Bradford, October 6, 1863, William Price to Bradford, October 12 and 24, 1863, and William Price to Madison Nelson, October 22, 1863, all in Governors Miscellaneous Papers (S1274), MSA.

24. Price to Bates, January 5, 1863, RG 60, Entry 9, Maryland Box 1.

25. Bates to Price, January 6, 1863, RG 60, microfilm M699, reel 8; also in *O.R.,* ser. 2, vol. 1, p. 667; *O.R.,* ser. 2, vol. 1, p. 748; *The Biographical Cyclopedia of Representative Men of Maryland and [the] District of Columbia* (Baltimore: National Biographical, 1879), 398; Lynda L. Crist et al., eds., *The Papers of Jefferson Davis,* 15 vols. (Baton Rouge: Louisiana State University Press, 1971–), 10:86, 484–89.

26. Price to Bates, January 16, 1863, RG 60, Entry 9, Maryland Box 2; Bates to Price, January 21, 1863, RG 60, microfilm M699, reel 8.

27. *Baltimore Sun,* May 6 and 7, 1863; *Baltimore County Advocate,* May 9, 1863.

28. Indictment of John Merryman, July 28, 1863, in NARA-MB. The 1861 indictment charged Merryman with treason by levying war against the United States and with treason by adherence to the rebels. In 1863, Price added "giving aid and comfort" to the charges of treason by adherence. In some ways, this change was logical as the Constitution specifies that one may commit treason by "adhering to their [the United States'] Enemies, giving them Aid and Comfort." The giving of "aid and comfort" is the "overt Act" that the Constitution requires to prove the crime of adherence. But Price worded the charge differently, stating that Merryman sought "to fulfill and bring into effect the said treason and traitorous adhering and giving aid and comfort." Aid and comfort, in Price's construction, seemed a distinct crime from adherence. Either way, charging an American with adherence conflicted with the view of many legal authorities at the time who held that a person could give aid and comfort only to a foreign enemy and thus not to the Confederacy. See, for example, Justice Stephen J. Field's opinion in *United States v. Greathouse et al.,* 2 Abbott's Rep. 372–73 (1863); Edward D.

Tittmann, "The Exploitation of Treason," *New Mexico Historical Review* 4 (April 1929): 136; *The American Annual Cyclopaedia and Register of Important Events of the Year 1864* (New York: Appleton, 1865), 773.

29. Price to Bates, October 15, 1862, RG 60, Entry 9, Maryland Box 1; Bates to Price, October 20, 1862, RG 60, microfilm M699, reel 7. These letters predate the second set of treason indictments but represent the frustrations Price and Bates experienced throughout the prosecution.

30. On the same day that the Habeas Corpus Act of 1863 was enacted, Congress adopted a law that would have allowed a circuit justice who was incapacitated to request another justice to preside over sessions of the circuit court in his absence. While this legislation did not compel a sick justice to find a replacement, it may have been intended as a nudge to convince Chief Justice Taney to have one of his brethren preside over the treason cases in Baltimore. See *An Act to Give Greater Efficiency to the Judicial System of the United States,* act of March 3, 1863, in 12 Stat. 768.

31. Taney to Campbell, March 18, 1863, Howard Family Papers (MS 469), Taney Collection, Box 10, MDHS.

32. In federal courts throughout the North, including in Baltimore, the administration also prosecuted handfuls of civilians who impeded the draft or encouraged desertion during the war. Unlike the Baltimore rioters, these civilians were indicted for lesser crimes than treason.

33. Peleg Sprague, "Charge to Grand Jury—Treason," 30 Fed. Cases 1039–42 (1861); Peleg Sprague, *What is Treason? A Charge Addressed by the Hon. Peleg Sprague, Judge of the U. S. District Court for the District of Massachusetts, to the Grand Jury, at the March Term, A.D., 1863. Printed for the Union League* (Salem, Mass.: Charles W. Swasey, 1863).

34. U.S. Constitution, art. 3, sec. 3 (1787); James Willard Hurst, *The Law of Treason in the United States: Collected Essays* (Westport, Conn.: Greenwood, 1971), 3–56; William Whiting, *The War Powers of the President, and the Legislative Powers of Congress in Relation to Rebellion, Treason and Slavery* (Boston: John L. Shorey, 1862), 94.

35. Whiting, *War Powers,* 94; George P. Fletcher, "The Case for Treason," *Maryland Law Review* 41 (1982): 197–205; *The Federalist* No. 43.

36. Bradley Chapin, *The American Law of Treason: Revolutionary and Early National Origins* (Seattle: University of Washington Press, 1964), 85–97; Thomas P. Slaughter, "'The King of Crimes': Early American Treason Law, 1787–1860," in *Launching the "Extended Republic": The Federalist Era,* ed. Ronald Hoffman and Peter J. Albert (Charlottesville: University Press of Virginia, 1996), 89–135; John Marshall to William Cushing, June 29, 1807, in Charles F. Hobson et al., eds., *The Papers of John Marshall,* 12 vols. (Chapel Hill: University of North Carolina Press, 1974–2006), 2:60–62. In the early nineteenth century, the federal courts also made a distinction between "public" and "private" resistance to a federal law. In other words, a person who violently resisted a federal statute in the hopes of making a profit or obtaining some other personal advantage should not be convicted of treason. Of course, the Baltimore rioters did actually attack a body of federal troops on their way to defend the national capital. This was an act of public aggression against the federal government that might be more reasonably classified as "levying war" than the localized resistance of the Whiskey Rebellion and the Northampton Insurrection. A more difficult problem for federal prosecutors would

be proving that the rioters were part of a treasonable conspiracy with the Confederacy, as the 1851 case against Castner Hanway would seem to require.

37. Bates and Lincoln both quoted in Randall, *Constitutional Problems,* 87–88.

38. Bates to R. J. Lackey, January 19, 1863, in *O.R.,* ser. 2, vol. 5, pp. 190–91.

39. That is precisely what happened four months after Bates wrote this letter, when Union general Ambrose Burnside arrested former Ohio congressman Clement Vallandigham. Democrats held indignation meetings throughout the North to protest Lincoln's habeas corpus policy. See chapter 4 for further discussion of the Vallandigham case.

40. Bates to Robert C. Schenck, January 6, 1863, Robert C. Schenck Papers, Box 2.2, University Archives, Miami University of Ohio, Miami, Ohio. Likewise, Radical Republican Henry Winter Davis called Giles "a notorious secessionist." See Davis to Lyman Trumbull, July 12, 1862, Lyman Trumbull Papers, LC.

41. *The Federalist* No. 74.

42. Former Indiana congressman Robert Dale Owen brought *The Federalist* No. 74 to Lincoln's attention. See Owen to Lincoln, September 30, 1863, Lincoln Papers.

43. Lincoln, "Proclamation of Amnesty and Reconstruction," December 8, 1863, in *CWL,* 7:53–56; Assistant Attorney General T. J. Coffey to Price, March 11, 1864, RG 60, microfilm M699, reel 8.

44. RG 21 (Records of the U.S. District Court for the District of Maryland), Baltimore Division, Criminal Records, Case Files, Box 17, NARA-P; Lincoln, "Proclamation about Amnesty," March 24, 1864, and "Proclamation Concerning Reconstruction," July 8, 1864, both in *CWL,* 7:269–70, 433–34; Coffey to Price, March 30, 1864, RG 60, microfilm M699, reel 8; *Baltimore American and Commercial Advertiser,* March 28, 1864.

45. At the beginning of the war, Attorney General Bates expressed doubt that the president possessed the authority to pardon someone prior to conviction. "Of course the President has no power to pre-examine the facts of a pending case in court, & the[reb]ly supersede the office of the Jury," wrote Bates to the U.S. attorney in Maryland. "The matter I think, belongs exclusively to the prosecuting attorney, who, while he will prosecute the guilty, with zealous vigor, will of course cease to prosecute whenever the innocence of the accused is apparent to him." See Bates to William Meade Addison, July 17, 1861, RG 60, microfilm M699, reel 6. Bates's view, however, was not historically correct. At the Constitutional Convention, Luther Martin had proposed that the pardon power be limited only to "after conviction," but James Wilson convinced him to withdraw the proposal because preconviction pardons might be necessary to secure witnesses for trials (as President Jefferson sought to do during the *Burr* treason trial). Thus, the Constitution does not limit the time at which a president may issue a pardon. It was not until Reconstruction that Radical Republicans in Congress began to question the power of the president to issue blanket amnesties without congressional approval and prior to conviction. See William F. Duker, "The President's Power to Pardon: A Constitutional History," *William and Mary Law Review* 18 (Spring 1977): 501–2, 513–21. For more on Lincoln's amnesty policy, see Robert J. Chandler, "The Release of the *Chapman* Pirates: A California Sidelight on Lincoln's Amnesty Policy," *Civil War History* 43 (June 1977): 129–43.

46. William A. Russ, Jr., "The Struggle between President Lincoln and Congress over Disfranchisement of Rebels (Part 1)," *Susquehanna University Studies* 3 (March 1947): 204; *In re Greathouse,* 10 Fed. Cases 1057 (1864).

47. Case file for Josiah Grindall, RG 21 (Records of the U.S. District Court for the District of Maryland), Baltimore Division, Criminal Records, Case Files, Box 14. In at least one earlier case, that of a Baltimore rioter named James McCartney, the attorney general left the issuance of a *nolle prosequi* "to the discretion of the U.S. District Attorney for Maryland," if the guilt of the accused was in doubt. See RG 204 (Records of the Office of the Pardon Attorney), Entry 7 (Docket of Pardon Cases, 1853–1923), Vol. A, p. 357; Edward Bates to William Meade Addison, July 17, 1861, RG 60, microfilm M699, reel 6.

48. Randall, *Constitutional Problems,* 75–78. In truth, the Lincoln administration did not rely on disloyalty statutes as much as Randall may have presumed. For example, Samuel Sterrett of Maryland was convicted by a military commission at Fort McHenry for corresponding with his father, who was in the rebel service. See Court-Martial Case File MM-1106. Sterrett should have been tried by a civil court under *An Act to Prevent Correspondence with Rebels,* act of February 25, 1863, in 12 Stat. 696. Moreover, as has already been shown, Lincoln could not have tried Merryman and the Baltimore rioters under the later disloyalty legislation since these laws were not on the books at the time that those Marylanders acted against the Union.

49. It was a rare accused traitor, like Aaron Burr in 1806, who would flee and forfeit his bond. Peter Charles Hoffer, *The Treason Trials of Aaron Burr* (Lawrence: University Press of Kansas, 2008), 56.

50. George P. Kane to William H. Seward, October 26, 1861, in *O.R.,* ser. 2, vol. 1, p. 656; Andrew S. Ridgely to Henry Stanbery, April 1, 1867, RG 60, Entry 9, Maryland Box 2; Samuel Mactier to Edwin M. Stanton, March 28, 1864, Lincoln Papers. Mactier's case was finally dismissed on November 4, 1868. See RG 21 (Records of the U.S. Circuit Court for the District of Maryland), Baltimore Division, Criminal Docket (1864–1903), vol. 1, NARA-P.

51. Price to James Speed, March 21, 1865, RG 60, Entry 9, Maryland Box 2.

52. RG 21 (Records of the U.S. District Court for the District of Maryland), Baltimore Division, Criminal Case Files, Box 20. Other Confederate soldiers, like Isaac R. Trimble, had been indicted in 1861 and 1863 for their actions in April 1861. See boxes 13 and 16. As a point of clarification, George H. Steuart (1828–1903) resigned his commission in the U.S. army to join the Confederate service, where he rose to the rank of brigadier general. His father, also George H. Steuart (1790–1867), was the general in the Maryland militia at the beginning of the Civil War who had ordered the Baltimore County Horse Guards to burn the railroad bridges. The elder Steuart was indicted for treason in the U.S. circuit court in Baltimore in 1861; the younger Steuart was indicted for treason when he returned home from the war in 1865. Neither man was ever prosecuted.

53. Ridgely to Henry Stanbery, April 1 and 4, 1867, RG 60, Entry 9, Maryland Box 2. See also Jonathan Truman Dorris, *Pardon and Amnesty under Lincoln and Johnson: The Restoration of the Confederates to Their Rights and Privileges, 1861–1898* (Chapel Hill: University of North Carolina Press, 1953), 120–21; Ulysses S. Grant to Andrew Johnson, April 2, 1866, and James Speed to William J. Jones, April 2, 1866, both in Bradley T. Johnson Papers, Box 2, Special Collections, University of Virginia, Charlottesville, Va.

54. RG 21 (Records of the U.S. Circuit Court for the District of Maryland), Baltimore Division, Criminal Docket (1864–1903), vol. 1, NARA-P; Ridgely to Stanbery, April 15, 1867, RG 60, Entry 9, Maryland Box 2; M. F. Pleasants to Ridgely, April 22, 1867, in NARA-MB.

55. Persons indicted for treason were excluded from President Johnson's proclamation of September 7, 1867 (15 Stat. 699), which offered full pardon to most classes of rebels; how-

ever, Johnson offered individual pardons to several of the rioters. See the case files for Philip Cashmyer and Samuel McCubbin, both in RG 21 (Records of the U.S. District Court for the District of Maryland), Baltimore Division, Criminal Case Files, Box 16, NARA-P.

56. Salmon P. Chase to Milton Sutliff, June 3, 1868, in John Niven et al., eds., *The Salmon P. Chase Papers,* 5 vols. (Kent, Ohio: Kent State University Press, 1993–98), 5:227; Ridgely to Stanbery, April 23, 1868, RG 60, Entry 9, Maryland Box 2; "By the President of the United States of America: A Proclamation," July 4, 1868, in 15 Stat. 702; RG 21 (Records of the U.S. Circuit Court for the District of Maryland), Baltimore Division, Criminal Docket (1864–1903), vol. 1, NARA-P; "By the President of the United States of America: A Proclamation," December 25, 1868, in 15 Stat. 711; Roy F. Nichols, "United States vs. Jefferson Davis, 1865–1869," *American Historical Review* 31 (January 1926): 266–84.

57. See, for example, the Democrats' position in the debate over the expulsion of Senator Jesse Bright of Indiana in the *Congressional Globe,* 37th Cong., 2nd sess., pp. 393–94, 397, 541–42, 649–50.

58. Price to James Speed, March 21, 1865, RG 60, Entry 9, Maryland Box 2.

59. Ibid.; Ridgely to Stanbery, April 15, 1867, RG 60, Entry 9, Maryland Box 2.

60. *U.S. v. Hodges* (1815), 26 Fed. Cases 332. One important difference between these cases is that Hodges was indicted for adherence to the enemy, whereas Merryman was indicted for both levying war and adherence.

61. Slaughter, "King of Crimes," 54–135.

62. Mactier to Stanton, March 28, 1864, Lincoln Papers. See also Frank Towers, ed., "Military Waif: A Sidelight on the Baltimore Riot of 19 April 1861," *Maryland Historical Magazine* 89 (Winter 1994): 429; William Meade Addison to Edward Bates, March 17, 1862, RG 60, Entry 9, Maryland Box 1.

CHAPTER 4

1. *Appendix to the Congressional Globe,* 37th Cong., 1st sess., p. 17 (Bayard); *Congressional Globe,* 37th Cong., 1st sess., p. 48 (Polk).

2. Edward Spencer to Anne Catherine Bradford Harrison, July 14, 1861, in Anna Bradford Agle and Sidney Hovey Wanzer, eds., "Dearest Braddie: Love and War in Maryland, 1860–61: Part 2," *Maryland Historical Magazine* 88 (Fall 1993): 343.

3. Mark E. Neely, Jr., *The Fate of Liberty: Abraham Lincoln and Civil Liberties* (New York: Oxford University Press, 1991), 26, 75–77. Neely points out that one-third of the military arrests of civilians in 1861 took place in Maryland; by 1863–64 Maryland's share had dropped to just under 14 percent.

4. Nathaniel P. Banks to Sir, July 13, 1861, RG 60, Entry 9 (Letters Received by the Attorney General, 1809–70), Maryland Box 1.

5. *Congressional Globe,* 37th Cong., 1st sess., p. 198; *New York Times,* July 8, 1861; *Chicago Tribune,* July 13, 1861.

6. *Congressional Globe,* 37th Cong., 1st sess., pp. 131–32, 198; *Chicago Tribune,* July 13 and 18, 1861. If the resolution had been adopted, May most likely would have lost his seat in the House. See *New York Times,* September 30, 1861.

7. *Chicago Tribune,* July 16, 1861; *Congressional Globe,* 37th Cong., 1st sess., pp. 131–32.

8. *Congressional Globe,* 37th Cong., 1st sess., pp. 196–98; *Congressional Serial Set,* 37th Cong., 1st sess., House Report No. 2.

9. *Congressional Globe,* 37th Cong., 1st sess., pp. 196–97.

10. Ibid., 198.

11. Ibid., 198–202.

12. Ibid., 367, 445.

13. Ibid., 367, 445, 448, 458.

14. *O.R.,* ser. 2, vol. 2, pp. 102, 225–29, 790–95. May was also accused of "loitering about" Baltimore "with other rebels" and "taking observations" of Fort McHenry. See Charles W. Mitchell, ed., *Maryland Voices of the Civil War* (Baltimore: Johns Hopkins University Press, 2007), 163.

15. *O.R.,* ser. 2, vol. 2, pp. 799–801.

16. Quoted in the *New York Times,* July 14, 1861.

17. *New York Times,* July 20, 1861.

18. H.R. 362, 37th Cong., 2nd sess.

19. In August 1861, Congress enacted legislation that declared that "all the acts, proclamations, and orders of the President . . . respecting the army and navy of the United States, and calling out or relating to the militia or volunteers from the States, are hereby approved and in all respects legalized and made valid, to the same intent and with the same effect as if they had been issued and done under the previous express authority and direction of the Congress of the United States." Some historians contend that this act legalized Lincoln's earlier suspensions of the writ of habeas corpus, although the language of the act does not signify that it does (except for, perhaps, in the cases of minors who enlisted in the service without a parent's consent). See *An Act to Increase the Pay of the Privates in the Regular Army and [of] the Volunteers in the Service of the United States, and for Other Purposes,* act of August 6, 1861, in 12 Stat. 326. Brian McGinty, for example, argues that in the act of August 6, 1861, "Congress also approved his suspension of habeas corpus." See Brian McGinty, *Lincoln & the Court* (Cambridge, Mass.: Harvard University Press, 2008), 304. In fact, Congress refused to adopt a joint resolution in August 1861 that would have specifically approved of Lincoln's suspension of the writ of habeas corpus, further underscoring that the act of August 6, 1861, was not intended to "approve" of Lincoln's earlier actions in regard to the Great Writ. For discussion of the failed resolution, see Mary Bernard Allen, "Joseph Holt: Judge Advocate General (1862–1875): A Study in the Treatment of Political Prisoners by the United States Government during the Civil War" (Ph.D. diss., University of Chicago, 1927), 10–16.

20. H.R. 362, 37th Cong., 2nd sess.

21. Henry Winter Davis to Lyman Trumbull, July 12, 1862, Lyman Trumbull Papers, LC.

22. H.R. 591, 37th Cong., 3rd. sess.; *Congressional Globe,* 37th Cong., 3rd sess., pp. 20–22, 165–66; *O.R.,* ser. 2, vol. 1, pp. 632–33, 664; George Clarke Sellery, "Lincoln's Suspension of Habeas Corpus as Viewed by Congress," *Bulletin of the University of Wisconsin* 1 (1907): 217–63; James G. Randall, "The Indemnity Act of 1863: A Study in the Wartime Immunity of Governmental Officers," *Michigan Law Review* 20 (April 1922): 589–96. Stevens did not believe the president possessed the constitutional authority to suspend the writ of habeas corpus and that Congress needed to expressly grant him that power. Other Republicans disagreed and

believed Stevens's bill was unnecessary. Most Republicans supported the Habeas Corpus Bill, either as a necessity or as a precautionary measure.

23. *Congressional Globe,* 37th Cong., 3rd sess., pp. 1158–59. Some Democrats also feared that the bill would be used to authorize the imprisonment of Democrats at elections and to diminish the criminal jurisdiction of the states. Delaware senator James A. Bayard privately wished that Delaware was strong enough to fight back against these intrusions on civil liberty. "Would to God we had the physical power of resistance in our small state but the attempt would be madness," Bayard wrote to his son. Bayard could only hope that New York or the states of the Old Northwest would rise up. See James A. Bayard to Thomas F. Bayard, December 16, 1862, January 31 and February 24, 1863, all in Thomas F. Bayard Papers, LC.

24. *Congressional Globe,* 37th Cong., 3rd sess., 542–43.

25. Ibid., 544–46; Patrick Henry, Speech in the House of Burgesses, May 29, 1765, in William Wirt Henry, comp., *Patrick Henry: Life, Correspondence and Speeches,* 3 vols. (New York: Scribner's, 1891), 1:86.

26. *Congressional Globe,* 37th Cong., 3rd sess., pp., 548–50.

27. *Liberator,* January 30, 1863; Henry M. Cannon to mother, January 29, 1863, letter listed on eBay (Auction No. 220518378446), sold December 8, 2009; *Congressional Globe,* 37th Cong., 3rd sess., pp. 552.

28. *Congressional Globe,* 37th Cong., 3rd sess., pp. 558–59, 584; Sidney George Fisher, diary entry for January 28, 1863, in Jonathan W. White, ed., *A Philadelphia Perspective: The Civil War Diary of Sidney George Fisher* (New York: Fordham University Press, 2007), 183; James A. Bayard to Thomas F. Bayard, December 18, 1862, and January 10 and 31, 1863, Thomas F. Bayard Papers, LC.

29. A month after Saulsbury's confrontation in the Senate, the Democrat-controlled legislature in Delaware passed a law in 1863 "to prevent illegal arrests" in the state by the Lincoln administration. In Delaware the governor could not veto any legislation adopted by the general assembly, so in response, Governor William Cannon, a Unionist, declared that he would not enforce the law. "The preservation of the Government is the highest duty of those charged with its administration; and the personal liberty of the individual is only to be regarded when compatible with its safety." Cannon conceded that citizens had the right to discuss political issues and peacefully assemble to seek the redress of grievances, "but there is a wide difference between the exercise of this right and the disloyal opposition which proceeds from sympathy with a public enemy." "The idea that the Government is bound to await the development of a conspiracy until the actors shall have perfected their plans and committed some overt act necessary to bring them within the technical definition of treason, is, to my mind, absurd. The object is not punishment, but prevention." If a citizen wished to avoid arrest, Cannon suggested he show unfailing and unequivocal loyalty to the national government. In the meantime, Cannon pledged to aid in the disclosure or arrest of "any one guilty of disloyal practices or treasonable designs against the Government." See "An Act to Prevent Illegal Arrests in this State," act of February 24, 1863, in *Laws of the State of Delaware, Passed at the Session of the General Assembly, Commenced and Held at Dover, on Tuesday, the Sixth Day of January A.D. 1863* (Wilmington: Henry Eckel, 1863), 288–90; *Philadelphia Press,* March 16, 1863.

30. The Senate passed the bill in the closing hours of the 37th Congress (literally, at 5:30 a.m. on March 3), in proceedings that historian James G. Randall called "a truly remarkable

struggle." Senate Democrats had been mounting an all-night filibuster to prevent passage of the bill but at some point after 5:00 a.m. they lost control of the floor and the Republicans voted to pass it. The Senators were so exhausted, and the parliamentary proceedings had become so muddled, that the Democrats did not even realize that it had been voted on. When one Republican claimed that it had passed, Senator Lazarus Powell replied: "No, it has not passed. I want the yeas and nays on its passage. It is not passed at all." When the presiding officer insisted that it had indeed passed, Powell responded, "By what kind of jockeying?" Later that day Powell claimed that the presiding officer "in a very low and very hurried manner asked those who were in favor of concurring in the report of the committee to say 'ay,'" but that he never asked for the nays. See Randall, "Indemnity Act," 593–95; *Congressional Globe,* 37th Cong., 3rd sess., p. 1490; *New York Times,* March 5, 7, 1863; *The Washington Despotism Dissected in Articles from the Metropolitan Record* (New York: Metropolitan Record, 1863), 12.

31. On February 19, 1863, Thaddeus Stevens called on Lincoln at the White House to see if Lincoln was "satisfied" with the Senate's amendments to Stevens's bill. Upon not being able to meet with the president, Stevens left him a note: "If I do not hear from you before 1. 'O clk I shall consider that you are content." It is unclear whether or how Lincoln replied to this note. See Stevens to Lincoln, February 19, 1863, in Beverly Wilson Palmer and Holly Byers Ochoa, eds., *The Selected Papers of Thaddeus Stevens,* 2 vols. (Pittsburgh: University of Pittsburgh Press, 1997), 1:370.

32. The text of the law did not explicitly condone Lincoln's earlier suspensions because Congress was divided over whether Lincoln's previous actions needed congressional sanction. Rather, the law stated, in rather ambiguous language, that the president "is authorized to suspend" the writ. For further discussion of the evolution of the statutory language, see Sellery, "Lincoln's Suspension as Viewed by Congress."

33. *An Act Relating to Habeas Corpus, and Regulating Judicial Proceedings in Certain Cases,* act of March 3, 1863, in 12 Stat. 755.

34. Lincoln to Erastus Corning and others, June 12, 1863, in *CWL,* 6:265; Allen, "Joseph Holt," 32; James A. Dueholm, "Lincoln's Suspension of the Writ of Habeas Corpus: An Historical and Constitutional Analysis," *Journal of the Abraham Lincoln Association* 29 (Summer 2008): 47–66.

35. It is a mistake to see the Habeas Corpus Act of 1863 as Congress giving Lincoln "broad discretion to suspend habeas," as some historians do. See, for example, McGinty, *Lincoln & the Court,* 306.

36. May did not take part in the vote on the passage of the Habeas Corpus Act. If he had been present, he would have likely joined the Democrats in voting against it because of the act's suspension-authorizing and indemnification provisions. See *House Journal,* 37th Cong., 3rd sess., pp. 51–52.

37. Henry Winter Davis to Lyman Trumbull, July 12, 1862, Lyman Trumbull Papers, LC.

38. This is not to suggest that Taney approved of the act as it was adopted, but that he assented to and possibly influenced the crafting of the provisions that placed military prisoners back into the federal judicial system.

39. To be precise, not all civilians tried by military tribunals were charged with treason or treason-related crimes, but many were. While some persons faced charges of "treason" proper, others were charged with disloyal practice, "acts of a treasonable character," aiding and abetting the enemy, sedition, disloyal language, "treason under the laws of war," en-

couraging rebellion, corresponding with the enemy, "publicly expressing sympathy with the enemies of the government," giving intelligence to the enemy, being an insurgent, disloyal conduct, and a host of other similar charges. While not technically "treason," charges of this nature essentially accused the defendant of being a traitor. Privately, Judge Advocate General Joseph Holt had written that "a general court martial has not jurisdiction of this crime [treason]." Perhaps Holt distinguished between courts-martial and military commission trials. See Joseph Holt to Francis Lieber, February 26, 1863 (L12345), Francis Lieber Papers, The Huntington, San Marino, Calif.

40. U.S. Constitution, art. 3, secs. 2 and 3 (1787); 5th and 6th amends. (1791); Max Farrand, ed., *The Records of the Federal Convention of 1787*, 3 vols. (New Haven, Conn.: Yale University Press, 1911), 2:348. In 1861, U.S. district judge John Cadwalader argued that enemies of the United States and prisoners of war could not seek relief from military captivity by a writ of habeas corpus—even when the writ was not suspended. See "Judge Cadwalader's Opinion in the Habeas Corpus Case at Baltimore Respecting George Cadwalader's Action Regarding a Prisoner," manuscript opinion in Cadwalader Collection, Series VI (Judge John Cadwalader), Box 264, HSP.

41. My interpretation is that prior to the adoption of the Habeas Corpus Act of 1863, Lincoln's suspension of the writ enabled the executive branch to detain civilians indefinitely but that when the period of suspension was ended they would either have to be released or brought before a civil court. For nineteenth-century arguments similar to mine, see the argument of Reverdy Johnson in *The Trial of the Alleged Assassins and Conspirators at Washington City, D.C., May and June, 1865, for the Murder of President Abraham Lincoln* (Philadelphia: T. B. Peterson & Brothers, 1865), 161, and *Ex parte Milligan*, 71 U.S. 125–26 (1866). For other perspectives, see Neely, *Fate of Liberty*, 32–38 and chap. 8; Herman Belz, *Abraham Lincoln, Constitutionalism, and Equal Rights in the Civil War Era* (New York: Fordham University Press, 1998), chap. 1, and Chief Justice Chase's concurring opinion in *Milligan*.

42. Neely, *Fate of Liberty*, 32–46; Lincoln, "Proclamation Suspending the Writ of Habeas Corpus," September 24, 1862, in *CWL*, 5:436–37; see also "Order Authorizing Arrests of Persons Discouraging Enlistments," August 8, 1862, in *O.R.*, ser. 3, vol. 2, pp. 321–22; "Order to Prevent Evasion of Military Duty and for the Suppression of Disloyal Practices," August 8, 1862, *O.R.*, ser. 2, vol. 4, pp. 358–59.

43. Art. 1, sec. 8, grants Congress the power "To constitute Tribunals inferior to the supreme Court" and "To make Rules for the Government and Regulation of the land and naval Forces." Art. 3, sec. 1, says that the judiciary of the United States "shall be vested in one supreme Court, and in such inferior Courts as the Congress may from time to time ordain and establish."

44. During the war, Congress first recognized the existence of military commissions in Section 5 of the Militia Act of 1862, but the act did not say anything about the nature or jurisdiction of these tribunals. See *An Act to Amend the Act Calling Forth the Militia to Execute the Laws of the Union, Suppress Insurrections, and Repel Invasions, approved February Twenty-Eighth, Seventeen Hundred and Ninety-Five, and the Acts Amendatory Thereof, and for Other Purposes*, act of July 17, 1862, in 12 Stat. 597.

45. *An Act Making an Appropriation for Completing the Defences of Washington, and for Other Purposes*, act of February 13, 1862, in 12 Stat. 340, and *An Act to Prevent and Punish Frauds upon the Government of the United States*, act of March 2, 1863, in 12 Stat. 697. Military

trials of civilians, significantly, violated the text of wartime legislation *that had been adopted by Republicans* to suppress the rebellion and enforce the draft. The Conspiracies Act of July 31, 1861, required conspirators against the government to face trial in the federal civil courts, while the Enrollment Act of March 3, 1863, stated that those resisting the draft or encouraging desertion "shall, upon legal conviction, be fined, at the discretion of any court having cognizance of the same." The Enrollment Act of 1864 added: "And in cases where such assaulting, obstructing, hindering, or impeding [of the draft] shall produce the death of such officer or other person [enforcing the draft], the offender shall be deemed guilty of murder, and, upon conviction thereof upon indictment in the circuit court of the United States for the district within which the offence was committed, shall be punished with death." Section 30 of the Enrollment Act of 1863 specifically limited the jurisdiction of military courts to members of the armed forces. It specified that crimes "shall be punishable by the sentence of a general court-martial or military commission, when committed by persons who are in the military service of the United States, and subject to the articles of war." See *An Act to Define and Punish Certain Conspiracies*, act of July 31, 1861, in 12 Stat. 284; *An Act for Enrolling and Calling Out the National Forces, and for Other Purposes*, act of March 3, 1863, in 12 Stat. 735–36; *An Act to Amend an Act Entitled "An Act for Enrolling and Calling Out the National Forces, and for Other Purposes," approved March Third, Eighteen Hundred and Sixty-Three*, act of February 24, 1864, in 13 Stat. 8.

46. Court-Martial Case File NN-3028; *Baltimore County Advocate* November 12, 1864. Hutchins was released from prison in December 1864. William Ives, a citizen of New York City, was also charged with violation of the laws of war and "treason under the laws of war" for working with Hutchins to procure the sword for Gilmor. He pleaded not guilty and was acquitted. See Court-Martial Case File NN-3080.

47. Court-Martial Case File NN-3030.

48. Court-Martial Case File MM-751.

49. Like Merryman, Cockey was indicted for treason in both 1861 and 1863 for burning railroad bridges on April 23, 1861. See RG 21 (Records of the U.S. District Court for the District of Maryland), Baltimore Division, Criminal Case Files (1841–78), Box 16, and General Records, Minutes (1790–1972), vol. for 1860–63.

50. Court-Martial Case File NN-2466.

51. Ibid.

52. Neely, *Fate of Liberty*, 32–50, 168–72. Some of the border state cases I have examined are Court-Martial Case Files II-476, KK-151, KK-825, KK-838, LL-475, LL-588, LL-2436, MM-15, MM-79, MM-147, MM-518, MM-1923, NN-3437, NN-3717, and NN-3853. Persons interested in brief overviews of military commission trials involving northern and border state women should consult Thomas P. Lowry, *Confederate Heroines: 120 Southern Women Convicted by Union Military Justice* (Baton Rouge: Louisiana State University Press, 2006), 1–75, 147–53, 160–67.

53. Court-Martial Case Files NN-2198, NN-2216, and NN-2277.

54. Jonathan W. White, "Canvassing the Troops: The Federal Government and the Soldiers' Right to Vote," *Civil War History* 50 (September 2004): 290–316; Joseph George, Jr., "The North Affair: A Lincoln Administration Military Trial, 1864," *Civil War History* 33 (September 1987): 199–218.

55. I am not including draftees in this number. Section 13 of the Conscription Act of 1863

permitted drafted men to be tried by courts-martial; however, Sections 24 and 25 required persons resisting or inhibiting the draft to be tried in civil courts.

56. George Turner, ed., *Civil War Letters from Soldiers and Citizens of Columbia County, Pennsylvania* (New York: American Heritage, 1996), 409–70; Court-Martial Case Files LL-2689, NN-2823, NN-3175, NN-3348, and NN-3365; Neely, *Fate of Liberty*, 174.

57. Thirteen men from Luzerne County were convicted by a military commission in January 1864 for resisting the draft as part of a secret society alternately called the "Buck Shots" and the "Golden Circle." They were sentenced to imprisonment at Fort Mifflin for the duration of the war. See Court-Martial Case File NN-1478. Rev. Alvah Rutan, an anti-abolitionist preacher in Luzerne County was arrested three times during the war for uttering disloyal sentiments; after his third arrest he was tried and convicted by a military commission and sentenced to imprisonment at Fort Mifflin. See John G. Freeze, *A History of Columbia County, Pennsylvania: From the Earliest Times* (Bloomsburg, Pa.: Elwell & Bittenbender, 1883), 408–12; Court-Martial Case File LL-2906; affidavits of William Forbes and Seth T. Dodson, September 9 and October 13, 1864, both in RG 393, Part 1, Entry 4663 (Departments of the Susquehanna and Pennsylvania, Judge Advocate: Letters and Reports Received, 1863–65), Box 2, NARA. In early 1865, three civilians from Clearfield County were convicted by a military commission for draft resistance and being members of a treasonable "Democratic Castle." See Court-Martial Case Files MM-1607, MM-1611, and OO-348; Robert M. Sandow, *Deserter Country: Civil War Opposition in the Pennsylvania Appalachians* (New York: Fordham University Press, 2009).

58. "General Orders No. 38," April 13, 1863, in *O.R.*, ser. 2, vol. 5, p. 480 (emphasis added). It will be remembered that the Constitution defines treason as an "overt Act."

59. "General Orders No. 9," April 15, 1863, in *O.R.*, ser. 2, vol. 5, p. 485. Compare with George M. Frederickson, *The Inner Civil War: Northern Intellectuals and the Crisis of the Union* (New York: Harper & Row, 1965), chap. 9.

60. Stephen E. Towne, "Killing the Serpent Speedily: Governor Morton, General Hascall, and the Suppression of the Democratic Press in Indiana, 1863," *Civil War History* 52 (April 2006): 51–53. Oliver P. Morton, Indiana's Republican governor, also complained to Lincoln that if Burnside's order could take effect "then the Act of Congress amounts to nothing." See Morton to Lincoln, May 30, 1863, Lincoln Papers.

61. Pugh quoted in George H. Porter, *Ohio Politics during the Civil War Period* (New York: Columbia University Press, 1911), 171 (emphasis added); Frank L. Klement, *The Limits of Dissent: Clement L. Vallandigham and the Civil War* (Lexington: University Press of Kentucky, 1970), 156–72. President Lincoln regretted the arrest and military trial of Vallandigham, but publicly he defended it. After a short period in the Confederacy, Vallandigham escaped to Windsor, Canada, where, in October 1863, he ran for governor of Ohio on the Democratic ticket. The exiled candidate was defeated in a landslide. The following year he returned to the United States, and in August 1864 he was a prominent "Peace" delegate at the Democratic National Convention.

62. *The Trial of Hon. Clement L. Vallandigham, by a Military Commission: and the Proceedings under His Application for a Writ of Habeas Corpus in the Circuit Court of the United States for the Southern District of Ohio* (Cincinnati: Rickey & Carroll, 1863), 263–64; *Ex parte Vallandigham*, 68 U.S. 243 (1863). Shortly after returning to the United States, Vallandigham

sent a check for $44 to the Supreme Court to pay the fee for his appeal. See Clement L. Val-
landigham to D.W. Middleton, September 17, 1864, RG 267 (Records of the Supreme Court
of the United States), Entry 31 (Records of the Office of the Clerk, General Correspondence,
1791–1941), Box 17, NARA.

63. Stephen E. Towne, "Worse than Vallandigham: Governor Oliver P. Morton, Lambdin P.
Milligan, and the Military Arrest and Trial of Indiana State Senator Alexander J. Douglas
during the Civil War," *Indiana Magazine of History* 106 (March 2010): 1–39; Court-Martial
Case Files LL-449, NN-3, and MM-1102; Lowry, *Confederate Heroines*, 151–53.

64. Jonathan W. White, ed., "The Civil War Disloyalty Trial of John O'Connell," *Ohio
Valley History* 9 (Spring 2009): 2–20. John O'Connell was not charged under General Orders
No. 38; his sentence was later commuted.

65. For an overview of these arrests and trials, see Frank L. Klement, *Dark Lanterns:
Secret Political Societies, Conspiracies, and Treason Trials in the Civil War* (Baton Rouge:
Louisiana State University Press, 1984), 151–217. Four of these cases culminated in the famous
postwar case *Ex parte Milligan,* which will be discussed in greater detail below. For other
instances of federal suppression of draft resistance in the Midwest, see Patrick J. Drouhard,
It Don't Look Right for the Times: The Factual History of the Holmes County Rebellion (Card-
ington, Ohio: Privately printed, 2005); Kenneth H. Wheeler, "Local Autonomy and Civil War
Draft Resistance: Holmes County, Ohio," *Civil War History* 45 (June 1999): 147–59; and Peter
J. Barry, "'I'll Keep Them in Prison Awhile . . .': Abraham Lincoln and David Davis on Civil
Liberties in Wartime," *Journal of the Abraham Lincoln Association* 28 (Winter 2007): 20–29.

66. In fact, these civil liberties issues became a matter of international consequence because many of those arrested claimed to be subjects of foreign governments. Military commission case files frequently contain letters from ambassadors and foreign ministers seeking
the release of foreign-born persons who had been convicted in American military courts. Records at the National Archives of the United Kingdom also contain related correspondence.

67. *Ex parte Merryman,* 17 Fed. Cases 149 (1861).

68. Neely concludes that most of the civilians detained by the military were not arrested
for political reasons; neither were they arrested to squelch anti-administration speech. To
the contrary, Neely argues that most of these arrests were intended to enforce conscription,
prevent border state civilians from assisting rebel soldiers and guerrillas, and inhibit trade
with the enemy. In short, these arrests and trials were not meant to stifle dissent but to aid the
Union war effort. Accordingly, even if Lincoln had not suspended the writ of habeas corpus,
"a majority of the arrests would have occurred" anyway. Neely, *Fate of Liberty,* 168, 233–34.

69. Lincoln to Erastus Corning and others, June 12, 1863, in *CWL,* 6:260–69; Lincoln to
Matthew Birchard and others, June 29, 1863, quoted in Neely, *Fate of Liberty,* 174.

70. Neely, *Fate of Liberty,* 174–75. Lincoln might have been less disingenuous if he had
issued something of a signing statement when he signed the Habeas Corpus Act into law,
similar to when he attached his veto message to his signing of the Second Confiscation Act.
In doing so, Lincoln could have tacitly approved of Congress's action in the matter while
affirming his belief that the president possessed the constitutional authority to suspend the
writ of habeas corpus and try civilians before military tribunals.

71. Holt to Stanton, June 9, 1863, in *O.R.,* ser. 2, vol. 5, pp. 765–66; Harold M. Hyman, *A
More Perfect Union: The Impact of the Civil War and Reconstruction on the Constitution* (New

York: Knopf, 1973), 254. The War Department sent few lists to the federal courts between 1863 and 1865, and those that were sent were often incomplete. The list Holt sent to Judge Cadwalader in Philadelphia, for example, included only two names—one Pennsylvanian imprisoned at Fort Delaware and one held at Fort McHenry. See Holt to John Cadwalader, June 9, 1863, RG 21 (Records of the U.S. District Court for the Eastern District of Pennsylvania), Habeas Corpus Cases (1791–1915), Box 3, NARA-P. The lists supplied by General Irvin McDowell to the federal judges in California were more thorough, but these lists were from the early postwar period. See Irvin McDowell to Ogden Hoffman, June 10, 1865, RG 21 (Records of the U.S. District Court for the Northern District of California), San Francisco, Case Papers, 1851–66, Box 2, National Archives at San Francisco.

72. Holt apparently later admitted that the War Department had been neglecting the provisions of the Habeas Corpus Act. See Joseph George, Jr., "Military Trials of Civilians under the Habeas Corpus Act of 1863," *Lincoln Herald* 98 (Winter 1996): 127.

73. *Congressional Globe,* 38th Cong., 2nd sess., p. 76.

74. Johnson argued that Congress was not the only branch of the government that possessed the authority to suspend the privilege of the writ of habeas corpus. See Reverdy Johnson, "Power of the President to Suspend the Habeas Corpus Writ," in *Rebellion Record: A Diary of American Events,* 12 vols., ed. Frank Moore (New York: G. P. Putnam, 1861–68), 2:185–93.

75. Benjamin F. Butler, *Butler's Book: Autobiography and Personal Reminiscences of Major-General Benjamin F. Butler* (Boston: A.M. Thayer, 1892), 234; Brad C. Steiner, *Life of Reverdy Johnson* (Baltimore: Norman, Remington, 1914), 50–57.

76. "Reverdy Johnson's Argument," in *Trial of the Alleged Assassins and Conspirators,* 158–65. Compare with Thomas Jefferson's complaints in the Declaration of Independence that King George III "has made Judges dependent on his Will alone, for the Tenure of their Offices, and the Amount and Payment of their Salaries," and that he had "depriv[ed] us, in many Cases, of the Benefits of Trial by Jury."

77. Quoted in James L. Swanson and Daniel R. Weinberg, *Lincoln's Assassins: Their Trial and Execution* (Santa Fe, N.M.: Arena Editions, 2001), 26.

78. William Davis Shipman to Samuel L. M. Barlow, July 12, 1865, Samuel L. M. Barlow Papers, The Huntington, San Marino, Calif. Shipman, a Democrat, was a federal judge in Connecticut. In the postwar period federal judges in other parts of the country—including Republican appointees—also began to express doubts about the legality of military trials of civilians. See Donald O. Dewey, ed., "Hoosier Justice: The Journal of David McDonald, 1864–1868," *Indiana Magazine of History* 62 (September 1966): 203–8.

79. Elizabeth D. Leonard, "Mary Surratt and the Plot to Assassinate Abraham Lincoln," in *The War Was You and Me: Civilians in the American Civil War,* ed. Joan E. Cashin (Princeton, N.J.: Princeton University Press, 2002), 301–5.

80. For competing interpretations of the Milligan affair, see Klement, *Dark Lanterns,* 91–244; Robert H. Churchill, *To Shake Their Guns in the Tyrant's Face: Libertarian Political Violence and the Origins of the Militia Movement* (Ann Arbor: University of Michigan Press, 2009), 107–44, and "Liberty, Conscription, and Delusions of Grandeur: The Sons of Liberty Conspiracy of 1863–1864," *Prologue* 30 (Winter 1998): 295–303.

81. *Ex parte Milligan,* 71 U.S. 107 (1866).

82. Ibid., 132. See also *The Federalist* No. 23, as well as Mark E. Neely, Jr., "The Constitution and Civil Liberties under Lincoln," in *Our Lincoln: New Perspectives on Lincoln and His World,* ed. Eric Foner (New York: W. W. Norton, 2008): 42–45.

83. 71 U.S. 109. Davis had, in fact, opposed Lincoln's internal security policies during the war and he privately informed Lincoln of his views; however, he acquiesced to Lincoln's wishes in a case in his circuit rather than make a public pronouncement on the habeas corpus issue while the nation was still at war. See Barry, "I'll Keep Them in Prison Awhile . . . ," 20–29.

84. Lincoln was an adherent to the idea of "departmental review" of the Constitution— that is, that each branch of the federal government was obligated to determine the meaning of the Constitution for itself. See his discussions of Andrew Jackson's 1832 bank veto and the power of judicial review in Lincoln, "Speech at Springfield, Illinois," June 26, 1857, and "First Inaugural Address—Final Text," March 4, 1861, both in *CWL,* 2:400–403, and 4:267–68. In a similar way, Lincoln claimed the authority to interpret the constitutional powers of the president when it came to the issue of emancipation. For example, when he revoked General David Hunter's military order emancipating slaves in South Carolina, Georgia, and Florida, Lincoln stated: "I further make known that whether it be competent for me, as Commander-in-Chief of the Army and Navy, to declare the Slaves of any state or states, free, and whether at any time, in any case, it shall have become a necessity indispensable to the maintenance of the government, to exercise such supposed power, are questions which, under my responsibility, I reserve to myself." See Lincoln, "Proclamation Revoking General Hunter's Order of Military Emancipation of May 9, 1862," May 19, 1862, in *CWL,* 5:222.

CHAPTER 5

1. John M. Read to Lyman Trumbull, February 13, 1863, Lyman Trumbull Papers, LC.

2. British jurist A.V. Dicey described indemnity laws "as the supreme instance of Parliamentary sovereignty" because they "are retrospective statutes which free persons who have broken the law from responsibility for its breach, and thus make lawful acts which when they were committed were unlawful." Dicey pointed out that some indemnity acts were "narrow" and others were "wide"—meaning that some laws offered "a very limited amount of protection to official wrongdoers" while in other cases the statutes protected government officials even for gross violations of the law. The Habeas Corpus Act of March 3, 1863, was patterned after the "narrow" indemnity statutes. The British Indemnity Act of 1801, for example, provided "a defence against actions or prosecutions in respect of anything done, commanded, ordered, directed, or advised to be done in Great Britain for apprehending, imprisoning, or detaining in custody any person charged with high treason or treasonable practices." The act, according to Dicey, would "cover any irregularity or merely formal breach of the law"; but acts done for "spite or extortion . . . would expose the offender to actions or prosecutions, and could not be justified under the terms of the Indemnity Act. Reckless cruelty to a political prisoner, or, still more certainly, the arbitrary punishment or the execution of a political prisoner, between 1793 and 1801 would, in spite of the Indemnity Act, have left every man concerned in the crime liable to suffer punishment." See A.V. Dicey, *Introduction to the Study of the Law of the Constitution* (Indianapolis: Liberty Classics, 1982), 142–45. For a discussion of

the Habeas Corpus Act of 1863 and the issue of federalism in the United States, see Harold M. Hyman, *A More Perfect Union: The Impact of the Civil War and Reconstruction on the Constitution* (New York: Knopf, 1973), 245–62.

3. See *Charles Howard v. George R. Dodge, Severn Teackle Wallis v. John E. Wool, Frank K. Howard v. John E. Wool, Henry M. Warfield v. John E. Wool, Thomas Sewell Jr. v. John E. Wool, Thomas H. Gardner v. John E. Wool, Thomas R. Rich v. John E. Wool,* and *A. D. Evans v. John E. Wool,* all listed in RG 21 (Records of the U.S. Circuit Court for the District of Maryland), Baltimore Division, General Records, Index to Judgments and Decrees (1790–1877), NARA-P; case files for these cases are held with the court's Law Records in RG 21. Three of these suits were originally instituted in the Maryland state courts and then removed to the federal circuit court in Baltimore.

4. *O.R.,* ser. 2, vol. 2, pp. 505–9; *CWL,* 5:193–94; Cameron to Lincoln, Thursday, April 17, 1862, Lincoln Papers; George A. Coffey to Edward Bates, May 7, 1862, RG 60, Entry 9 (Letters Received by the Attorney General, 1809–70), Pennsylvania Box 2; Benjamin H. Brewster to William H. Seward, April 16, 1862, Seward to Brewster, April 18, 1862, and Seward to Edward Bates, April 18, 1862, all in RG 60, Entry 9, Department of State Box 3; Simon Cameron to George Cadwalader, April 17, 1862, Cadwalader Collection, Series VII (General George Cadwalader), Box 411, HSP; George Cadwalader to Simon Cameron, April 17, 1862, Simon Cameron Papers, HSDC; Benjamin H. Brewster to Simon Cameron, April 19, 1862, Edwin M. Stanton Papers, LC.

5. Cameron to Lincoln, April 17, 1862, Lincoln Papers; Lincoln quoted in James G. Randall, "The Indemnity Act of 1863: A Study in the Wartime Immunity of Governmental Officers," *Michigan Law Review* 20 (April 1922): 592; Edward Bates, diary entry for April 21, 1862, in Howard K. Beale, ed., *The Diary of Edward Bates, 1859–1866* (Washington, D.C.: Government Printing Office, 1933), 252.

6. Thaddeus Stevens's initial bill would have declared all civil and criminal prosecutions against the president and his subordinates "discharged and made void." The final legislation, however, merely removed such suits from the state to federal courts and made orders from the president grounds for defense in such prosecutions. See H.R. 591, 37th Cong., 3rd sess.

7. Baltimore City Superior Court, transcript of *Merryman v. Cadwalader.* The state and federal case papers for the first *Merryman v. Cadwalader* case are in RG 21 (Records of the U.S. Circuit Court for the District of Maryland), Merryman Box, NARA-P (hereafter NARA-MB); William Schley to Edwin M. Stanton, July 28, 1863, RG 107, microfilm M221 (Letters Received by the Secretary of War: Main Series, 1801–70), reel 231. Cadwalader owned significant real estate in Harford County, Maryland.

William Schley, a prominent member of the Baltimore bar, had been an antebellum Whig who never joined another political party after the demise of the Whig Party in the 1850s. In 1863, he served as defense counsel for alleged traitor Hazel B. Cashell (Cashell's case is described in chapter 3). In 1864, he was a presidential elector on the Democratic ticket, although he did not join the Democratic Party. See *Baltimore Sun,* December 23, 1863, March 16 and November 2, 1864.

8. Shortly after Pierce Butler sued Simon Cameron for damages in April 1862, Cameron's friend and attorney, Benjamin H. Brewster, suggested that Cameron lobby Congress for statutory protection from this type of litigation. Brewster recommended several elements

that should be contained in the legislation, including a provision for the removal of damages suits from the state to the federal courts. "This is essential," wrote Brewster. "First for protection. Second to prevent various and conflicting adjudications on the points raised in such suits which if the State Courts are allowed to have concurrent or exclusive jurisdiction will lead to a sure state of injustice." See Brewster to Cameron, April 19, 1862, Stanton Papers, LC.

9. *An Act Relating to Habeas Corpus, and Regulating Judicial Proceedings in Certain Cases,* act of March 3, 1863, in 12 Stat. 755; Cadwalader to Cameron, March 3, 1863, Cameron Papers, HSDC.

10. Curiously, the Maryland state court records do not mention the Habeas Corpus Act as a reason for removal of the case; they only cite the federal courts' diversity jurisdiction.

11. RG 21 (Records of the U.S. Circuit Court for the District of Maryland), Baltimore Division, General Records, Dockets (1790–1877), Trials, April Term 1864, case no. 32, NARA-P; William Schley to George Cadwalader, March 9, 1864, Cadwalader Collection, Series VII (General George Cadwalader), Box 442, HSP. Schley also served as General Wool's attorney in the suits against Wool (see Epilogue).

12. See chapter 4. Suspected traitors under indictment in other northern states also took the oath under Lincoln's proclamation of December 8, 1863. See *U.S. v. Edward L. Hughes,* 1 Bond's Rep. 574. In this case, the U.S. Circuit Court for the Southern District of Ohio held that Lincoln's second proclamation could not negate the oath that an indicted traitor had already taken under the first proclamation.

13. I searched the Records of the Office of the Pardon Attorney in RG 204, Entry 1 (Pardon Case Files, 1853–1946), Entry 7 (Docket of Pardon Cases, 1853–1923), Entry 12 (Lists of Pardon Cases, 1861–65), Entry 13 (Index to Pardon Cases, 1853–89), Entry 17 (Indexes to Requisitions for Pardon Warrants, 1861–71), and Entry 28 (Miscellaneous Material, 1865, 1881–84, 1901), all at Archives II, but did not find any records related to Merryman. This does not mean that he did not pursue amnesty, however. He might have communicated his wish for pardon directly to U.S. attorney William Price either verbally or in writing, in which case such a request might be impossible to locate today.

14. Assistant Attorney General T. J. Coffey to Price, March 11, 1864, RG 60, microfilm M699 (Letters Sent by the Department of Justice: General and Miscellaneous, 1818–1904), reel 8 (emphasis in the original).

15. Lincoln later commented on the need for this shift in policy: "During the year many availed themselves of the general provision, and many more would, only that the signs of bad faith in some led to such precautionary measures as rendered the practical process less easy and certain." See Lincoln, "Annual Message to Congress," December 6, 1864, in *CWL,* 8:152.

16. Lincoln's shift in policy—to exclude rebels and traitors who were under indictment in the federal courts—could have had a significant effect on his reconstruction policy in the South. In June 1864, for example, there were 2,014 rebels indicted for treason in the U.S. Circuit Court for the Eastern District of Tennessee. These rebels would have been eligible for pardon under Lincoln's December 1863 proclamation but were now excluded by his March 1864 proclamation. A thirty-eight-page list enclosing the names of each person indicted for treason in the Eastern District of Tennessee is enclosed in Crawford W. Hall to James Speed, March 1, 1866, RG 60, Entry 9, Tennessee Box 1.

Scholars have not paid much attention to Lincoln's March 1864 proclamation. Those who have written about it argue that Lincoln issued it to withdraw "the privilege for prisoners of war or Confederates under parole in the South." See William C. Harris, *With Charity for All: Lincoln and the Restoration of the Union* (Lexington: University Press of Kentucky, 1997), 147. While it is true that the proclamation did exclude paroled rebel soldiers and Confederate prisoners of war from the amnesty, an understanding of the Maryland treason cases reveals the fuller significance of the proclamation—that Lincoln also intended it to apply to traitors in the North and that he did not want indicted traitors, like Merryman, to be able to receive amnesty under the December 1863 proclamation. The March 1864 proclamation excluded "persons who . . . are in military, naval or civil confinement or custody, or under bonds or on parole of the civil, military or naval authorities or agents of the United States as prisoners of war or persons detained for offences of any kind, either before or after conviction, and that, on the contrary, it does apply only to those persons who being yet at large and free from any arrest, confinement or duress, shall voluntarily come forward and take the said oath with the purpose of restoring peace and establishing the national authority." See *CWL,* 7:269–70.

The best book on Reconstruction policy formation, Herman Belz's *Reconstructing the Union: Theory and Policy during the Civil War* (Ithaca, N.Y.: Cornell University Press, 1969), does not mention the second amnesty proclamation. Nor do most other works that discuss Lincoln's Proclamation of Amnesty and Reconstruction. Yet the policy Lincoln put in place in March 1864—of excluding persons indicted in the federal courts from blanket amnesty—remained the policy of the executive branch until Andrew Johnson's Christmas Pardon of 1868. By that time, as we saw in chapter 3, there was only one indicted traitor remaining in the United States.

17. RG 21 (Records of the U.S. Circuit Court for the District of Maryland), Baltimore Division, Law Records, Case Files (1790–1911), Box 106, NARA-P.

18. *Seventh Annual Report of the President and Directors of the Northern Central Railway Co. to the Stockholders, for the Year 1861* (Baltimore: James Lucas & Son, 1862), 10; *State of Maryland v. Northern Central Railway Company,* 18 Md. 193 (1862); Thomas S. Alexander to Cameron, May 5, 1863, Cameron Papers, HSDC. On April 17, 1863, the Northern Central's board of directors began discussing the possibility of filing a lawsuit to recover damages for the losses the company had incurred in April 1861. See Northern Central Railway Company, Board of Directors, Minute Books (1854–1949), Manuscript Group 286 (Penn Central Railroad Collection), Pennsylvania State Archives, Harrisburg, Pa.

19. Baltimore County Circuit Court, Judgment Docket No. 7 (Civil Docket, CM171), May 1863 term, p. 27, MSA; *Baltimore County Advocate,* May 23, 1863. Baltimore Unionist David Creamer, who had served as the foreman of the federal grand jury that indicted Merryman in 1861, sent his notes from the grand jury hearings to the War Department because he thought they "may be of use to the Northern Central Railway Co. in the suit brought by it against John Merryman." Creamer's willingness to send his notes to the War Department is particularly ironic since we saw in chapter 3 that a grand juror—quite possibly Creamer—had been unwilling to give his notes to U.S. attorney William Price to assist in the prosecution of the treason cases. Creamer's letters to the War Department of May 29, 1863, and June 14, 1869, are described in RG 107, microfilm M22 (Registers of Letters Received by the Office of the Secretary of War: Main Series, 1800–1870), reels 106 and 131. Copies of Creamer's notes are available at LC and MDHS.

20. RG 21 (Records of the U.S. District Court for the District of Maryland), Baltimore Division, Criminal Case Files (1841–78), Box 16, and General Records, Minutes (1790–1972), vol. for 1860–63. And, as we saw in chapter 4, Cockey also was convicted by a military commission for aiding Confederate soldiers during Jubal Early's raid into Maryland in July 1864.

21. Alexander to Cameron, September 19, 1863, Cameron Papers, LC. According to a June 21, 1861, report in the *Baltimore Sun,* Merryman had offered from prison "to raise means, from his own resources and those of his friends, to pay for the rebuilding of the bridges."

22. I have searched extensively for the outcome of this case but have been unable to find it. The 1865 volume of the Baltimore City Superior Court's "Cases Instituted" (C1497-14) has two entries for the case but neither one signifies that any proceedings were held in it. The court's Judicial Record volume for 1864–76 (C201-6) and Judicial Docket for 1854–68 (T584-1) do not mention it. Unfortunately, the volume of the Judgment Docket (T570-3) from this period is missing the pages for cases beginning with the letters M and N so that it is impossible to tell whether or how the case was finally settled. The Superior Court's Rough Minutes (C251-6) from 1865 and 1866 make no mention of cases before the court; the case also does not appear in the volume of "Cases Instituted" for 1866 (C1497-15). All previously mentioned records are held at MSA. I have also used ProQuest and NewsBank to search the *Baltimore Sun* for any mention of the case after it was transferred to the Baltimore City Superior Court, and I have searched the "Proceedings of the Courts" section of the *Baltimore American and Commercial Advertiser* (on microfilm) from January to May 1865 but saw no mention of the case. On July 27, 1866, attorney J. Mason Campbell read a report "on the position of the suit against John Merryman" to the board of the Northern Central Railway Company, but the board laid the report on the table. Unfortunately, the report is no longer among the company's papers and the minute books make no mention of the report's content. See Manuscript Group 286, Pennsylvania State Archives.

23. *Grason,* 194–95.

24. It will be recalled from chapters 1 and 3 that other members of the Baltimore County Horse Guards claimed similar motives.

25. John Merryman to Simon Cameron, May 21, 1863, in Cameron Papers, HSDC. I have kept the spelling, grammar, and punctuation as close to the original as possible.

26. It is not clear to what Merryman is referring here.

27. James Donald Cameron (1833–1918), the son of Simon Cameron, served as vice president of the Northern Central Railway Company from 1861 to 1863 and as president from 1863 to 1874 (some of the railroad's *Annual Reports* list him as John D. Cameron). He later served as secretary of war under President Ulysses S. Grant, from 1876 to 1877 and as a Republican in the U.S. Senate from 1877 to 1897.

28. Columbus O'Donnell (1797–1873) was a businessman, banker, and railroad developer in Baltimore. Court records reveal that O'Donnell posted bond for George Cadwalader both times that John Merryman sued him in the Harford County Circuit Court. It will be recalled from chapter 1 that O'Donnell delivered a secessionist speech in Baltimore on April 19, 1861.

29. Johns Hopkins (1795–1873) was a prominent entrepreneur and philanthropist in Baltimore.

30. John Clark, a lottery broker and banker in Baltimore, was president of the Citizens' National Bank from 1850 until his death in 1867.

31. For more information on this episode, see George William Brown, *Baltimore and the Nineteenth of April, 1861: A Study of the War* (Baltimore: Johns Hopkins University Press, 1887), 61.

32. William Colder (some sources say Calder) of Harrisburg, Pa., served on the board of directors for the Northern Central Railroad.

33. The Know Nothings, or Native American Party, was a secretive, nativist political party that arose in the 1850s. Merryman had been a Whig prior to the demise of the Whig Party in the early 1850s. He became a Democrat in the mid-1850s in opposition to the rise of the Know Nothings in Maryland. In 1855, Merryman ran for the Maryland House of Delegates but was defeated by the Know Nothing candidate in Baltimore County. About that same time he was elected president of the Baltimore County Board of Commissioners. *Biographical Cyclopedia of Representative Men of Maryland and [the] District of Columbia* (Baltimore: National Biographical, 1879), 312–13; *Baltimore Sun,* November 16, 1881; Guy Edison Kagey, *Sherwood Church: Sketches of the History of Sherwood Parish, Cockeysville, Baltimore County, Maryland, 1830–1930* (Baltimore: Read-Taylor, 1930), 37. For more information on prewar disputes in Baltimore between the Democrats and Know Nothings, see Frank Towers, *The Urban South and the Coming of the Civil War* (Charlottesville: University of Virginia Press, 2004).

34. Thomas S. Alexander (1801–71) also argued other cases for the Northern Central Railway Co. For example, he represented the railroad with J. Mason Campbell in *Canton Company of Baltimore v. Northern Central Railway Company,* 21 Md. 389 (1864).

35. Archibald Stirling, Jr. (1832–92), a Unionist, was city counselor of Baltimore City from 1858 to 1863 and U.S. attorney for the District of Maryland from 1869 until 1886. In 1864, he served as a delegate to the state constitutional convention in Maryland.

36. Richard J. Gittings (1830–82) was elected the state's attorney for Baltimore County in 1855 and served until January 1864.

37. Erwin Stanley Bradley, *Simon Cameron, Lincoln's Secretary of War: A Political Biography* (Philadelphia: University of Pennsylvania Press, 1966), 36–39, 116–22; Daniel J. Curran, "Polk, Politics, and Patronage: The Rejection of George W. Woodward's Nomination to the Supreme Court," *Pennsylvania Magazine of History and Biography* 121 (July 1997): 163–99; Mark E. Neely, Jr., *The Union Divided: Party Conflict in the Civil War North* (Cambridge, Mass.: Harvard University Press, 2002), 50–55.

38. Bradley, *Simon Cameron,* 53–56, 201; Robert L. Gunnarsson, *The Story of the Northern Central Railway: From Baltimore to Lake Ontario* (Sykesville, Md.: Greenberg, 1991), 29, 49–52; Samuel R. Kamm, *The Civil War Career of Thomas A. Scott* (Philadelphia: University of Pennsylvania Press, 1940), 9.

39. *The American Farmer* 10 (March 1855): 284; *Fifth Annual Report of the President and Directors of the Northern Central Railway Co. to the Stockholders, for the Year 1859* (Baltimore: James Lucas & Son, 1860), 2. Merryman is not listed among the stockholders in the company's ledger, although the ledger appears to have been compiled later in the nineteenth century, excluding earlier stockholders who no longer held stock in the company. See Manuscript Group 286, Pennsylvania State Archives.

40. See Merryman to Cameron, April 16, 1860, and January 14, 1861, Cameron Papers, HSDC.

41. John S. Gittings to Cameron, December 28, 1863, Cameron Papers, HSDC.

42. *John W. Davis v. Simon Cameron, John W. Davis v. Northern Central Railway Company, Charles Howard v. Simon Cameron, Charles Howard v. Northern Central Railway Company, William H. Gatchell v. Simon Cameron,* and *William H. Gatchell v. Northern Central Railway Company,* case numbers 42–47, all in RG 21 (Records of the U.S. Circuit Court for the District of Maryland), Baltimore Division, Law Records, Case Files, in Boxes 103–4, NARA-P.

43. Alexander to Cameron, September 19, 1863, Cameron Papers, LC.

44. Cameron to Lincoln, April 17, 1862, and October 25, 1863, both in Lincoln Papers; Cameron to Ira Harris, May 3, 1862, Gratz Collection, HSP; Cameron to Salmon P. Chase, May 5, 7, 1862, and January 7, 1863, all in Chase Papers, HSP; Cameron to Lincoln, December 22, 1862, Stanton Papers, LC.

45. Alexander to Cameron, October 24, 1863, and Cameron to Lincoln, October 25, 1863, both in Lincoln Papers.

46. Nathaniel Thayer to Edward Bates, November 3, 1863, RG 60, Entry 9 (Letters Received by the Attorney General, 1809–70), Maryland Box 2.

47. Alexander to Robert C. Schenck, August 27, 1863, RG 393 (Records of United States Army Continental Commands), Part 1, Middle Department and 8th Army Corps, Entry 2343 (Letters Received), Box 1, NARA; Alexander, Treason Memo, [1863], Cameron Papers, HSDC; Alexander, Memorandum regarding Witnesses, [1863], RG 21 (Records of the U.S. Circuit Court for the District of Maryland), Baltimore Division, Law Records, Case Files (1790–1911), Box 104, NARA-P; Cameron to Seward, November 21, 1863, RG 107, microfilm M221, reel 234.

48. *Baltimore Sun,* November 3, 1863; Cameron to Lincoln, November 1 and 2, 1863, Lincoln Papers.

49. *Baltimore Sun,* November 16, 1863; see also cases 42–47 in Law Records (see n. 42 above). At the same time that the Baltimore police commissioners were suing Simon Cameron, they also instituted proceedings against the new pro-Union government in Baltimore. In February 1862 one of the commissioners attempted to collect the pay that he would have earned during the time he was incarcerated in military prison, but the new city officials refused to pay him. The other commissioners and he sued the city for their salaries. U.S. attorney William Price argued the city's case, while former mayor George William Brown represented the police commissioners. On December 11, 1863, the Maryland Court of Appeals (the state's highest court) ruled that the police commissioners were owed their salaries since it was "uncontrollable events"—and not negligence—that had kept them from doing their duties. See *The Mayor and City Council of Baltimore, et al., v. Charles Howard, et al.,* in 20 Md. 335 (1863). I thank George Liebmann for bringing this case to my attention.

50. William Price to Edward Bates, November 3, 1863, RG 60, Entry 9, Maryland Box 2. Price's logic here was similar to that employed by Attorney General Bates in his July 5, 1861, opinion on Lincoln's suspension of habeas corpus. See Edward Bates, "Suspension of the Privilege of the Writ of Habeas Corpus," July 5, 1861, in *Official Opinions of the Attorneys General of the United States,* 43 vols. (Washington, D.C.: W. H. and O. H. Morrison, 1852–1996), 10:74–92.

51. William H. Seward to E. R. Meade, January 16, 1863, in *O.R.,* ser. 2, vol. 2, p. 1302. In October 1863, one justice of the New York Supreme Court, sitting in chambers, decided that the Habeas Corpus Act was unconstitutional and that the suit could not be removed to the

federal courts. In March 1864 the Supreme Court of New York reversed that decision. Jones's suit against Seward remained on the books in a federal court in New York until 1872. "The death of Mr. Seward interrupted my suit," recalled Jones. "His attorney had offered mine $5,000 to withdraw my suit, and he declined because I had sued for $50,000. Thus the case ended." John Carl Parish, *George Wallace Jones* (Iowa City: State Historical Society of Iowa, 1912), 246–47; 17 Abbott's Rep. 377, 3 Grant's Rep. (Pa.) 431; *New York Times,* June 20, October 10, 22, 1863, and February 5, March 16, June 25, 1864.

52. Quoted in Mark E. Neely, Jr., *The Fate of Liberty: Abraham Lincoln and Civil Liberties* (New York: Oxford University Press, 1991), 23.

53. Dennis A. Mahony, *The Prisoner of State* (New York: Carleton, 1863), 399–400; *Congressional Globe,* 37th Cong., 3rd sess., 37. George Bickley, the founder of the Knights of the Golden Circle, also had to sign an oath pledging not to prosecute any government officials for his arrest in order to be released—and this was several years after the passage of the Habeas Corpus Act, thus signifying that the officers overseeing his incarceration did not trust the Habeas Corpus Act to serve as adequate protection. See Frank L. Klement, *Dark Lanterns: Secret Political Societies, Conspiracies, and Treason Trials in the Civil War* (Baton Rouge: Louisiana State University Press, 1984), 219.

54. *Baltimore Sun,* October 28, 1864; *Hodgson v. Millward,* 3 Grant's Rep. (Pa.) 406 (1863); William Millward to John P. Usher, February 12, 1863, RG 60, Entry 58 (Letters Received Relating to Judiciary Accounts, 1849–89), Box 587, Archives II.

55. *New York Times,* April 27, 1867; *McCall v. McDowell,* 1 Deady's Rep. 238, 263 (1867); Klement, *Dark Lanterns,* 228–32; *McCormick and Others v. Humphrey,* 27 Ind. 144 (1866); *Milligan v. Hovey,* 17 Fed. Cases 380 (1871). In at least one case, the Habeas Corpus Act of 1863 was applied to a civil dispute between two citizens. See *Mitchell v. Clark,* 110 U.S. 633 (1884).

56. Howard K. Beale, ed., *Diary of Gideon Welles: Secretary of the Navy under Lincoln and Johnson,* 3 vols. (New York: W.W. Norton, 1960), 2:206.

EPILOGUE

1. *Laws of the State of Maryland, Made and Passed at a Special Session of the General Assembly, Held at Frederick, April 26, 1861* (Annapolis: Elihu S. Riley, 1861), resolution 13. Historian Jean H. Baker has argued that, prior to the November 1861 elections, the Maryland general assembly was controlled by Democrats who were loyal to the Union but critical of the Lincoln administration's actions in their state. "Viewing their role as that of watchful critics, not secessionists," writes Baker, "Democrats denied the right of the legislature to pass an ordinance of secession. . . . Unquestionably loyal to the Union, Democrats were nonetheless critical of Lincoln's war policies." See Jean H. Baker, *The Politics of Continuity: Maryland Political Parties from 1858 to 1870* (Baltimore: Johns Hopkins University Press, 1973), 55–56. The pro-Confederate resolutions and laws adopted between April and August 1861 cast some doubt upon Baker's interpretation. My interpretation of the Maryland legislature during this time is more in line with Charles Branch Clark, "Politics in Maryland during the Civil War" (Ph.D. diss., University of North Carolina, 1940), 158–95.

2. Resolutions 4, 12, 13, 14, and 15, and *An Act to Relieve the Mayor and Members of the*

Board of Police of the City of Baltimore, and All Persons Who Acted under Their Orders, in Their Efforts to Maintain Peace and Good Order, and Prevent Further Strife on and after the Occurrences of the Nineteenth of April, Eighteen Hundred and Sixty-one, in said City, from Prosecution for, or in Consequence of Their Acts of Obedience to said Orders,* act of May 8, 1861, chap. 8, all in *Laws of the State of Maryland* (1861).

3. Maryland, *An Act to Make Valid the Qualification of John Merryman, as First Lieutenant of the Baltimore County Horse Guards,* act of June 18, 1861, in ibid., chap. 49; Maryland, *An Act to Repeal An Act Making Valid the Qualification of John Merryman, as First Lieutenant of the Baltimore County Home Guards,* act of January 4, 1862, in *Laws of the State of Maryland, Made and Passed at a Session of the General Assembly Begun and Held at the City of Annapolis on the Third Day of December, 1861, and Ended on the Tenth Day of March, 1862* (Annapolis: Thomas J. Wilson, 1862), 18.

4. Maryland, *An Act to Amend Article Forty-three of the Code of Public General Laws, Relating to Habeas Corpus,* act of February 1, 1862, and *An Act to Amend Section Two Hundred and Two of Article Thirty of the Code of Public General Laws, Relating to Crimes and Punishments, by Defining Treason, and Providing for the Punishment of Treason and Other Kindred Offences,* act of March 6, 1862, both in *Laws of the State of* Maryland (1862), 47–48, 250–54; Maryland constitution, art. 1, sec. 4 (1864).

5. Mark E. Neely, Jr., "'Seeking a Cause of Difficulty with the Government': Reconsidering Freedom of Speech and Judicial Conflict under Lincoln," in *Lincoln's Legacy: Ethics and Politics,* ed. Phillip Shaw Paludan (Urbana: University of Illinois Press, 2008), 52; R. M. T. Hunter to William L. Yancey, P. A. Rost, and A. D. Mann, July 29, 1861, in *Official Records of the Union and Confederate Navies in the War of the Rebellion,* 30 vols. (Washington, D.C.: Government Printing Office, 1894–1922), ser. 2, vol. 3, p. 228–29; Jefferson Davis, "Speech at Richmond," June 1, 1861, and letter to Joseph E. Davis, June 18, 1861, both in Lynda L. Crist et al., eds., *The Papers of Jefferson Davis,* 15 vols. (Baton Rouge: Louisiana State University Press, 1971–), 7:184, 203. Unlike Lincoln, Davis waited to suspend the writ of habeas corpus until after the Confederate Congress passed authorizing legislation. See Mark E. Neely, Jr., *Southern Rights: Political Prisoners and the Myth of Confederate Constitutionalism* (Charlottesville: University Press of Virginia, 1999), 37.

6. Some versions change "touch" to "torch."

7. James Ryder Randall, *Maryland, My Maryland and Other Poems* (Baltimore: John Murphy, 1908), 17–20; Stephen W. Sears, *Landscape Turned Red: The Battle of Antietam* (New York: Ticknor & Fields, 1983), 72; James M. McPherson, *Crossroads of Freedom: Antietam* (New York: Oxford University Press, 2002), 95.

8. James Ryder Randall, "There's Life in the Old Land Yet!" song sheet, American Song Sheets, ser. 1, vol. 9, and "John Merryman" song sheet, Civil War Song Sheets, ser. 2, vol. 1, both in Rare Book and Special Collections Division, Library of Congress.

9. Taney to Franklin Pierce, June 12, 1861, in "Some Papers of Franklin Pierce, 1852–1862," *American Historical Review* 10 (January 1905): 368; John William Wallace to D. W. Middleton, October 27, 1864, RG 267 (Records of the Supreme Court of the United States), Entry 31 (Records of the Office of the Clerk, General Correspondence, 1791–1941), Box 17, NARA; Philip G. Auchampaugh, ed., "A Great Justice on State and Federal Power: Being the Thoughts of Chief Justice Taney on the Federal Conscription Act (An Undelivered Opinion)," *Tyler's Quarterly*

Magazine 18 (1936): 72–87 (some of the original draft opinions are in Box 9 of the Perine Family Papers at MDHS); Carl Brent Swisher, *Roger B. Taney* (New York: Macmillan, 1935), 570–72; Don E. Fehrenbacher, *Slavery, Law, and Politics: The Dred Scott Case in Historical Perspective* (New York: Oxford University Press, 1981), 298; George Templeton Strong, diary entry for October 13, 1864, in Allan Nevins and Milton Halsey Thomas, eds., *The Diary of George Templeton Strong*, 4 vols. (New York: Macmillan, 1952), 3:500–501; William Blair Lord and Henry M. Parkhurst, eds., *The Debates of the Constitutional Convention of the State of Maryland*, 3 vols. (Annapolis: Richard P. Bayly, 1864), 3:1925–26.

10. H.R. 748, 38th Cong., 2nd sess.; *Congressional Globe*, 38th Cong., 2nd sess., pp. 666, 671–72, 742, 1012–17; H.R. 3788, 42nd Cong., 3rd sess.; *An Act Providing for Busts of the Late Chief Justice Roger Brooke Taney and of Samuel Portland Chase, to be Placed in the Supreme Court Room of the United States*, act of January 29, 1874, in 18 Stat. 6.

11. Maryland, *An Act to Restore to Full Citizenship, and the Right to Vote and Hold Office, All Persons Who May be Deprived Thereof by the Provisions Contained in the Fourth Section of the First Article of the Constitution of this State*, act of January 24, 1867, and *An Act to Repeal the Act of the January Session, Eighteen Hundred and Sixty-four, Chapter Two Hundred and Eighty-two Entitled, An Act to Add the Following Section to the Fortieth Article of Public General Laws Requiring Jurors to Take the Oath of Allegiance*, act of March 23, 1867, both in *Laws of the State of Maryland, Made and Passed at a Session of the General Assembly, Begun and Held at the City of Annapolis, on the 2nd Day of January, 1867, and Ended on the 23rd Day of March, 1867* (Annapolis: Henry A. Lucas, 1867), 18–20, 346–47; Maryland, *An Act to Repeal Sub-section eight, Sub-section Eleven, Sub-section twelve, and Sub-section Thirteen of Article Thirty of the Code of Public General Laws, Title "Crimes and Punishments," Sub-title "Treason," Being Parts of an Act Passed at the January Session, March Sixth, in the Year Eighteen Hundred and Sixty-two, Chapter Two Hundred and Thirty-five, Entitled "An Act to Amend Section Two Hundred and Two of Article Thirty of the Code of Public General Laws, Relating to "Crimes and Punishments," and Providing for the Punishment of Treason, and Other Kindred Offences*, act of April 11, 1874, in *Laws of the State of Maryland, Made and Passed at a Session of the General Assembly, Begun and Held at the City of Annapolis, on the Seventh Day of January, 1874, and Ended on the Sixth Day of April, 1874* (Annapolis: S. S. Mills & L. F. Colton, 1874), 574; Maryland Constitution, Declaration of Rights, art. 44; art. 3, sec. 55 (1867). Other states followed suit. West Virginia, for example, copied the "necessity" language from Maryland in its 1872 constitution and also forbid the suspension of habeas corpus. See West Virginia constitution, art. 1, sec. 3; art. 3, sec. 11 and 12 (1872).

12. John Merryman to Simon Cameron, June 7, 1861, RG 107, microfilm M492 (Letters Received by the Secretary of War: Irregular Series, 1861–66), reel 9.

13. Longnecker was the clerk of the Circuit Court of Baltimore County (a state court) and was also the publisher of the *Baltimore County American*. Longnecker later claimed that he had been intimidated by members of the Baltimore County Horse Guards in April 1861. See *Grason*, 80–83, 273–76.

14. *Baltimore County Advocate*, September 6, 1862; for the arresting officer's account of what happened, as well as the testimony of Longnecker and one of the men arrested, see *Grason*, 20, 159–64.

15. *Grason*, 20, 159–64.

16. John E. Wool to Henry Wager Halleck, September 13, 14, and 17, 1862, John Ellis Wool Papers, New York State Library, Albany, N.Y. Wool was not specifically discussing Merryman and the other midnight partygoers in these letters; he was complaining about the large number of arrests being made in Maryland based only on suspicion of disloyalty, of which Merryman and his friends were eighteen. For purposes of clarification: the arrest of the partygoers had been done under the supervision of William A. Van Nostrand. Van Nostrand had been police marshal of Baltimore since April 1862; on September 1, 1862 (the same day as the midnight arrests at John White's house), Wool appointed Van Nostrand "civil provost-marshal for the Eighth Army Corps, Middle Department." James McPhail, the "military" provost marshal for the state of Maryland, had previously been appointed by the War Department. Wool did not wish to be held liable for the actions of someone he had not appointed, but the overarching principle still applied in the case of Merryman and his party-going friends. Wool did not want to be sued by civilians who had been arrested for "disloyalty." See *O.R.*, ser. 1, vol. 19, pt. 2, pp. 236, 286–87, 304. Despite General Wool's misgivings about Provost Marshal McPhail, McPhail would go on to attain some measure of fame as one of the successful officers in the manhunt to capture several of the Lincoln assassination conspirators.

17. It should be noted that this episode was also about five months before John Merryman's first suit against General Cadwalader.

18. The plaintiffs against General Wool included Maryland legislators Severn Teackle Wallis and Henry M. Warfield; newspaperman Frank Key Howard; Thomas Sewell, Jr.; the clerk of the Baltimore City Criminal Court, Thomas H. Gardner; Thomas R. Rich, who was an aide to Unionist governor Augustus W. Bradford; and Alexander D. Evans. See RG 21 (Records of the U.S. Circuit Court for the District of Maryland), Baltimore Division, General Records, Index to Judgments and Decrees (1790–1877), NARA-P; William Schley to William Whiting, March 21, 1863, RG 107, microfilm M492, reel 34.

19. Neal A. Brooks and Eric G. Rockel, *A History of Baltimore County* (Towson, Md.: Friends of the Towson Library, 1979), 241, 244; *Baltimore County Advocate*, October 18, November 8, 1862; *Baltimore Sun*, July 11, 1863; Charles W. Mitchell, ed., *Maryland Voices of the Civil War* (Baltimore: Johns Hopkins University Press, 2007), 198.

20. Bradley T. Johnson, "The Ride around Baltimore," *Philadelphia Weekly Times*, December 27, 1879, reprinted in Peter Cozzens and Robert I. Girardi, eds., *The New Annals of the Civil War* (Mechanicsburg, Pa.: Stackpole, 2004), 439; John W. McGrain, *From Pig Iron to Cotton Duck: A History of Manufacturing Villages in Baltimore County* (Towson, Md.: Baltimore County Public Library, 1985), 37.

21. *The Biographical Cyclopedia of Representative Men of Maryland and [the] District of Columbia* (Baltimore: National Biographical, 1879), 313; Francis B. Culver, "Merryman Family," *Maryland Historical Magazine* 10 (September 1915): 293, 297; *Baltimore County Advocate*, January 30, 1864.

22. *Baltimore Sun*, April 23, 1863; *Baltimore County Advocate*, September 19, October 3, 1863.

23. *Baltimore Sun*, November 16, 1881; *Biographical Cyclopedia*, 313; George W. Howard, *The Monumental City: Its Past History and Present Resources* (Baltimore: J. D. Ehlers, 1873), 691; James McHenry Howard, "Ridgely Family History," unpublished memoir (ca. 1894), typescript by Helen West Ridgely, Ridgely Family Papers (MS 1001), FC1–2, Folder 165, HAMP 21686, Hampton National Historic Site, National Park Service, Towson, Md.

24. Northern Central Railway Company, Board of Directors, Minute Books (1854–1949), Manuscript Group 286 (Penn Central Railroad Collection), Pennsylvania State Archives, Harrisburg, Pa.

25. *Baltimore Sun,* November 16, 1881.

26. *Ibid.,* May 17, 1978. The purchase agreement permitted Mrs. John Merryman Franklin to continue living at Hayfields for up to ten years after the date of the sale. It was rumored that the land was sold at $5,000 per acre.

27. *Baltimore Sun,* May 4, 16, July 21, August 1, September 6, 18, 19, November 14, 1979; September 5, October 28, 1980; January 17, April 28, 1981; November 14, 1984.

28. Dissent of Scalia in *Hamdi v. Rumsfeld,* 542 U.S. 562 (2004). In addition to the works listed in the Bibliography, one can find hundreds of law review articles and notes discussing *Ex parte Merryman* that were published over the past decade by searching HeinOnline's "Journals Library."

29. Lincoln, "Proclamation Calling Militia and Convening Congress," April 15, 1861, in *CWL,* 4:331–33.

30. Consider that William Meade Addison indicted about sixty Baltimoreans in 1861 but that William Price chose to re-indict only one quarter of them in 1863.

31. Grier quoted in James G. Randall, *Constitutional Problems under Lincoln,* revised ed. (Urbana: University of Illinois Press, 1964), 90–93. According to Randall, "This illustrates the attitude of a practical-minded judge toward the efforts which a puzzled and well-meaning district attorney was making to prosecute some of the treason cases."

32. Joseph Holt to Francis Lieber, February 26, 1863 (L12345), Francis Lieber Papers, The Huntington, San Marino, Calif.

33. Lincoln to Albert G. Hodges, April 4, 1864, in *CWL,* 7:281. In this passage, Lincoln was defending his policy of military emancipation, but his argument can equally be applied to his policies on civil liberties. Lincoln did not disregard the Constitution, as other presidents may have done, or as some of his detractors claim he did. FDR's attorney general, Francis Biddle, once said that "The Constitution has not greatly bothered any wartime President." Quoted in William H. Rehnquist, *All the Laws but One: Civil Liberties in Wartime* (New York: Knopf, 1998), 191. But such an argument does not exactly apply to Lincoln. Throughout his life—whether in defense of his position that Congress could legislate regarding slavery in the territories, his view of why he could not emancipate slaves in 1861, why he could free them in 1863, or why he believed that the Constitution did not explicitly say who could suspend the writ of habeas corpus—Lincoln almost invariably rooted his arguments in the text of the Constitution.

34. In *The Federalist* No. 23, Alexander Hamilton argued that the powers of the federal government were unlimited in national security matters. Of course, Hamilton wrote this prior to the adoption of the Bill of Rights.

35. Lincoln to Erastus Corning and others, June 12, 1863, in *CWL,* 6:260–69.

36. For discussions of the high rate of treason and disloyalty cases that never went to trial or that ended in acquittals, see Patrick J. Drouhard, *It Don't Look Right for the Times: The Factual History of the Holmes County Rebellion* (Cardington, Ohio: Privately printed, 2005); Kellee Green Blake, "Aiding and Abetting: Disloyalty Prosecutions in the Federal Civil Courts of Southern Illinois, 1861–1866," *Illinois Historical Journal* 87 (Summer 1994): 103;

Edward D. Tittmann, "The Exploitation of Treason," *New Mexico Historical Review* 4 (April 1929): 128–45; Kellee L. Blake, "Ten Firkins of Butter and Other 'Traitorous' Aid" *Prologue* 30 (Winter 1998): 288–93. In addition to Maryland, I have examined treason cases in the federal courts in California, Pennsylvania, West Virginia, Virginia, Tennessee, Ohio, and the District of Columbia. Most cases either never went to trial or ended in acquittal.

37. The Supreme Court of Indiana declared the Habeas Corpus Act of 1863 unconstitutional in 1863, but the Supreme Court of the United States upheld the act (except for one provision that has not been discussed in this book) in several suits that extended into the 1870s and 1880s. In regards to the 1866 act, historian James G. Randall noted: "This punishment of State judges for acts done in a judicial capacity was attacked during the congressional debate as a violation of those well-known principles of jurisprudence which give to the judge an independent, impartial character and protect him from personal consequences as a result of the performance of judicial functions." See James G. Randall, "The Indemnity Act of 1863: A Study in the Wartime Immunity of Governmental Officers," *Michigan Law Review* 20 (April 1922): 596–612; *New York Times*, July 7, 1864; Edward Bates to A. Q. Keasby, April 29, 1863, RG 60, microfilm M699 (Letters Sent by the Department of Justice: General and Miscellaneous, 1818–1904), reel 8; Reuben Gold Thwaites, ed., *Civil War Messages and Proclamations of Wisconsin War Governors* ([Madison]: Wisconsin History Commission, 1912), 166; Dennis K. Boman, *Lincoln and Citizens' Rights in Civil War Missouri: Balancing Security and Freedom* (Baton Rouge: Louisiana State University Press, 2011), 235–37; *Beckwith v. Bean*, 98 U.S. 266 (1878); *Mitchell v. Clark*, 110 U.S. 633 (1884).

38. Smith D. Atkins to Lyman Trumbull, February 11, 1863, Lyman Trumbull Papers, LC; William Schley to Edwin M. Stanton, December 27, 1862, RG 107, microfilm M492, reel 34.

39. Padilla's suit is only for $1 and lawyers' fees. But the legal costs could, of course, reach the hundreds of thousands of dollars.

40. Yoo wrote an op-ed in the *Wall Street Journal*, January 19, 2009 (accessed through ProQuest) in which he argued that lawsuits like this will have a detrimental effect on government officials who are charged with protecting the country: "It is easy to understand why CIA agents, who are working on the front lines to protect the nation from attack, are so concerned about their legal liability that they have taken out insurance against lawsuits. . . . Worrying about personal liability will distort the thinking of federal officials, who should be focusing on the costs and benefits of their decisions to the nation as a whole, not to their own pockets." On June 20, 2009, the editorial board of the *Washington Post* (accessed through ProQuest) remarked that Padilla's suit against Yoo was "troubling" and "could have a chilling effect on the ability of government lawyers to give candid, good-faith advice for fear of being held personally liable."

41. John C. Underwood to William T. Otto, July 8, 1868, RG 60, Entry 58 (Letters Received Relating to Judiciary Accounts, 1849–89), Box 694.

Bibliography

PRIMARY SOURCES

Archival and Manuscript Sources

Dauphin County Historical Society, Harrisburg, Pa.
    Simon Cameron Papers
Duke University, Department of Special Collections, Durham, N.C.
    Nathaniel P. Banks Papers
eBay, Inc.
    Henry M. Cannon Letters. Auction No. 220518378446. Sold December 8, 2009.
Hampton National Historic Site, Towson, Md.
    Ridgely Family Papers
Historical Society of Pennsylvania, Philadelphia, Pa.
    Cadwalader Family Papers
    Salmon P. Chase Papers
    Simon Gratz Collection
    Society Miscellaneous Collection
    Society Small Collection
Johns Hopkins University, Special Collections, Baltimore, Md.
    Merryman-Crane Family Papers
Library of Congress, Manuscript Division, Washington, D.C.
    Nathaniel P. Banks Papers
    Edward Bates Papers
    Thomas F. Bayard Papers
    Simon Cameron Papers
    Salmon P. Chase Papers
    David Creamer Diaries
    Reverdy Johnson Papers
    Abraham Lincoln Papers (American Memory)
    William H. Seward Papers

Edwin M. Stanton Papers
Thaddeus Stevens Papers
Lyman Trumbull Papers
Maryland Historical Society, Baltimore, Md.
Civil War Papers (MS 1860)
Harry Gilmor Papers (MS 1288)
Howard Family Papers (MS 469)
James Alfred Pearce Papers (MS 1384)
John Wilson Heard Papers (MS 2132)
Merryman Family Papers (MS 2285)
Perine Family Papers (MS 645)
Maryland State Archives, Annapolis, Md.
Baltimore City Criminal Court, Docket Book (C1814)
Baltimore City Superior Court, Cases Instituted (C1497)
Baltimore City Superior Court, Judgment Docket (T570)
Baltimore City Superior Court, Judicial Docket (T584)
Baltimore City Superior Court, Judicial Record (C201)
Baltimore County Circuit Court, Judgment Docket (CM171)
Governor's Miscellaneous Papers (S1274)
Miami University of Ohio, University Archives, Miami, Ohio
Robert C. Schenck Papers
National Archives and Records Administration, Washington, D.C.
RG 21, Records of the United States District Court for the District of Columbia
RG 46, Records of the United States Senate
RG 107, Records of the Office of the Secretary of War
RG 109, War Department Collection of Confederate Records
RG 153, Records of the Office of the Judge Advocate General (Army)
RG 233, Records of the United States House of Representatives
RG 267, Records of the Supreme Court of the United States
RG 393, Records of United States Army Continental Commands
National Archives at College Park, Md.
RG 56, General Records of the Department of the Treasury
RG 60, General Records of the Department of Justice
RG 204, Records of the Office of the Pardon Attorney
National Archives at Philadelphia
RG 21, Records of the U.S. Circuit Court for the District of Maryland
RG 21, Records of the U.S. District Court for the District of Maryland
RG 21, Records of the U.S. Circuit Court for the Eastern District of
Pennsylvania
RG 21, Records of the U.S. District Court for the Eastern District of
Pennsylvania

National Archives at San Francisco
    RG 21, Records of the U.S. District Court for the Northern District of
        California
National Archives of the United Kingdom, Kew, U.K.
    Records of the Foreign Office
New York State Library, Albany, N.Y.
    John Ellis Wool Papers (SC 15361)
Pennsylvania State Archives, Harrisburg, Pa.
    Penn Central Railroad Collection (Manuscript Group 286)
Princeton University, Special Collections, Firestone Library, Princeton, N.J.
    Augustus W. Bradford Papers
    Benjamin H. Brewster Papers
The Huntington, San Marino, Calif.
    Francis Lieber Papers
    Samuel L. M. Barlow Papers
University of Delaware, Special Collections, Newark, Del.
    Willard Saulsbury Papers
University of Virginia, Special Collections, Charlottesville, Va.
    Bradley T. Johnson Papers
U.S. Army Military History Institute, Carlisle, Pa.
    Arnold Family Papers
    Civil War Miscellaneous Collection
    Civil War Times Illustrated Collection
    Harrisburg Civil War Round Table Collection
    Joseph Barlow Collection
    Lowry Hinch Papers
    Pardee-Robison Collection
    Thomas Stone Collection
    Michael Winey Collection

Newspapers

Illinois
    Chicago Tribune (ProQuest)
Maryland
    Baltimore American and Commercial Advertiser
    Baltimore Sun (ProQuest and NewsBanks)
    Baltimore, The South
    Towsontown, *Baltimore County Advocate*
Massachusetts
    The Liberator (ProQuest)

Michigan
  Detroit Free Press (ProQuest)
New York
  Brooklyn Daily Eagle (Brooklyn Public Library)
  New York Daily Tribune
  New York Evening Post
  New York Independent
  New York Times (ProQuest)
  New York Weekly Journal of Commerce
  New York World
  Wall Street Journal (ProQuest)
Ohio
  Cincinnati Daily Gazette
  Columbus Crisis
Pennsylvania
  Franklin Repository (Penn State Digital Collections)
  Philadelphia Inquirer
  Philadelphia, *North American and United States Gazette*
  Philadelphia Press (Penn State Digital Collections)
  Pittsburgh Daily Commercial
  Waynesboro, *Village Record* (Penn State Digital Collections)
Washington, D.C.
  Evening Star
  National Intelligencer
  National Republican
  Washington Post (ProQuest)

Constitutional Documents

Farrand, Max, ed. *The Records of the Federal Convention of 1787.* 3 vols. New Haven, Conn.: Yale University Press, 1911.
Lord, William Blair, and Henry M. Parkhurst, eds. *The Debates of the Constitutional Convention of the State of Maryland, Assembled at the City of Annapolis, Wednesday, April 27, 1864.* 3 vols. Annapolis: Richard P. Bayly, 1864.
U.S. Constitution (1787)

Congressional Documents

Appendix to the Congressional Globe, 37th and 38th Congresses
Congressional Globe, 36th, 37th, and 38th Congresses
Congressional Serial Set, 37th, 38th, and 39th Congresses

House of Representatives Bills and Resolutions
Journal of the House of Representatives, 37th and 38th Congresses
Senate Bills and Resolutions
Senate Journal, 37th and 38th Congresses
U.S. Statutes at Large, vols. 1–18

Music and Poetry

American Song Sheets, Rare Book and Special Collections Division, Library of
    Congress (American Memory).
Barrett, Faith, and Cristanne Miller, eds. *"Words for the Hour": A New Anthology of
    American Civil War Poetry.* Amherst: University of Massachusetts Press, 2006.
Melville, Herman. *Battle-Pieces and Aspects of the War.* New York: Harper & Broth-
    ers, 1866.
Randall, James Ryder. *Maryland, My Maryland and Other Poems.* Baltimore: John
    Murphy, 1908.

Official Documents

Delaware. *Laws of the State of Delaware, Passed at the Session of the General As-
    sembly, Commenced and Held at Dover, on Tuesday, the Sixth Day of January
    A.D. 1863.* Wilmington: Henry Eckel, 1863.
Historic American Buildings Survey. "Hayfields Farm Buildings, Worthington Val-
    ley, Cockeysville Vicinity, Baltimore County, MD." Survey Number HABS
    MD-15. Prints and Photographs Division, Library of Congress.
Maryland. *Laws of the State of Maryland, Made and Passed at a Special Session of
    the General Assembly, Held at Frederick, April 26, 1861.* Annapolis: Elihu S.
    Riley, 1861.
———. *Laws of the State of Maryland, Made and Passed at a Session of the General
    Assembly Begun and Held at the City of Annapolis on the Third Day of Decem-
    ber, 1861, and Ended on the Tenth Day of March, 1862.* Annapolis: Thomas J.
    Wilson, 1862.
———. *Laws of the State of Maryland, Made and Passed at a Session of the General As-
    sembly, Begun and Held at the City of Annapolis, on the 2nd Day of January, 1867,
    and Ended on the 23rd Day of March, 1867.* Annapolis: Henry A. Lucas, 1867.
———. *Laws of the State of Maryland, Made and Passed at a Session of the General
    Assembly, Begun and Held at the City of Annapolis, on the Seventh Day of
    January, 1874, and Ended on the Sixth Day of April, 1874.* Annapolis: S. S. Mills
    & L. F. Colton, 1874.
Maryland General Assembly. *Documents of the General Assembly, 1861.* Annapolis:
    E. S. Riley, 1861.

———. *Documents of the General Assembly, 1864.* Annapolis: Richard P. Bayly, 1864.

———. *Documents of the General Assembly, 1865.* Annapolis: Richard P. Bayly, 1865.

———. *Report of the Adjutant General of Maryland, to the General Assembly, Special Session, 1861.*

Official Opinions of the Attorneys General of the United States. 43 vols. Washington, D.C.: W.H. and O.H. Morrison, 1852–1996.

Official Records of the Union and Confederate Navies in the War of the Rebellion. 30 vols. Washington, D.C.: Government Printing Office, 1894–1922.

U.S. Census Bureau. Eighth Census (1860). *Maryland Slave Schedule.* Washington, D.C., 1864.

War of the Rebellion: A Compilation of the Official Records of the Union and Confederate Armies. 128 vols. Washington, D.C.: Government Printing Office, 1880–1901.

Published Primary Sources

Agle, Anna Bradford, and Sidney Hovey Wanzer, eds. "Dearest Braddie: Love and War in Maryland, 1860–61: Part 1." *Maryland Historical Magazine* 88 (Spring 1993): 73–88.

———. "Dearest Braddie: Love and War in Maryland, 1860–61: Part 2." *Maryland Historical Magazine* 88 (Fall 1993): 337–58.

The American Annual Cyclopaedia and Register of Important Events. 14 vols. New York: D. Appleton, 1862–75.

"An Eyewitness to the Baltimore Riot, 19th April, 1861." *Maryland Historical Magazine* 53 (December 1958): 402–3.

Angle, Paul M., ed. *By These Words: Great Documents of American Liberty.* New York: Rand McNally, 1954.

Auchampaugh, Philip G., ed. "A Great Justice on State and Federal Power: Being the Thoughts of Chief Justice Taney on the Federal Conscription Act (An Undelivered Opinion)." *Tyler's Quarterly Magazine* 18 (1936): 72–87.

Bain, William E., ed. *B&O in the Civil War, from the Papers of Wm. Prescott Smith.* Denver: Sage, 1966.

Basler, Roy P., et al., eds. *The Collected Works of Abraham Lincoln.* 9 vols. New Brunswick, N.J.: Rutgers University Press, 1953–55.

Beale, Howard K. ed. *Diary of Edward Bates.* Washington, D.C.: Government Printing Office, 1933.

———. *Diary of Gideon Welles: Secretary of the Navy under Lincoln and Johnson.* 3 vols. New York: W. W. Norton, 1960.

Brown, George William. *Baltimore and the Nineteenth of April, 1861: A Study of the War.* Baltimore: Johns Hopkins University Press, 1887.

Brownson, Orestes A. *The American Republic: Its Constitution, Tendencies and Destiny.* 1865, reprint; Wilmington, Del.: ISI Books, 2003.

Burlingame, Michael, and John R. Turner Ettlinger, eds. *Inside Lincoln's White House: The Complete Civil War Diary of John Hay.* Carbondale: Southern Illinois University Press, 1997.

Butler, Benjamin F. *Butler's Book: Autobiography and Personal Reminiscences of Major-General Benjamin F. Butler.* Boston: A. M. Thayer, 1892.

Cary, George W., and James McClellan, eds. *The Federalist: The Gideon Edition.* Indianapolis: Liberty Fund, 2001.

Catton, Bruce, ed. "Brother *against* Brother." *American Heritage* 12 (April 1961): 4–7, 89.

Cole, Donald B., and John J. McDonough, eds. *Witness to the Young Republic: A Yankee's Journal, 1828–1870.* London: University Press of New England, 1989.

Cox, Samuel Sullivan. *Eight Years in Congress, from 1857 to 1865: Memoir and Speeches.* New York: D. Appleton, 1865.

Cozzens, Peter, and Robert I. Girardi, eds. *The New Annals of the Civil War.* Mechanicsburg, Pa.: Stackpole, 2004.

Crist, Lynda Lasswell, et al., eds. *The Papers of Jefferson Davis.* 15 vols. (projected). Baton Rouge: Louisiana State University Press, 1971–present.

Dewey, Donald O., ed. "Hoosier Justice: The Journal of David McDonald, 1864–1868." *Indiana Magazine of History* 62 (September 1966): 175–232.

[Dutton, Henry]. "Writ of Habeas Corpus." *American Law Register* 9 (October 1861): 705–17.

Freidel, Frank, ed. *Union Pamphlets of the Civil War, 1861–1865.* 2 vols. Cambridge, Mass.: Harvard University Press, 1967.

Frost, Robert W., and Nancy D. Frost, eds. *Picket Pins and Sabers: The Civil War Letters of John Burden Weston.* Ashland, Ky.: Economy Printers, 1971.

Henry, William Wirt, comp. *Patrick Henry: Life, Correspondence and Speeches.* 3 vols. New York: Scribner's, 1891.

Hobson, Charles F., et al., eds. *The Papers of John Marshall.* 12 vols. Chapel Hill: University of North Carolina Press, 1974–2006.

Howard, Frank Key. *Fourteen Months in American Bastiles.* Baltimore: Kelly, Hedian & Piet, 1863.

Johnston, Gertrude K., ed. *Dear Pa—And So It Goes.* Harrisburg: Business Service Co., 1971.

[Johnston, James F.] *Suspending Power and the Writ of Habeas Corpus.* Philadelphia: John Campbell, 1862.

Kurland, Philip B., and Ralph Lerner, eds. *The Founders' Constitution.* 5 vols. Indianapolis: Liberty Fund, 1987.

Laas, Virginia J., ed. *Wartime Washington: The Civil War Letters of Elizabeth Blair Lee.* Urbana: University of Illinois Press, 1991.

Mahony, Dennis A. *The Prisoner of State.* New York: Carleton, 1863.

Marks, Bayly Ellen, and Mark Norton Schatz, eds. *Between North and South: A*

Maryland Journalist Views the Civil War. Rutherford, N.J.: Fairleigh Dickinson University Press, 1976.

Marshall, Jessie Ames, comp. *Private and Official Correspondence of Gen. Benjamin F. Butler: During the Period of the Civil War.* 5 vols. Norwood, Mass.: Plimpton Press, 1917.

Mitchell, Charles W., ed. *Maryland Voices of the Civil War.* Baltimore: Johns Hopkins University Press, 2007.

Moore, Frank, ed. *The Rebellion Record: A Diary of American Events.* 12 vols. New York: G. P. Putnam, 1861–68.

Nevins, Allan, and Milton Halsey Thomas, eds. *The Diary of George Templeton Strong, 1835–1875.* 4 vols. New York: Macmillan, 1952.

Niven, John, et al., eds. *The Salmon P. Chase Papers.* 5 vols. Kent, Ohio: Kent State University Press, 1993–98.

Palmer, Beverly Wilson, and Holly Byers Ochoa, eds. *The Selected Papers of Thaddeus Stevens.* 2 vols. Pittsburgh, Pa.: University of Pittsburgh Press, 1997.

Pease, Theodore Calvin, and James G. Randall, eds. *The Diary of Orville Hickman Browning.* 2 vols. Springfield: Illinois State Historical Library, 1925.

Robinson, Edward Ayrault. "Some Recollections of April 19, 1861." *Maryland Historical Magazine* 27 (December 1932): 274–79.

Rowe, Kenneth E., ed. "David Creamer and the Baltimore Mob Riot, April 19, 1861." *Methodist History* 13 (1975): 61–64.

Rowland, Dunbar, ed. *Jefferson Davis, Constitutionalist: His Letters, Papers and Speeches.* 10 vols. Jackson: Mississippi Department of Archives and History, 1923.

"Some Papers of Franklin Pierce, 1852–1862." *American Historical Review* 10 (January 1905): 350–70.

Thwaites, Reuben Gold, ed. *Civil War Messages and Proclamations of Wisconsin War Governors.* [Madison]: Wisconsin History Commission, 1912.

Towers, Frank, ed. "Military Waif: A Sidelight on the Baltimore Riot of 19 April 1861." *Maryland Historical Magazine* 89 (Winter 1994): 427–46.

"Treason. Can the Crime of Treason Be Committed against One of the United States?" *American Law Magazine* 8 (January 1845): 318–50.

The Trial of Hon. Clement L. Vallandigham, by a Military Commission: and the Proceedings under His Application for a Writ of Habeas Corpus in the Circuit Court of the United States for the Southern District of Ohio. Cincinnati: Rickey & Carroll, 1863.

The Trial of the Alleged Assassins and Conspirators at Washington City, D.C., May and June, 1865, for the Murder of President Abraham Lincoln. Philadelphia: T. B. Peterson & Brothers, 1865.

Turner, George, ed. *Civil War Letters from Soldiers and Citizens of Columbia County, Pennsylvania.* New York: American Heritage, 1996.

The Washington Despotism Dissected in Articles from the Metropolitan Record. New York: Metropolitan Record, 1863.

White, Jonathan W., ed. "A Pennsylvania Judge Views the Rebellion: The Civil War Letters of George Washington Woodward." *Pennsylvania Magazine of History and Biography* 129 (April 2005): 290–316.

———. *A Philadelphia Perspective: The Civil War Diary of Sidney George Fisher.* New York: Fordham University Press, 2007.

———. "The Civil War Disloyalty Trial of John O'Connell." *Ohio Valley History* 9 (Spring 2009): 2–20.

Pamphlets

Addison, William Meade. *United States vs. John W. Heard: A Citizen of Maryland. Defence of the Prisoner before a Military Commission, at Fort McHenry, Md. Charged with Recruiting Troops in the Federal Lines for the Confederate Army. September, 1863.* Baltimore: Murphy, 1863.

Binney, Horace. *The Privilege of the Writ of Habeas Corpus under the Constitution.* Philadelphia: C. Sherman & Son, 1862.

Bradford, Augustus. *Inaugural Address of Hon. Augustus Bradford, Governor of Maryland; Delivered in the Senate Chamber, before the Senate and House of Delegates, January 8, 1862.* Annapolis: Thomas J. Wilson, 1862.

Field, R. S. *A Charge to the Grand Jury of the United States for the District of New Jersey, April 21, 1863.* Trenton: State Gazette & Republican Print, 1863.

Irving, Henry P. *Argument of H. P. Irving in the Circuit Court of the United States, in and for the District of California. July Term, 1866. Before Hon. Judge Deady. John McCall, Plaintiff, vs. Charles D. Douglass, and Irvin McDowell, Defendants.* N.p., [1866].

Maryland Agricultural College. *First Circular of the Maryland Agricultural College.* Baltimore: Samuel Sands Mills, 1859.

———. *Second Circular of the Maryland Agricultural College.* Washington, D.C.: Henry Polkinhorn, 1860.

———. *Circular of the Maryland Agricultural College.* Baltimore: John Murphy, 1863.

———. *Circular of the Maryland Agricultural College.* Baltimore: John Murphy, 1864.

———. *Catalogue of the Maryland Agricultural College, Prince George's County, for the Years 1865–6.* Baltimore: John Murphy, 1865.

May, Henry. *Speeches of the Hon. Henry May, of Maryland, Delivered in the House of Representatives, at the Third Session of the Thirty-Seventh Congress.* Baltimore: Kelly, Hedian & Piet, 1863.

Northern Central Railway Company. *Fifth Annual Report of the President and Directors of the Northern Central Railway Co. to the Stockholders, for the Year 1859.* Baltimore: James Lucas & Son, 1860.

————. *Seventh Annual Report of the President and Directors of the Northern Central Railway Co. to the Stockholders, for the Year 1861.* Baltimore: James Lucas & Son, 1862.

Parker, Joel. *Habeas Corpus and Martial Law: A Review of the Opinion of Chief Justice Taney, in the Case of John Merryman.* Philadelphia: John Campbell, 1862.

Price, William. *The Position of Maryland: Letter of William Price, Esq., of Baltimore.* Baltimore: John Murphy, [1861].

Sanford, Miles. *Treason and the Punishment it Deserves: A Sermon Founded on Ezra 7:26, and Preached before the Berkshire Baptist Association, at its Thirty-Fifth Anniversary at Sandisfield, Wednesday Evening, October 8, 1862.* Boston: J. M. Hewes, 1862.

Smith, Gerrit. *No Treason in Civil War: Speech of Gerrit Smith, at Cooper Institute, New-York, June 8, 1865.* New York: American News Company, 1865.

Spooner, Lysander. *No Treason: The Constitution of No Authority.* 1870, reprint; Larkspur, Colo.: Pine Tree Press, 1966.

Sprague, Peleg. *What is Treason? A Charge Addressed by the Hon. Peleg Sprague, Judge of the U.S. District Court for the District of Massachusetts, to the Grand Jury, at the March Term, A.D., 1863. Printed for the Union League.* Salem, Mass.: Charles W. Swasey, 1863.

Treason and Rebellion: Being in Part the Legislation of Congress and of the State of California thereon, Together with the Recent Charge by Judge Field, of the U.S. Supreme Court, Delivered to the Grand Jury in Attendance at the June Term, Eighteen Hundred and Sixty-Three, of the U.S. Circuit Court for the Northern District of California. San Francisco: Towne & Bacon, 1863.

Wallis, Severn Teackle, and John Sherman. *Correspondence between S. Teackle Wallis, Esq., of Baltimore, and the Hon. John Sherman, of the U.S. Senate: Concerning the Arrest of Members of the Maryland Legislature, and the Mayor and Police Commissioners of Baltimore, in 1861.* Baltimore: Kelly, Hedian & Piet, 1863.

Whiting, William. *The War Powers of the President, and the Legislative Powers of Congress in Relation to Rebellion, Treason and Slavery.* Boston: John L. Shorey, 1862.

Periodicals and Almanacs

The American Farmer
American Law Register
Monthly Law Reporter
The Old Guard: A Monthly Journal, Devoted to the Principles of 1776 and 1787
Tribune Almanac and Political Register

Court Reports

Abbott's Reports (U.S. District and Circuit Court cases)
Bond's Reports (U.S. District and Circuit Courts for the Southern District of Ohio)
Cadwalader's Cases (Pennsylvania, federal cases)
Deady's Reports (California and Oregon, federal cases)
Federal Cases (U.S. District and Circuit Court cases)
Grant's Reports (Supreme Court of Pennsylvania)
Hayward and Hazleton's District of Columbia Reports
Indiana Reports
Maryland Reports
New York Reports
Ohio Reports
U.S. Reports (Supreme Court of the United States)

SECONDARY SOURCES

Books

Baker, Jean H. *The Politics of Continuity: Maryland Political Parties from 1858 to 1870.* Baltimore: Johns Hopkins University Press, 1973.
———. *Affairs of Party: The Political Culture of Northern Democrats in the Mid-Nineteenth Century.* Ithaca, N.Y.: Cornell University Press. Reprint, New York: Fordham University Press, 1998.
Bates, Samuel P. *History of Pennsylvania Volunteers, 1861–5.* 5 vols. Harrisburg, Pa.: B. Singerly, 1869–71.
Belz, Herman. *Reconstructing the Union: Theory and Policy during the Civil War.* Ithaca, N.Y.: Cornell University Press, 1969.
———. *A New Birth of Freedom: The Republican Party and Freedmen's Rights, 1861–1866.* Westport, Conn.: Greenwood, 1976.
———. *Emancipation and Equal Rights: Politics and Constitutionalism in the Civil War Era.* New York: W.W. Norton, 1978.
———. *Abraham Lincoln, Constitutionalism, and Equal Rights in the Civil War Era.* New York: Fordham University Press, 1998.
Biographical Cyclopedia of Representative Men of Maryland and [the] District of Columbia. Baltimore: National Biographical, 1879.
Blair, William. *Virginia's Private War: Feeding Body and Soul in the Confederacy, 1861–1865.* New York: Oxford University Press, 1998.
———. *Why Didn't the North Hang Some Rebels?: The Postwar Debate over Punishment for Treason.* Milwaukee, Wis.: Marquette University Press, 2004; re-

printed in *More than a Contest between Armies: Essays on the Civil War Era*, ed. James A. Marten and A. Kristen Foster, 189–218. Kent, Ohio: Kent State University Press, 2008.

Bogue, Allan G. *The Earnest Men: Republicans of the Civil War Senate*. Ithaca, N.Y.: Cornell University Press, 1981.

Boman, Dennis K. *Lincoln and Citizens' Rights in Civil War Missouri: Balancing Security and Freedom*. Baton Rouge: Louisiana State University Press, 2011.

Bradley, Erwin Stanley. *Simon Cameron, Lincoln's Secretary of War: A Political Biography*. Philadelphia: University of Pennsylvania Press, 1966.

Brooks, Neal A., and Eric G. Rockel. *A History of Baltimore County*. Towson, Md.: Friends of the Towson Library, 1979.

Burlingame, Michael. *Abraham Lincoln: A Life*. 2 vols. Baltimore: Johns Hopkins University Press, 2009.

Callcott, George H. *A History of the University of Maryland*. Baltimore: Maryland Historical Society, 1966.

Carnahan, Burrus M. *Lincoln on Trial: Southern Civilians and the Law of War*. Lexington: University Press of Kentucky, 2010.

Carso, Brian F., Jr. *"Whom Can We Trust Now?": The Meaning of Treason in the United States, from the Revolution through the Civil War*. Lanham, Md.: Lexington Books, 2006.

Chapin, Bradley. *The American Law of Treason: Revolutionary and Early National Origins*. Seattle: University of Washington Press, 1964.

Churchill, Robert H. *To Shake Their Guns in the Tyrant's Face: Libertarian Political Violence and the Origins of the Militia Movement*. Ann Arbor: University of Michigan Press, 2009.

Curtis, Michael Kent. *Free Speech, "The People's Darling Privilege": Struggles for Freedom of Expression in American History*. Durham, N.C.: Duke University Press, 2000.

Davis, Stanton Ling. *Pennsylvania Politics, 1860–1863*. Cleveland, Ohio: Western Reserve University Bookstore, 1935.

Dicey, A.V. *Introduction to the Study of the Law of the Constitution*. 1915 ed., reprint; Indianapolis: Liberty Classics, 1982.

Dorris, Jonathan Truman. *Pardon and Amnesty under Lincoln and Johnson: The Restoration of the Confederates to Their Rights and Privileges, 1861–1898*. Chapel Hill: University of North Carolina Press, 1953.

Drouhard, Patrick J. *It Don't Look Right for the Times: The Factual History of the Holmes County Rebellion*. Cardington, Ohio: Privately printed, 2005.

Duker, William F. *A Constitutional History of Habeas Corpus*. Westport, Conn.: Greenwood Press, 1980.

Egnal, Marc. *Clash of Extremes: The Economic Origins of the Civil War*. New York: Hill & Wang, 2009.

Farber, Daniel A. *Lincoln's Constitution.* Chicago: University of Chicago Press, 2003.

Fehrenbacher, Don E. *Slavery, Law, and Politics: The Dred Scott Case in Historical Perspective.* New York: Oxford University Press, 1981.

Fields, Barbara Jeanne. *Slavery and Freedom on the Middle Ground: Maryland during the Nineteenth Century.* New Haven, Conn.: Yale University Press, 1985.

Frederickson, George M. *The Inner Civil War: Northern Intellectuals and the Crisis of the Union.* New York: Harper & Row, 1965.

Freeze, John G. *A History of Columbia County, Pennsylvania: From the Earliest Times.* Bloomsburg, Pa.: Elwell & Bittenbender, 1883.

Green, Michael S. *Freedom, Union, and Power: Lincoln and His Party during the Civil War.* New York: Fordham University Press, 2004.

Grimsley, Mark. *The Hard Hand of War: Union Military Policy toward Southern Civilians, 1861–1865.* New York: Cambridge University Press, 1995.

A Guide to the Preservation of Federal Judges' Papers. 2nd ed. Washington, D.C.: Federal Judicial Center, 2009.

Gunnarsson, Robert L. *The Story of the Northern Central Railway: From Baltimore to Lake Ontario.* Sykesville, Md.: Greenberg, 1991.

Hamilton, Daniel W. *The Limits of Sovereignty: Property Confiscation in the Union and the Confederacy during the Civil War.* Chicago: University of Chicago Press, 2007.

Harper, Robert S. *Lincoln and the Press.* New York: McGraw-Hill, 1951.

Harris, William C. *With Charity for All: Lincoln and the Restoration of the Union.* Lexington: University Press of Kentucky, 1997.

Hobson, Charles F. *The Aaron Burr Treason Trial.* Washington, D.C.: Federal Judicial Center, 2006.

Hoffer, Peter Charles. *The Treason Trials of Aaron Burr.* Lawrence: University Press of Kansas, 2008.

Hollandsworth, James G., Jr. *Pretense of Glory: The Life of General Nathaniel P. Banks.* Baton Rouge: Louisiana State University Press, 1998.

Howard, George W. *The Monumental City: Its Past History and Present Resources.* Baltimore: J. D. Ehlers, 1873.

Hurst, James Willard. *The Law of Treason in the United States: Collected Essays.* Westport, Conn.: Greenwood, 1971.

Hyman, Harold M. *Era of the Oath: Northern Loyalty Tests during the Civil War and Reconstruction.* Philadelphia: University of Pennsylvania Press, 1954.

———. *A More Perfect Union: The Impact of the Civil War and Reconstruction on the Constitution.* New York: Knopf, 1973.

Kagey, Guy Edison. *Sherwood Church: Sketches of the History of Sherwood Parish, Cockeysville, Baltimore County, Maryland, 1830–1930.* Baltimore: Read-Taylor, 1930.

Kamm, Samuel R. *The Civil War Career of Thomas A. Scott.* Philadelphia: University of Pennsylvania Press, 1940.

Klement, Frank L. *The Copperheads in the Middle West.* Chicago: University of Chicago Press, 1960.

———. *The Limits of Dissent: Clement L. Vallandigham and the Civil War.* Lexington: University of Kentucky Press, 1970.

———. *Dark Lanterns: Secret Political Societies, Conspiracies, and Treason Trials in the Civil War.* Baton Rouge: Louisiana State University Press, 1984.

Lawson, Melinda. *Patriot Fires: Forging a New American Nationalism in the Civil War North.* Lawrence: University Press of Kansas, 2002.

Levy, Leonard W. *Jefferson and Civil Liberties: The Darker Side.* Cambridge, Mass.: Harvard University Press, 1963.

Lewis, Walker. *Without Fear or Favor: A Biography of Chief Justice Roger Brooke Taney.* Boston: Houghton Mifflin, 1965.

Lowry, Thomas P. *Confederate Heroines: 120 Southern Women Convicted by Union Military Justice.* Baton Rouge: Louisiana State University Press, 2006.

McGinty, Brian. *Lincoln & the Court.* Cambridge, Mass.: Harvard University Press, 2008.

McGrain, John W. *From Pig Iron to Cotton Duck: A History of Manufacturing Villages in Baltimore County.* Towson, Md.: Baltimore County Public Library, 1985.

———. *An Agricultural History of Baltimore County, Maryland.* Perry Hall, Md.: Accent Printers, 1990.

McPherson, James M. *Crossroads of Freedom: Antietam.* New York: Oxford University Press, 2002.

———. *Tried by War: Abraham Lincoln as Commander in Chief.* New York: Penguin Press, 2008.

Moore, Kathleen Dean. *Pardons: Justice, Mercy, and the Public Interest.* New York: Oxford University Press, 1989.

Neely, Mark E., Jr. *The Fate of Liberty: Abraham Lincoln and Civil Liberties.* New York: Oxford University Press, 1991.

———. *Southern Rights: Political Prisoners and the Myth of Confederate Constitutionalism.* Charlottesville: University Press of Virginia, 1999.

———. *The Union Divided: Party Conflict in the Civil War North.* Cambridge, Mass.: Harvard University Press, 2002.

Neff, Stephen C. *Justice in Blue and Gray: A Legal History of the Civil War.* Cambridge, Mass.: Harvard University Press, 2010.

Nolan, J. Bennett. *Lafayette in America: Day by Day.* Baltimore: Johns Hopkins University Press, 1934.

Parish, John Carl. *George Wallace Jones.* Iowa City: State Historical Society of Iowa, 1912.

Porter, George H. *Ohio Politics during the Civil War Period.* New York: Columbia University Press, 1911.

Radcliffe, George L. P. *Governor Thomas H. Hicks of Maryland and the Civil War.* Baltimore: Johns Hopkins University Press, 1901.

Ragsdale, Bruce A. *Ex parte Merryman and Debates on Civil Liberties during the Civil War.* Washington, D.C.: Federal Judicial Center, 2007.

Randall, James G. *Constitutional Problems under Lincoln.* Revised ed. Urbana: University of Illinois Press, 1964.

Rehnquist, William H. *All the Laws but One: Civil Liberties in Wartime.* New York: Knopf, 1998.

Rosen, Jeffrey. *The Most Democratic Branch: How the Courts Serve America.* New York: Oxford University Press, 2006.

Samito, Christian G. *Changes in Law and Society during the Civil War and Reconstruction.* Carbondale: Southern Illinois University Press, 2009.

Sanders, Alvin H. *The Story of the Herefords.* Chicago: Breeder's Gazette, 1914.

Sandow, Robert M. *Deserter Country: Civil War Opposition in the Pennsylvania Appalachians.* New York: Fordham University Press, 2009.

Scharf, J. Thomas. *History of Maryland from the Earliest Period to the Present Day.* 3 vols. Baltimore: John B. Piet, 1879.

———. *History of Baltimore City and County.* Philadelphia: Louis H. Everts, 1881.

———. *History of Philadelphia, 1609–1884.* 3 vols. Philadelphia: L. H. Everts, 1884.

Scott, Sean A. *A Visitation of God: Northern Civilians Interpret the Civil War.* New York: Oxford University Press, 2011.

Sears, Stephen W. *Landscape Turned Red: The Battle of Antietam.* New York: Ticknor & Fields, 1983.

Siegel, Martin. *The Supreme Court in American Life, Volume 3: The Taney Court, 1836–1864.* Millwood, N.Y.: Associated Faculty Press, 1987.

Silbey, Joel H. *A Respectable Minority: The Democratic Party in the Civil War Era, 1860–1868.* New York: W.W. Norton, 1977.

Simon, James F. *Lincoln and Chief Justice Taney: Slavery, Secession, and the President's War Powers.* New York: Simon & Schuster, 2006.

Smith, Adam I. P. *No Party Now: Politics in the Civil War North.* New York: Oxford University Press, 2006.

Smith, Craig R. *Silencing the Opposition: Government Strategies of Suppression.* Albany: State University of New York Press, 1996.

Steiner, Brad C. *Life of Reverdy Johnson.* Baltimore: Norman, Remington, 1914.

Stone, Geoffrey R. *Perilous Times: Free Speech in Wartime, From the Sedition Act of 1798 to the War on Terrorism.* New York: W. W. Norton, 2004.

Swanson, James L., and Daniel R. Weinberg. *Lincoln's Assassins: Their Trial and Execution.* Santa Fe, N.M.: Arena Editions, 2001.

Swisher, Carl Brent. *Roger B. Taney.* New York: Macmillan, 1935.

———. *The Oliver Wendell Holmes Devise History of the Supreme Court of the United States, Vol. V: The Taney Period.* New York: Macmillan, 1974.

Syrett, John. *The Civil War Confiscation Acts: Failing to Reconstruct the South.* New York: Fordham University Press, 2005.

Thomas, Benjamin P., and Harold M. Hyman. *Stanton: The Life and Times of Lincoln's Secretary of War.* New York: Knopf, 1962.

Toomey, Daniel Carroll. *The Civil War in Maryland.* Baltimore: Toomey Press, 1983.

Towers, Frank. *The Urban South and the Coming of the Civil War.* Charlottesville: University of Virginia Press, 2004.

Trimble, David C. *Furious, Insatiable Fighter: A Biography of Major General Isaac Ridgeway Trimble, C.S.A.* Lanham, Md.: University Press of America, 2005.

Tucker, Leslie R. *Major General Isaac Ridgeway Trimble: Biography of a Baltimore Confederate.* Jefferson, N.C.: McFarland, 2005.

Tyler, Samuel. *Memoir of Roger Brooke Taney, LL.D., Chief Justice of the Supreme Court of the United States.* Baltimore: J. Murphy, 1872.

Urofsky, Melvin I. *A March of Liberty: A Constitutional History of the United States.* New York: Knopf, 1988.

Wagandt, Charles L. *The Mighty Revolution: Negro Emancipation in Maryland, 1862–1864.* Baltimore: Johns Hopkins University Press, 1964.

Weber, Jennifer L. *Copperheads: The Rise and Fall of Lincoln's Opponents in the North.* New York: Oxford University Press, 2006.

Wheeler, Russell R., and Cynthia Harrison. *Creating the Federal Judicial System,* 3rd ed. Washington, D.C.: Federal Judicial Center, 2005.

Whittington, Keith E. *Constitutional Construction: Divided Powers and Constitutional Meaning.* Cambridge, Mass.: Harvard University Press, 1999.

Wiecek, William M. *Liberty under Law: The Supreme Court in American Life.* Baltimore: Johns Hopkins University Press, 1988.

Williams, Frank J. *Judging Lincoln.* Carbondale: Southern Illinois University Press, 2002.

Williams, Thomas J. C. *A History of Washington County Maryland.* 2 vols. 1906, reprint; Baltimore: Regional Publishing, 1968.

Wilson, Douglas L. *Lincoln's Sword: The Presidency and Power of Words.* New York: Knopf, 2006.

Yoo, John. *Crisis and Command: A History of Executive Power from George Washington to George W. Bush.* New York: Kaplan, 2009.

Articles and Book Chapters

Andrews, Matthew Page. "Passage of the Sixth Massachusetts Regiment through Baltimore, April 19, 1861." *Maryland Historical Magazine* 34 (1919): 60–76.

Barry, Peter J. "'I'll Keep Them in Prison Awhile . . .': Abraham Lincoln and David Davis on Civil Liberties in Wartime." *Journal of the Abraham Lincoln Association* 28 (Winter 2007): 20–29.

Bestor, Arthur. "The American Civil War as a Constitutional Crisis." *American Historical Review* 69 (January 1964): 327–52.

Blake, Kellee Green. "Aiding and Abetting: Disloyalty Prosecutions in the Federal Civil Courts of Southern Illinois, 1861–1866." *Illinois Historical Journal* 87 (Summer 1994): 95–108.

Blake, Kellee L. "Ten Firkins of Butter and Other 'Traitorous' Aid." *Prologue* 30 (Winter 1998): 288–93.

Chandler, Robert J. "The Release of the *Chapman* Pirates: A California Sidelight on Lincoln's Amnesty Policy." *Civil War History* 43 (June 1977): 129–43.

———. "Crushing Dissent: The Pacific Coast Tests Lincoln's Policy of Suppression, 1862." *Civil War History* 30 (September 1984): 235–54.

———. "Fighting Words: Censoring Civil War Journalism in California." *California Territorial Quarterly* 51 (September 2002): 4–17.

Chapin, Bradley. "Colonial and Revolutionary Origins of the American Law of Treason." *William and Mary Quarterly* 17 (January 1960): 3–21.

Chesnut, W. Calvin. "Address by Judge W. Calvin Chesnut: History of the Federal Courts in Maryland." *Report of the Forty-First Annual Meeting of the Maryland State Bar Association* 41 (1936): 63–89.

Churchill, Robert H. "Liberty, Conscription, and Delusions of Grandeur: The Sons of Liberty Conspiracy of 1863–1864." *Prologue* 30 (Winter 1998): 295–303.

Clemens, Andrew. "Hereford Farmhouse." *History Trails* 7 (Spring 1973): 9–12.

Cotter, Thomas F. "The Merryman Affair." *History Trails* 24 (Winter 1989–90): 5–8.

Culver, Francis B. "Merryman Family." *Maryland Historical Magazine* 10 (June 1915): 176–85.

———. "Merryman Family." *Maryland Historical Magazine* 10 (September 1915): 286–99.

Curran, Daniel J. "Polk, Politics, and Patronage: The Rejection of George W. Woodward's Nomination to the Supreme Court." *Pennsylvania Magazine of History and Biography* 121 (July 1997): 163–99.

Curry, Leonard P. "Congressional Democrats: 1861–1863." *Civil War History* 12 (September 1966): 213–29.

Davis, Erick F. "The Baltimore County Horse Guard." *History Trails* 10 (Winter 1975–76): 5–8.

Delaplaine, Edward S. "Chief Justice Roger B. Taney—His Career at the Frederick Bar." *Maryland Historical Magazine* 13 (September 1918): 109–42.

Downey, Arthur T. "The Conflict between the Chief Justice and the Chief Executive: *Ex parte Merryman*." *Journal of Supreme Court History* 31 (2006): 262–78.

Dueholm, James A. "Lincoln's Suspension of the Writ of Habeas Corpus: An Historical and Constitutional Analysis." *Journal of the Abraham Lincoln Association* 29 (Summer 2008): 47–66.

Duker, William F. "The President's Power to Pardon: A Constitutional History." *William and Mary Law Review* 18 (Spring 1977): 475–538.

Everett, Edward G. "The Baltimore Riots, April, 1861." *Pennsylvania History* 24 (October 1957): 331–42.

Faulkner, Robert K. "John Marshall and the Burr Trial." *Journal of American History* 53 (September 1966): 247–58.

Fletcher, George P. "The Case for Treason." *Maryland Law Review* 41 (1982): 197–205.

George, Joseph, Jr. "The North Affair: A Lincoln Administration Military Trial, 1864." *Civil War History* 33 (September 1987): 199–218.

———. "Military Trials of Civilians under the Habeas Corpus Act of 1863." *Lincoln Herald* 98 (Winter 1996): 126–38.

Halbert, Sherrill. "The Suspension of the Writ of Habeas Corpus by President Lincoln." *American Journal of Legal History* 2 (April 1958): 95–116.

Henderson, Dwight F. "Treason, Sedition, and Fries' Rebellion." *American Journal of Legal History* 14 (October 1970): 308–18.

"Historical Concept of Treason: English, American." *Indiana Law Journal* 35 (1959–60): 70–80.

Jackson, Jeffrey D. "The Power to Suspend Habeas Corpus: An Answer from the Arguments Surrounding *Ex Parte Merryman*." *University of Baltimore Law Review* 34 (2004–5): 11–54.

Klugewicz, Stephen M. "'The First Martyrs': The Sixth Massachusetts and the Baltimore Riot of 1861." *Southern Historian* 20 (Spring 1999): 5–24.

Leek, J. H. "Treason and the Constitution." *Journal of Politics* 13 (November 1951): 604–22.

Leonard, Elizabeth D. "Mary Surratt and the Plot to Assassinate Abraham Lincoln." In *The War Was You and Me: Civilians in the American Civil War,* ed. Joan E. Cashin, 286–309. Princeton, N.J.: Princeton University Press, 2002.

Melton, Tracy Matthew. "The Lost Lives of George Konig Sr. & Jr., A Father-Son Tale of Old Fell's Point." *Maryland Historical Magazine* 101 (Fall 2006): 332–61.

Merryman, Nicholas Bosley. "Hayfields History." *History Trails* 19 (Winter 1984–85): 5–8.

Mitchell, Charles W. "'The Whirlwind Now Gathering': Baltimore's Pratt Street Riot and the End of Maryland Secession." *Maryland Historical Magazine* 97 (Summer 2002): 203–32.

Neely, Mark E., Jr. "The Constitution and Civil Liberties under Lincoln." In *Our Lincoln: New Perspectives on Lincoln and His World,* ed. Eric Foner, 37–61. New York: W. W. Norton, 2008.

———. "'Seeking a Cause of Difficulty with the Government': Reconsidering Freedom of Speech and Judicial Conflict under Lincoln." In *Lincoln's Legacy: Ethics and Politics,* ed. Phillip Shaw Paludan, 48–66. Urbana: University of Illinois Press, 2008.

Nichols, Roy F. "United States vs. Jefferson Davis, 1865–1869." *American Historical Review* 31 (January 1926): 266–84.

Randall, James G. "The Indemnity Act of 1863: A Study in the Wartime Immunity of Governmental Officers." *Michigan Law Review* 20 (April 1922): 589–613.

Ridgway, Whitman D. "Fries in the Federalist Imagination: A Crisis of Republican Society." *Pennsylvania History* 67 (Winter 2000): 141–60.

Russ, William A., Jr. "The Struggle between President Lincoln and Congress over Disfranchisement of Rebels (Part 1)." *Susquehanna University Studies* 3 (March 1947): 177–205.

Sellery, George Clarke. "Lincoln's Suspension of Habeas Corpus as Viewed by Congress." *Bulletin of the University of Wisconsin* 1 (1907): 217–85.

Simon, Walter G. "The Evolution of Treason." *Tulane Law Review* 35 (June 1961): 669–704.

Slaughter, Thomas P. "'The King of Crimes': Early American Treason Law, 1787–1860." In *Launching the "Extended Republic": The Federalist Era*, ed. Ronald Hoffman and Peter J. Albert, 54–135. Charlottesville: University Press of Virginia, 1996.

Snyder, Timothy R. "'Making No Child's Play of the Question': Governor Hicks and the Secession Crisis Reconsidered." *Maryland Historical Magazine* 101 (Fall 2006): 304–31.

Tap, Bruce. "'Union Men to the Polls, and Rebels to Their Holes." *Civil War History* 46 (March 2000): 24–40.

Tittmann, Edward D. "The Exploitation of Treason." *New Mexico Historical Review* 4 (April 1929): 128–45.

Towers, Frank. "'A Vociferous Army of Howling Wolves': Baltimore's Civil War Riot of April 19, 1861." *Maryland Historian* 23 (Fall/Winter 1992): 1–27.

Towne, Stephen E. "Killing the Serpent Speedily: Governor Morton, General Hascall, and the Suppression of the Democratic Press in Indiana, 1863." *Civil War History* 52 (April 2006): 41–65.

———. "Worse than Vallandigham: Governor Oliver P. Morton, Lambdin P. Milligan, and the Military Arrest and Trial of Indiana State Senator Alexander J. Douglas during the Civil War." *Indiana Magazine of History* 106 (March 2010): 1–39.

Vorenberg, Michael. "The Chase Court, 1864–1873: Cautious Reconstruction." In *The United States Supreme Court: The Pursuit of Justice*, ed. Christopher Tomlin, 103–21. Boston: Houghton Mifflin, 2005.

Wagandt, Charles L. "Election by Sword and Ballot: The Emancipationist Victory of 1863." *Maryland Historical Magazine* 59 (June 1964): 143–64.

Wheeler, Kenneth H. "Local Autonomy and Civil War Draft Resistance: Holmes County, Ohio." *Civil War History* 45 (June 1999): 147–59.

White, Jonathan W. "Canvassing the Troops: The Federal Government and the Soldiers' Right to Vote." *Civil War History* 50 (September 2004): 290–316.

———. "'Sweltering with Treason': The Civil War Trials of William Matthew Merrick." *Prologue* 39 (Summer 2007): 26–36.

———. "'Words Become Things': Free Speech in Civil War Pennsylvania." *Pennsylvania Legacies* 8 (May 2008): 18–23.

Wiecek, William M. "The Reconstruction of Federal Judicial Power, 1863–1875." *American Journal of Legal History* 13 (October 1969): 333–59.

———. "The Great Writ and Reconstruction: The Habeas Corpus Act of 1867." *Journal of Southern History* 36 (November 1970): 530–48.

Wiser, Vivian. "Improving Maryland's Agriculture, 1840–1860." *Maryland Historical Magazine* 64 (Summer 1969): 105–32.

Yoo, John. "*Merryman* and *Milligan* (and *McCardle*)." *Journal of Supreme Court History* 34 (2009): 243–60.

Zornow, William Frank. "Treason as a Campaign Issue in the Re-election of Lincoln." *Abraham Lincoln Quarterly* 5 (June 1949): 348–63.

Dissertations and Theses

Allen, Mary Bernard. "Joseph Holt: Judge Advocate General (1862–1875): A Study in the Treatment of Political Prisoners by the United States Government during the Civil War." Ph.D. diss., University of Chicago, 1927.

Bailey, James C. "American Bastille?: Fort McHenry and Civil Liberty, 1861–1862." M.A. thesis, University of Maryland at Baltimore County, 2007.

Clark, Charles Branch. "Politics in Maryland during the Civil War." Ph.D. diss., University of North Carolina, 1940.

Index